A David Huddle Reader

The Bread Loaf Series of Contemporary Writers

DAVID HUDDLE

A David Huddle
READER

SELECTED

PROSE AND POETRY

Middlebury College Press and University of Vermont
Published by University Press of New England
Hanover and London

MIDDLEBURY COLLEGE PRESS AND UNIVERSITY OF VERMONT
Published by University Press of New England,
Hanover, NH 03755
© 1994 by David Huddle
Printed in the United States of America   5 4 3 2 1

CIP data appear at the end of the book

FOR MY MOTHER

who read to me

Contents

Contents

A Bread Loaf Contemporary

A T A T I M E when the literary world is increasingly dominated by commercial formulas and concentrated financial power, there is a clear need to restore the simple pleasures of reading: the experience of opening a book by an author you know and being delighted by a completely new dimension of her or his art, the joy of seeing an author break free of any formula to reveal the power of the well written word. The best writing, many authors affirm, comes as a gift; the best reading comes when the author passes that gift to the reader, a gift the author could imagine only by taking risks in a variety of genres including short stories, poetry, and essays.

As editors of The Bread Loaf Series of Contemporary Writers we subscribe to no single viewpoint. Our singular goal is to publish writing that moves the reader: by the beauty and lucidity of its language, by its underlying argument, by its force of vision. These values are celebrated each summer at the Writers' Conference on Bread Loaf Mountain in Vermont and in each of these books.

We offer you the Bread Loaf Contemporary series and the treasures with which these authors have surprised us.

Robert Pack
Jay Parini

A David Huddle Reader

Introduction: Confessions of a
Multi-Genre Writer

What It Feels Like from the Inside

A M O N G M Y P O E M S , stories, and essays, there are many more similarities than differences; finally my various works are "all of a piece." For me, writing an essay has always felt a lot like writing a story, which has always felt a lot like writing a poem. Adding the poetic line to the other elements of composition raises my blood pressure a notch—as might occur when I drive from a two-lane highway onto an interstate—but from the inside, writing in all three genres feels essentially the same. The destination is an arrangement of words that yields something true and interesting about human experience.

Though I've been seriously trying to write for half my fifty years of life, I've only recently begun to comprehend what now seems to me the most basic and obvious artistic principle: *Works of art are the mere by-product of an artist's work.*

My mother had a saying that she recited to me on various occasions of my childhood that contains the same notion: *Do the best you can, and angels can do no better.*

The basic task of an artist is to receive, understand, and attempt to realize the instruction of his or her inner life. The muscle an artist works to develop most is that of intuition. The most purely creative aspect of esthetic activity involves trying to discover the integrity of the thing-being-made—trying in the making of a thing to determine what its ideal form is to be.

Brenda Ueland, in *If You Want to Write*, puts it this way: *But we must try to find our True Conscience, our True Self, the very Center, for this is the only first-rate choice-making center. Here lies all originality, talent, honor, truthfulness, courage and cheerfulness. Here only lies the ability to choose the good and the grand, the true and the beautiful.*

In attempting to journey toward "the very Center," I produce poems, stories, and essays. Or I produce failed pieces of writing. One morning I write a poem that goes far beyond any level of achievement I could have imagined for myself. Another morning I produce drivel unworthy of the cheapest greeting card. *What* I produce is beside the point. The journey is the point.

I may even begin working with the hope of becoming famous and making a lot of money but then find myself lost in the work, pursuing a minor character into a subplot of extremely dense language, imagery, and psychology, and devote a year to producing an obscure novel that no publisher on the planet would dream of publishing. I've begun writing with a bad idea, become absorbed in the project, and produced work that surprised and pleased me. I've begun writing with the very highest esthetic principles firmly in mind but never managed to reach my deepest level of concentration, and therefore produced writing of very low quality.

Because when I begin, I can't anticipate how it's going to turn out, I must simply try to give myself wholly to the task, do the best I can to carry it out with sustained and intense attention, and hope that what I write will turn out to be valuable. If it doesn't turn out well, then I have to resist being discouraged.

One ruthlessly basic principle can be located in such an unpredictable endeavor: the *only* chance I have of producing art proceeds from my attempting "to find . . . the very Center."

There is no other way.

I think of Picasso, struck by inspiration at the end of an excellent lunch, brilliantly arranging the fishbones on his plate.

I think of Gulley Jimson, the impoverished genius of Joyce Cary's *The Horse's Mouth*, conniving—against common sense and his own well-being as well as the well-being of the woman he loves—to paint the crazy stuff he needs to paint.

I think of my daughter, a college sophomore with a paper on Milton to write for class the next day, spending the night writing a poem about the perfidiousness of the male gender.

And I think of myself writing a 500-page novel about a middle-aged professor of English who incidentally writes poems: When I finished it, I saw clearly that the novel was a failure, but I liked my protagonist's poems. I stole the good ones and published them in my book *The Nature of Yearning*.

Recently I set forth to write a short poem because I'd had a request from a literary festival that wanted to do a letter-press printing of a poem of mine for a broadside. The former owner of the press had sold off most of the print, and so my poem had to be no longer than 18 lines. Over the course of a couple of weeks of attempting to write an 18-line poem, I wrote four poems, of 37, 38, 34, and 32 lines.

I don't mean to say that all art—or even all of my art—is quirky in its origins. Sometimes I sit down to write a short poem, and that's exactly what I do, I write a short poem, and maybe it's a keeper. But I've certainly had the experience of trying to write a poem and after a number of attempts, seeing that it's actually a story I need to write. At least half of the various pieces I've written were conceived of in drastically different forms than what they actually turned out to be.

What I produce is usually not what I have in mind when I begin. Along the way, I pass through a phase of work, in which genre, length, tone, theme, almost all identifiable aspects of the piece are *in-process*, or *as yet to be determined*. I think that phase of the work must be the fiery matrix of art-making. It's what feels good—or dangerous or scary or satisfying—about writing. It's when all extraneous concerns drop away, when my concentration becomes absolute, and when I am wholly given over to the thing I am trying to make. It's what I imagine Brenda Ueland means by "the very Center." It is the purest kind of writing. If you sneaked up behind me when I was in this "state" and asked me what I was working on, I would have to journey back to you through the whole history of civilization before I would be able to give you an answer: "Oh, I guess it's an essay," I'd say. "I'm not yet sure what it is."

Even when I've finished them, some of the pieces I've written can't make up their minds about their identities. "A Dream with No Stump Roots In It," the title story of my first book, was composed in lines of poetry, and for a long while I kept it that way in a poetry manuscript I was sending out. I was also sending out, at the same time, a manuscript of a collection of stories that included the prose version of the same piece. The latter was what was accepted for publication; thus, "Stump Roots" achieved its definition as a story.

When I sent "Do You Wanna Dance?" to Dave Smith at *The Southern Review*, he wrote back to say that if it was a story, he had some problems with it, but if it was an essay, he liked it and wanted to publish it. That was when I decided "Do You Wanna Dance?" was most likely an essay.

I've always been charmed by that famous question someone allegedly asked Robert Creeley during a poetry reading: *Is that a real poem, or did you just make that up?* Like most poets, I appreciate the question because it so nakedly reveals the kind of bafflement many people feel when they are confronted with a work of art. But I like the metaphysical dimension of the question: Just what the hell are these things that come out of my computer, my typewriter, my pen, my brain, my heart? Looks like a poem? Well, let's call it a poem. Looks like a story? Well . . . And so on. But that thing-made-out-of-language that proceeded from my inner life—or passed through my inner life on its way—onto the page has its own integrity aside and apart from whatever name we give it. Whether we call it poem, story, essay, truck, rutabaga, or ocarina finally matters only to the extent its being named diminishes our anxiety about living with it. Is that a real *Langsamherzbaumgeschuz* or did you just make it up?

Though it is of considerably less importance to me, I've pursued tennis for just about as long as I have writing. In my early years, I was a racquet-flinger, a bigtime cusser, and a tantrum-thrower of the first rank. Nowadays I'll unleash the occasional *phooey* or *darn*, but for the most part I play serenely—and just about as well as a person of my ability might play. My principle is a variation of the one I've discovered about writing: *Tennis points [or games or sets or matches or lifetime records] are the mere by-product of a tennis player's play.* On every point, I try to run hard, watch the ball, take strong strokes, anticipate, read the shots that are coming back at me, and make smart decisions. I try to go all out, and I try to concentrate and completely give myself over to the play. I win some points, I lose some, it doesn't matter which; what matters is that I'm *there*—as completely as I possibly can be—in the flow of the game, trying to play the best I can.

I feel the same way about my writing—or I'm learning to feel that way: Whether I write a poem, a story, an essay, or a novel matters only incidentally. Whether it's short or long, lofty or vulgar, funny or sad, whether I make a lot of money or none at all, whether my writing brings me love, hatred, admiration, or contempt—all these things matter only slightly compared with that first principle: Am I trying as hard as I can in my art to reach the truth? Am I journeying toward "the very Center"?

4

ESSAYS

From *The Writing Habit* (1992)

Let's Say You Wrote Badly This Morning

> *. . . don't feel bad, Ramos*
> *What's done is did*
> *That's all right, son*
> *Ya git another chance tomorrer.*
>
> —MICHAEL CASEY, "The Company Physical
> Combat Proficiency Test Average," *Obscenities*

IN SEPTEMBER 1986, I had a novel rejected. In October of the same year, I had that rejection on my mind as I watched the American and National League baseball playoffs. A new television set allowed me to see what I had never really noticed before, the facial expressions of the players. What particularly intrigued me was how batters look when they strike out and how pitchers look when they give up a home run.

In that incredible American League fifth game, just after the Red Sox substitute center fielder Dave Henderson, with two strikes and two balls on him, had hit that ninth inning homer, the camera switched to a close-up of Angels relief pitcher Donnie Moore. I have never seen such visible anguish. Moore is a veteran, a man who gives the appearance of being quiet, proud, and possessed of a great deal of hard-earned skill. There was in his face at that moment the sign of a crushed spirit. I wondered how Donnie Moore could ever make himself pitch to another batter.

Getting my novel rejected was not at all similar to what I imagine was Donnie Moore's experience of pitching a ninth-inning, game-winning home-run ball to Dave Henderson. My publisher, David Godine, gave me the bad news in straightforward fashion as he and

7

I drove home from a day's fishing on the Lamoille River in Vermont. Godine had sat on the manuscript for eight months, time enough for me to imagine many and various scenarios of his discussing the book with me. The rosiest of these fantasies had him writing me a check on the spot for a six-figure advance; the bleakest had me committing suicide right in front of him upon hearing that he didn't want to publish the book.

In actual fact, the news was much worse than I expected—not only did Godine not want to publish the novel himself, he also thought it would be a dreadful mistake for me to let anyone publish the novel—but my feelings were not even vaguely suicidal. I think I'd known for a long while that my novel was weak. Consciously I'd hoped that an editor might be able to give me suggestions so that I could revise it to make it a good novel. Unconsciously I think I wanted somebody to tell me to put the thing away. In this regard Godine obliged my deepest desires. Earlier in the day he'd also caught more fish than I had.

I figure I worked on the novel for an average of about three hours a day for 10 months—let's say I had about 900 hours of writing time invested in that 307-page manuscript. That's not counting the time I spent thinking about it while I walked around or lapsed into a reverie over it while driving to the grocery store or solved some difficult problem in it with my subconscious mind while I slept.

As novels go, mine was written pretty efficiently. Ten years is not an outrageous amount of time for a writer to work on a book— Hannah Green, my old teacher at Columbia, gave that much of her life (say, conservatively, about 11,000 writing hours) to *The Dead of the House*, and Ralph Ellison apparently has been working on his second novel for more than twenty years. But Ann Beattie is said to have done one of her novels in about a month, and one can imagine Isaac Asimov starting a book on Monday and mailing the finished manuscript to his publisher the following Monday.

In my adult life I've written something in the neighborhood of forty or fifty short stories, of which I've published maybe twenty-five. There are only a few stories I still have on hand—ones that haven't found a home—that I can remember with any clarity. Usually when they aren't much good, I recognize that after they've gathered a couple of rejections, and I either revise them or put them away.

But this is the first novel I've ever written, and my immediate plan for it is to put it away. My theory about these matters is that if there's anything worthwhile in that manuscript, it will stick in my mind enough to send me back to the novel in a year or two. If there isn't anything worthwhile there, then I'll forget all about it and let the manuscript gather dust.

In consigning this manuscript to a desk drawer, I am comforted by the behavior of baseball players. There are *no* pitchers who do not give up home runs, there are *no* batters who do not strike out. There are *no* major league pitchers or batters who have not somehow learned to survive giving up home runs and striking out. That much is obvious.

What seems to me less obvious is how these "failures" must be digested, or put to use, in the overall experience of the player. A jogger once explained to me that the nerves of the ankle are so sensitive and complex that each time a runner sets his foot down, hundreds of messages are conveyed to the runner's brain about the nature of the terrain and the requirements for weight distribution, balance, and muscle-strength. I'm certain that that ninth-inning home run that Dave Henderson hit off Donnie Moore registered complexly and permanently in Moore's mind and body. The next time Moore faced Henderson or faced a similar circumstance, his pitching was informed by his awful experience of October 1986. Moore's continuing baseball career depended to some extent on his converting that encounter with Henderson into something useful for his pitching. I can also imagine such an experience destroying an athlete, registering in his mind and body in such a negative way as to produce a debilitating fear.

There are a few examples of writers who for one reason or another were stopped in their work. The Fugitive poet and critic John Crowe Ransom stopped writing original verse in his mid-thirties, though he tinkered with his old poems, making little changes here and there, for the rest of his life. After the publication of *Gone With the Wind*, Margaret Mitchell devoted her writing energy to answering her fan mail. A few years ago a young man named John Kennedy Toole drove to Milledgeville, Georgia, to commit suicide after his novel had been turned down a number of times; that book, *A Confederacy of Dunces*, was posthumously published to considerable acclaim. And will somebody please tell me what has happened to Harper Lee, author of nothing since her wonderful *To Kill a Mockingbird*?

However sturdy the human body may be, it is also immensely delicate. Any little malfunction—say, for example, one ever-so-slightly damaged nerve in an ankle—can cause the apparatus to break down significantly: The unhittable 95 m.p.h. fastball can become the immensely hittable 83 m.p.h. not-so-fastball. For an athlete to perform well, he must be able to extend himself out into a territory in which he is immensely vulnerable.

One of the many ways in which athletes and artists are similar is that, unlike accountants or plumbers or insurance salesmen, they must perform at an extraordinary level of excellence if they are to achieve even a small success. They must also be willing to extend themselves irrationally in order to achieve that level of performance. A writer doesn't have to write all-out all the time, but he or she must be ready to write all-out any time the story requires it. Hold back and you produce what just about any literate citizen can produce, a "pretty good" piece of work. Like the cautious pitcher, the timid writer can spend a lifetime in the minor leagues.

And what more than failure—the strike out, the crucial home run given up, the manuscript criticized and rejected—is more likely to produce caution or timidity? An instinctive response to painful experience is to avoid the behavior that produced the pain. To function at the level of excellence required for survival, writers like athletes must go against instinct, must absorb their failures and become stronger, must endlessly repeat the behavior that produced the pain.

It's not merely a matter of putting the failed work behind you and going on; what you must do is convert the energy of a failed past work into usable energy for present and future work. Consider the hypothetical case of Donnie Moore having to pitch to Dave Henderson again in a crucial situation: Instead of simply putting the 1986 experience behind him, Moore, according to my theory, could convert his memory of the 1986 home run into pitching brilliantly to Henderson. Not only would Moore have "learned from his experience," he would also have been charged with the energy of it.

Easy to say: Put failure to use. How does one do it? One notion I can offer has to do with what I'll call "esthetic luck"—a sibling of "athletic luck."

Esthetic luck is random and two-headed. No writer, no matter how accomplished, can be certain when sitting down to work that the results of extreme effort will be writing of high quality. One can school oneself in the literature of one's tradition, train oneself to a high level of technical skill, construct ideal working circumstances of time and place, regularly come to the writing desk rested, alert, and in good health, achieve a state of brutal self-honesty, open one's mind to every possibility of concept and language, and nevertheless write one lousy line after another. Conversely (and perversely) one may pick up a napkin in a bar to make a few notes and suddenly find oneself writing fabulous stuff. The odds of writing well are a great deal better if the writer is well prepared, but there's never a guarantee of good writing.

If production is the first of the two heads of esthetic luck, then the second is reception: Even if one has the good fortune to complete a fine piece of writing, there's a good chance it will go unrecognized by anyone else. Fine poems and stories and novels are rejected all the time. The story goes that *Catcher in the Rye* was turned down by twenty publishing houses before it found a taker. A much-admired poet acquaintance of mine says that while the best journals accept some of her work, they usually reject what she knows to be the best poems in any sheaf she submits to them. My opinion is that fine work can always find someone to recognize its value, but some looking is usually required. A strong manuscript may have to be sent to fifty editors before it reaches the one who recognizes its value. But it takes a pretty tough-skinned writer to send a work out again after the forty-ninth rejection.

There's a story that someone once asked the poet Richard Wilbur how he dealt with rejection slips and he confessed that he didn't know because he'd never received one. This seems to me such a necessary anecdote that if it didn't already exist we'd have to invent it. If esthetic luck is truly random—meaning that no matter what we do we can't assure ourselves we'll write well and that even if we write well we can't count on anyone's recognizing our achievement—it stands to reason that somebody somewhere would have to harvest nothing but good fortune.

What I think is valuable about understanding the crazy nature of esthetic luck is that it can be just as encouraging as it is discouraging. Understanding esthetic luck is the key to serenity for a writer. Let's say you wrote badly this morning, and the mail brought you a rejection slip for a sheaf of poems and an insulting note paper-clipped to a returned short story and another note from an editorial assistant at a publishing house explaining that somehow the manuscript of your novel has been misplaced, they're sorry they've taken a year to let you know this, but that the editor you sent it to in the first place has been fired, and so there's no need, really, to send them another copy. Lots of sensible people would take such a morning as a clear sign that there are better ways to spend one's time than in trying to write well. But our ideally serene writer will read the same evidence to make the opposite case: If your luck is bad today, the odds are improved that you'll get good luck tomorrow.

Esthetic luck is the major argument in favor of working through a process of revising a piece of writing through many drafts. If you're a supremely talented artist and you hit a very lucky day, then maybe you can write a poem or story or chapter of a novel that needs no revision. If you're a regular writer with your appointed portion of esthetic luck, you'll need to come at the piece again and again. I like to think of revision as a form of self-forgiveness: you can allow yourself mistakes and shortcomings in your writing because you know you're coming back later to improve it. Revision is the way you cope with the bad luck that made your writing less than excellent this morning. Revision is the hope you hold out for yourself to make something beautiful tomorrow though you didn't quite manage it today. Revision is democracy's literary method, the tool that allows an ordinary person to aspire to extraordinary achievement.

Revision of course is not an option for athletes. In my opinion, baseball players would be able to offer more testimony to the capriciousness of athletic luck than the players of any other game. My most outrageous notion on this matter is that the crazy luck of baseball accounts for the significance of its players' spitting: To spit is to change one's chemistry, to cast out the immediate past, to set oneself to face the future. In their thinking, batters and pitchers must proceed in a logical manner: They consider the scouting reports and the opinions of their coaches and fellow players; they consider "the last time up," along with the history they have shared in all their previous encounters; they make adjustments; they spit for luck.

In the overall balance of esthetic luck, by my calculations, the bad outweighs the good by a ratio of about 17 to 1, but the good nevertheless exists. Somebody who worked hard for years with little visible success suddenly gets a contract and publishes a fine book that is well-reviewed and that almost makes it to *The New York*

Times bestseller list; this somebody wins prizes and fellowships, receives invitations to lecture. For every version of this happy story, there are seventeen hard-working literary citizens who have given a considerable portion of their lives to the practice of their art, every one of them with artistic gifts in various stages of development. All seventeen have had the experience of writing well on a regular basis; not one of them has had much success at publishing.

Something at issue here is a peculiarly American misconception about talent, that either you have it or you don't—if you have it, performance is an effortless matter for you, and if you don't have it, you're hopeless. One of the most destructive archetypes of the American consciousness is "The Natural," the person who can do something perfectly without even trying; a sibling of "The Natural" is "The Discovery," a person who finds out he or she has this perfect ability or who is discovered by an expert to have it. From experience, I can tell you that the most common motivating factor for people attending the Bread Loaf Writers' Conference is to find out whether or not they "have what it takes."

What the great American game of baseball seems to me to demonstrate most obviously is that those who "have what it takes" must nevertheless work hard at their craft all the time and that many who might have been judged not to "have what it takes," through hard work at their craft, can also perform well. Recent years of World Series and league championship games have shown us great hitters and pitchers hitting and pitching badly while players we've never heard of perform beautifully. What veteran baseball players and writers know is that constantly working hard will produce a respectable batting or earned run average, a stack of pages of substantial literary value, an acceptance from a good journal.

I am not describing a method of achieving happiness. I am describing a necessary and healthy way for a few people to carry out their lives; happiness has nothing to do with it. What seems to me the only legitimate goal of any would-be writer is to achieve a circumstance of ongoing work, the serenity to carry out the daily writing and revising of what poems, stories, or novels are given you to write. On those occasions when your serenity seems about to collapse, I recommend that you step out into your back yard and vigorously spit.

FIRST EPILOGUE

In September, 1987, I returned to my novel manuscript to attempt a revision. About halfway through reviewing the manuscript, I realized that it was indeed a novel I didn't want to work on any more and didn't want ever to publish. I put it away permanently.

SECOND EPILOGUE

After "Let's Say You Wrote Badly This Morning" appeared in the January 31, 1988, issue of *The New York Times Book Review*, I found the letters of response I received to be uncommonly moving and illuminating. Relevant excerpts from these letters are as follows:

I wonder if you know Branch Rickey's famous comment: "Luck is the residue of design."

I have always felt that the greatest baseball players (i.e. Willie Mays) are those who are able to give themselves over most fully to the game in the present moment. It may be called "instinct," or it may be called artistic absorption (i.e. Willie Mays in centerfield or at the plate or on the base paths).

—David Moats
Rutland, Vermont

Let me offer you a quote by Phil Niekro. During Niekro's first season with the Yankees, a *Times* reporter asked him the key to baseball longevity. Niekro mentioned, of course, his knuckleball, but he also said that his attitude played a major role in providing himself with such a long career. "I try to accept my losses without being defeated," Niekro said.

—Jim Tackach
Bristol, Rhode Island

I think I will go outside and spit
Until I get the hang of it;
Then I will write far into the night
Until I get the damned thing right
And if I do not get the hang of it
I'll just go outside and take another spit!

—Sarge Sterling
Philadelphia, Pennsylvania

As a baseball fan and the author of a novel that has recently been rejected by nearly as many houses as 'Catcher in the Rye,' and as the son of a novelist who has been working on his third novel for the past 28 years, let me say . . . after all is said and done, I think spitting in the backyard might be the ultimate solution.

—Thomas Sancton
New York, New York

Your terms "esthetic luck" and "athletic luck" should be expanded to include "scientific luck." My mentor, Fritz Lipmann (Nobelist, 1953), asked me a penetrating question before accepting me as a graduate student in his laboratories at Rockefeller University—"How lucky are you?" My answer is obvious by the fact that I spent a decade with Lipmann.

At a recent memorial symposium for Fritz in Berlin the issue of "luck" surfaced again and again. Werner Maas of NYU medical center recalled an outing with Freda and Fritz Lipmann in the Adirondacks the weekend in October before Lipmann received the call from Stockholm. Fritz disappeared into a field of clover as Werner and Freda impatiently hiked on. He caught up with them thirty minutes later with a four leaf clover in hand and talked excitedly about how lucky he always was in the lab and the field!

—Peter Pennett
Gainesville, Florida

I went into my 9 a.m. freshman comp class and had all my students vigorously spit. It was messy, but it did change the chemistry of the class.

—Cathryn Amdahl
Pullman, Washington

And also baseball bears witness to the small *victories* that go unmarked, in life or in writing. The way Henderson danced around the bases—that's the way I feel when words work, when a line in a poem seems just right. Whether or not I will have the "esthetic luck" to share the words with a larger audience, the elation of that particular moment goes unmarked and unshared—unlike baseball, where we can all witness Henderson's glee.

—Wendy Mnookin
Chestnut Hill, Massachusetts

. . . so far as I'm concerned the only similiarity between writers and athletes is that they both scratch their privates in public.

—Fred Bruning
Long Island, New York

Your article appeared two days after I received a most damning review of what I felt to be an excellent research proposal (I am a chemist). I have been silently slinking through the hallway between my office and lab, fearful that a colleague may stop me and ask what my score was.

. . . I must not, as I was tempted to do, ignore the damning review letter. I must continue to write proposals, and they must be clearly and well written. The critique I received must fuel the fires of my efforts. And each morning, before I begin, I shall go out to the loading dock of our lab facility for a good spit.

—Clare Biswas
Beltsville, Maryland

I remember the look on Moore's face, too. Somebody just knocked off my new manuscript of poems this very morning. I just stepped outside the office and harked up a might gob. You are right! It works. Onward!

—Paul Zimmer
Iowa City, Iowa

I erred, though, following your advice a couple of evenings later. It was −25, the drifts were high, my aim was off, and the spittle damn near broke my toe!

—Lee Richardson-Ross
Concord, Vermont

On Thursday of this week I received a rejection slip from *The Atlantic* for the first short story I have ever sent out. It has taken me four years to feel I was ready to send one and it took them three months to decide they didn't like it . . . .

I now think I will purchase a bucket for every room in my house, labeled SPIT.

—Judy Darke Delogu
Portland, Maine

I am a cardiologist. I [have] take[n] care of desperately ill, fragile patients all my working life. I have patients die every week, and sometimes several; and this is quite typical for cardiologists. And let me agree with you, ". . . what seems to me less obvious is how these 'failures' must be digested . . ." I don't know how I go on, or how anyone "takes the hit," as we say in medicine; how someone can literally walk away from a cooling body in one room and be 100% ready to give one's best when one walks into the next room. Something complex registers on the mind and body of Donnie Moore when his pitch is swatted into the bleachers; and something complex gets registered on our minds when we attend the post-mortem examinations of those of our cases which end unfavorably. Yet we go on; and I am quite a cheerful and vigorous physician.

If a ballplayer consistently hit .400, he'd be in Cooperstown. If I hit .400, I'd be in prison.

—Name Withheld

Warren [Spahn] told me the following story: the once-Boston Braves wound up spring training one year by playing a game, in Boston, against the Red Sox. Spahn faced Ted Williams once and struck him out with a letter high fast ball over the outside corner. Afterward, Williams and Spahn chatted and Ted remarked, as they parted, "By the way, that fast ball you got me on was a great pitch."

Several years later, Spahn faced Williams again, this time in a clutch situation with men on base, late in the All Star game. Warren told me he did not consciously remember Williams' earlier comments, but Warren's subconscious knew just which pitch to throw, and he threw it. As Williams trotted around the bases after he belted the game-winning home run, he was grinning at Spahn; puzzled at first, the light bulb lit up, and Warren yelled, "You Son-of-a-Bitch, you set me up!" Williams laughingly acknowledged it.

—Harvey J. Blumenthal
Tulsa, Oklahoma

THIRD EPILOGUE

From page B-12 of *The New York Times* of July 20, 1989: "A Ball Player's Life Turns on a Home Run," by Michael Levy:

It was one pitch in one game during the course of a successful 13-year professional baseball career. But some of Donnie Moore's friends and teammates say that ever since he threw that pitch, giving up a home run that cost the California Angels an important playoff game in 1986, Moore had been on a downward spiral.

According to those interviewed, the spiral was forged by a complicated mixture of marital problems, financial strains, and the inevitable decline in athletic ability that comes with age. Moore was 35 years old and had been released by a minor league baseball team when, on Tuesday afternoon, he argued with his wife in the kitchen of their suburban Anaheim home, pulled a pistol, shot her three times and then killed himself.

"I think insanity set in," said Dave Pinter, Moore's longtime agent. "He could not live with himself after Henderson hit the home run. He kept blaming himself."

The Writing Habit

T H E M A J O R difficulty a writer must face has nothing to do with language: it is finding or making the circumstances that make writing possible. The first project for a writer is that of constructing a writing life.

Achievement in writing requires many hours and many pages of concentrated effort. That work must be carried out in a sustained fashion: A writer must be able to carry what has been learned from one day's writing into the next, from one week's writing into the next, and so on. Significant accomplishment in writing depends on growth. A writer's development depends on being able to write regularly and without distraction.

The actual details of writing lives differ with the personalities of individual writers. I remember a lecture given by the novelist Don Bredes, a very down-to-earth man, in which he set forth what he thought were the requirements of a writing circumstance. Shelves, he said, were necessary, in order to set out one's manuscripts, supplies, and reference materials. A phone immediately at hand was necessary so that one would not be ripped away from one's desk when the phone rang in another part of the house. A window with a view was necessary, but I don't remember if Don thought one's desk should face toward the window or away from it. And a plant, preferably a cactus, was necessary. I haven't remembered why Don thought one needed a plant—probably something to do with the benign influence of a low-profile living presence.

In her memoir of her father, Susan Cheever describes the young John Cheever putting on a suit and tie each morning, riding the elevator down to a basement storage room of their Manhattan apartment building, taking off his trousers and hanging them up with his coat to prevent wrinkling, and in his boxer shorts sitting down to his writing desk for his day's work. The established Cheever claimed to have written each of his later books in a different room of his Ossining, New York, home.

Eleanor Ross Taylor has written an intriguing description of the poet Randall Jarrell, apparently a very sociable man, keeping a writing pad and pen with him in his home, and writing intermittently all through his day, while entertaining visitors and tending to domestic duties.

I have had various writing circumstances, some of them refined to a state of high peculiarity. The most productive of them came together in the winter of 1978 when I lived alone in a cottage beside a small lake. I rose at sun-up, did fifteen minutes of calisthenics, showered, made coffee and ate a light breakfast. Then I worked at "fresh" writing, beginning around seven or seven-thirty. I tried not to excuse myself before eleven, though if momentum was with me, it was o.k. to stay later. My output for those hours was three to six pages of fresh prose each morning. I composed on a portable electric typewriter, the humming of which always seemed to me like very good company. I used canary yellow "second sheets" for that first draft material. My desk faced a large window that overlooked a woodsy hillside where I had set out bird food. For some reason I took to lighting a large "patio lantern" candle when I sat down to work and to blowing it out when I felt I had finished for the morning.

Those months of living beside Lake St. Clair were the one period of my life when I have been a runner, or more accurately a jogger. My run was my reward for having worked through my morning hours. Just as I had had to work up to my three or four hours of fresh writing a day, I had gradually to increase my running distance. The road around Lake St. Clair is a very hilly 2.3 miles long. When I began running in early February, I could trot only about a quarter of the way around it without stopping to walk—and I would always walk the rest of the way around, often picking up my pace again after I'd caught my breath. When I left Lake St. Clair in mid-May I was jogging (vigorously) around it twice without stopping. On the run I occasionally saw a pileated woodpecker, a blue heron, wild turkeys, and various other birds.

When I returned from jogging, I did some stretching, took a shower, and fixed myself a light lunch. For the first time in the day, I listened to the radio; I neither read, nor was I tempted to read, any newspapers during my lakeside tenure. After washing my lunch and breakfast dishes, I was in my "free period." I could do whatever I wanted. Whatever I wanted was almost always to read for a while and then to take a nap.

A few words here about naps: I'm convinced that naps are an essential part of a writing life, that they "clean" the brain by discharging the clutter and allowing the subconscious to address some of the central issues of the morning's writing. If I know I want to do some more writing in the afternoon, I'll always try to schedule that session immediately after a nap. It's rare for me to try to accomplish fresh writing in the afternoon, but I often try to carry out revisions if I have at least an hour or more of afternoon time available to me.

When I woke from a nap at Lake St. Clair, I had the delicious sensation of having nothing pressing to do and not having to hurry with whatever I chose to do. Most often I simply lay in bed, letting my mind wander as it would. Because I had minimum distraction there, whatever I was writing was what I thought about most of the time. It wasn't long after I awaked from my nap that I would turn to my manuscript; usually I'd be curious about the pages I'd written that morning and want to check them out. Of course, as I read, I reached for a pen to make corrections, changes, notes, and it wasn't uncommon for me to find myself again sitting before the typewriter, relighting my candle, retyping the morning's pages, perhaps even proceeding into a page of "fresh writing" without consciously deciding to do so. These afternoon writing sessions usually lasted only an hour or two, but I always considered them a bonus. Because my writing days became so productive, I felt more and more virtuous while I lived at Lake St. Clair.

At the end of an afternoon work session, I rewarded myself with a walk around the lake. I made myself walk slowly and try to observe my surroundings as carefully as I could. The world itself seemed especially charged with energy; it became an intense presence in my life. I was primarily interested in birds—I'd bought a field guide and begun keeping a list of the birds I saw—but I also became a student of the landscape, the variety and quality of light in different weathers and at different times of day. I suspect that the attention I paid to the world of my 2.3-mile walks around Lake St. Clair was of benefit to me in my writing. The fiction I wrote during those months seems to me informed by the world's presence and to articulate an intense connection between my characters and the world around them.

In the evenings I listened to the radio—jazz or classical music. Sometimes I worked on my writing. Evening work sessions were rare and likely to come about only if I was trying to complete a finished draft of a story and what had to be done was merely typing clean copy. Mostly I read, because reading had become unusually exciting to me: I felt as if I were reading on two levels, for the usual pleasure of poetry and narrative and also for my writerly education. In the works of other authors, I was able to observe technical achievement that I thought would be of eventual use in my own work.

I got sleepy early. It was rare that I didn't turn out my bedside light by ten or ten thirty. I went to sleep thinking about the writing I'd accomplished and about the work I meant to do the next morning. The telephone did ring now and then, and I had visitors, visitors I wanted and ones I didn't want. But what I had most of the time at Lake St. Clair was solitude, which instructed me: the more of it I had, the more I learned to make use of it. When a writing life is in good order, as mine was then, everything is relevant to it; every detail of one's day has a connection to one's writing.

I have been a resident of artists' colonies at Yaddo and the Virginia Center for the Creative Arts; on some occasions I have been able to work better at those places than at home, but in my best colony experience I've been only about fifty percent as productive as I was at Lake St. Clair. The obvious difference is that colonies have a social life that I felt I had to attend; I was guaranteed solitude during the day, but in the evenings I ate with the other colonists, I chatted after dinner, I made friends, and so on. This social life can be a healthy influence in a writing life, especially if two writers begin exchanging manuscripts and criticism. Along with valuable friendship, a writer can also find inspiration and illumination from visual artists and composers. But finally a social life is a distraction. Instead of having the evening hours to compose yourself, to let your mind wander back to the writing, you become involved with others. In the morning, when there should be no obstacles between self and work, you find you're reviewing last night's conversation.

Lake St. Clair was a temporary situation for me brought about by the luckily converging circumstances of a sabbatical leave from teaching at the University of Vermont, an NEA Fellowship that paid the bills for it, and a wife who for those months was willing to look after herself and our daughter. I have often wondered how different things would have been if I had thought of it as my permanent circumstance. Would all that solitude have seemed so luxurious then, or would it have seemed a punishment, a burden, an entrapment? Would I have found my work so fulfilling if I had believed it must take the place of my family? I don't think my writing would be helped by being permanently without the company of family and friends. Most likely I was able to put my solitude to such excellent use because I knew there would be an end to it.

When I left the lake, I had come to think of myself as a kind of esthetic saint. I had lost weight. I was in excellent physical condition. I had stripped my life down to what was essential to me. I had accomplished a greater quantity and a higher quality of writing than I ever had before. I had established a meaningful connection between myself and the natural world. I felt this exhilarating rightness to my life. I felt certain that I would be able to transport the habits I had formed into my "regular life," which now (from my saintly viewpoint) seemed cluttered, distracting, piggish, physically and esthetically unhealthy.

The disintegration took about a week. If I did my early morning calisthenics anywhere in the house, I made such a clatter that I woke my wife and daughter. My wife had to go to work and my daughter had to go to day-care; their preparations necessarily disturbed my concentration on my work. Near my house there was nowhere to run or walk without encountering traffic and carbon monoxide. In the house, everywhere I looked, there were little chores that needed doing, dishes to be washed, toys to be picked up, stacks of magazines to straighten, bills to pay, a screen with a hole in it, a borrowed book that needed to be returned. The phone rang more often now that I was back in my own community. I played tennis, I met a friend for lunch, I attended a surprise birthday party. I snacked between meals. I watched TV. In short, I drifted away from my writing life. My Lake St. Clair habits were not transportable.

Before and after my tenure at Lake St. Clair, I was a sporadic writer—if I had something I was working on, I worked at it until I finished it; then I didn't write again until something else pressed me urgently enough to begin it and pursue it. For periods of as long as a year, I wrote nothing. I had a rationale worked out about being a sporadic writer: I wasn't a factory, and it was only because of a national assembly-line mentality that American writers felt obligated to churn out books. Who needed another piece of writing anyway? If I wasn't writing, it probably meant I had nothing worthwhile to say. And so on. But my Lake St. Clair experience demonstrated to me what it felt like to have a real writing life, to have something that held my attention over a period of time, to have ongoing, deeply fulfilling work. I have never been able to duplicate that experience, but because I had it that once, it gave me something to aspire to again. I've gotten better and better at constructing a writing life for myself in the midst of my "regular life." I don't have any remarkable secrets about it, but I do have what I think are a few useful concepts.

To write well one must use one's "good hours" for one's writing. My good hours are the first three or four of my day. If I want to use them for my writing, that means I have to get up early and start writing before other demands are made on me. A few people I know have their good hours late at night, and that's when they should be writing. A poet I know warms up slowly; she finds her good hours to begin around mid or late morning.

Since I teach school for a living and since much of the work of my teaching involves reading and responding to student manuscripts, I find that I have to use my "next-best hours" (late morning or afternoons) for that work. But responding to student manuscripts is almost always in direct competition with my own writing for my good hours; I have to be clever to manage a heavy teaching load with a productive writing schedule. On a day when I teach my first class at 9:25 and I have a dozen student stories to respond to, I'll need to get up at 4:00, be at the writing desk by 4:45, work on my own writing until 6:00, write my responses until 8:30, and get to my office by 9:15.

Along with using my good hours for my writing, I've learned more about how to use my less-good hours for clearing the way for efficient use of my writing time. I'm a house-husband, which means that I have cooking, laundry, cleaning, and child-care duties to attend to, and like most writers I am very distractable; house-husbanding can devour my good writing hours if I let it. But nowadays my motto is that everything has to get done sometime, and the trick is to make sure that my writing always comes first. Taking a break from my writing, I can wash the dishes because doing that little task is just distracting enough to give me a new "take" on whatever it is I'm working on. Putting away laundry can often be a very useful fifteen-minute writing break. I can pay my bills while my printer is typing up a manuscript. What I understand better and better is how to clear the way to my good hours with my writing. Before I go to bed I try to have my little computer, with its battery charged, waiting for me, preferably with the document I'm working on ready to come up on the screen when I switch it on. I want my reading glasses right where I can find them, my coffee thermos clean, and the room straightened up. If I have bills to pay or letters that need to be answered, I want them neatly stashed where they won't catch my eye first thing when I sit down to write.

Robert Hass's poem "Measure" uses the phrase "the peace of the writing desk." These words accurately describe my own experience. My writing time is when I set my life in order. I examine my life through the act of writing. Although I try to sell most of my writing, my first desire for it is that it be as truthful and beautiful as I can make it out of what I know and think and feel. Therefore writing is to me a kind of meditation. It isn't a purely spiritual activity, but it is one in which my spirit is nourished. Writing has become so essential for my daily life that I feel denied if I miss a day of "the peace of the writing desk."

When I tell people that I get up at 4:30 or 5:00 to do my writing, they often praise my discipline, but now that my writing life has been established, discipline has nothing to do with it. Getting up to do my writing requires no more discipline than sitting down to eat a meal or going to bed at night to get some sleep. It's natural and necessary.

Flux has never been an easy principle for me to understand or to incorporate into my life. My make-up is conservative. My instinctive way of doing things is to try to get them just right and then to keep them that way. Some nasty lessons have taught me that I had better give flux its due. Thus it was silly of me to try to import my Lake St. Clair writing habits into the life I lived in my home with my family. Instead of becoming frustrated because I couldn't repeat my successful methods, a more intelligent course of action would have been to try to discover the different writing habits that would work in that different situation.

Cheever needed different rooms of his house because at different times of his life, he was a different writer and was writing different books. Learning to understand and monitor one's own writerly needs is the main project of a writer's education. Beginning writers almost always feel that they have to learn the secrets that all successful writers have mastered. They think they need to take possession of something outside themselves. Writing teachers are often frustrated because they can't make students see how they're looking away from the place where the real secrets are located. The elements of a writer's making are within the individual, and they are different with each individual. Each writer makes his own habit.

I write well at 5:30 a.m. sitting in an easy chair with a portable computer in my lap, a coffee thermos and a cup by my chair, and Glenn Gould playing Bach's "Well-Tempered Klavier" on the stereo. Across town, a little later, Alan Broughton will be sitting at his desk in his study using a pencil and a legal pad for his first draft, which he will later in the day type into his word processor because he can't read his handwriting if he lets it sit untranslated" more than a few hours. And even later, between classes, in his office at St. Michael's College, John Engels will be furiously annotating the manuscript of a poem he printed out yesterday. He will completely dismantle and reassemble his poem in the minutes available to him between conversations with students and colleagues who drop by to see him.

The options are various. If you're a would-be writer, what you need to find out is not how someone else works but how you are inclined to work. You have to determine your good hours, the writing tools and the writing environment that best suit you, the limitations you can overcome, and the best methods for dealing with the limitations you can't overcome.

You also have to become aware of your inclinations toward laziness, dishonesty, glibness, and other personal foibles. You have to become skillful at outwitting those negative aspects of your character. For instance, I know I am inclined to send manuscripts out before they're really ready to be submitted any place—before they're finished. I haven't been able to correct this failure, but I've gotten so I can delay my sending out a manuscript by giving copies of it to certain friends of mine to read and respond to it before I make up a "final copy." The more friends who give me responses to a manuscript, the more drafts I'll run it through. The help of peers is essential to most of the writers I know. To discuss our work, I meet with two other writers about every three weeks; we try to bring fresh writing or significant revisions to our meetings. We try to be very tough-minded in our responses to each other's work. Not only are these other two writers helpful to me as critics; they also inspire me to work regularly in hopes of producing something they will appreciate.

Like most writers, I'm a highly skilled procrastinator. I've had to develop the appropriate counter-skills. One of my more successful counter-procrastinating techniques is the bend-and-snap-back move: I'll tell myself yes, I really do need a break right now, but the only way I can justify it is by using it to accomplish some little task that might distract me from writing tomorrow morning.

These maneuvers of self against self for the good of getting my work done are not unlike similar moves I've learned for improving the writing itself. For instance, I have come to understand that I am weak when it comes to portraying female characters as whole human beings. My natural, porcine inclination is toward second-rate versions of characters like Hemingway's Maria, Faulkner's Eula Varner Snopes, Nabokov's Lolita, and Terry Southern's Candy. My more responsible writing self must always be questioning and arguing with this lesser Huddle. The tension is a healthy one for my writing; my female characters get so much of both the porcine and the responsible varieties of my attention, that in a few instances I've been able to create portraits of women who have both sexual force and emotional-intellectual complexity. And I count myself lucky that I'm able to write across gender even as well as I have been able to do so far.

Managing contraries within the self is an ability that must be cultivated by a writer, both in and out of the work. Your natural inclinations are often less than admirable, but rather than trying to eliminate them from your personality, you can learn how to change them into positive elements of your writing. Thus you can convert your inclination toward distraction and procrastination into habits that will clear the way toward using your good hours for concentrated writing. Thus you can transform your inclination toward fantasizing about wish-fulfilling female characters into the creation of appealingly whole human beings. Such alchemy is still possible in a well-constructed writing life.

Once you understand that your negative qualities can be put to use both inside and outside your writing, you can begin to be kind to yourself. No longer necessary are those lectures, "You lazy such and such, you took a nap when you should have been writing, you can't write about women, you sent out that story too soon, you..." Instead of flailing away like that, you can become crafty, learn how to use your whole self in your writing.

Hemingway had a rule that has been especially useful for my work. He thought you ought to stop writing for the day at a point where you knew what you were going to do next. I like that notion just as it stands—often at the end of my morning's writing session, I will make a few notes about what I think ought to come next. I also think a writer needs to stop work with a little bit of energy left. I feel good when I've written enough to be tired, but if I've written myself into a state of exhaustion, I don't feel so eager to get back to work the next day.

Hemingway's quitting-time axiom is one version of what seems to me a basic principle of the writing life: You must nourish the "on-goingness" of your work. Sometimes I convince myself that what is crucial is to finish this piece or that piece of writing, that the only thing that matters is to get this manuscript in the mail. But a real writing life is nothing so desperate as all that, not something you do merely for a day or a month or a year. Stories, poems, essays, and books are the by-product of a writing life; they are to be cherished, but they separate themselves from their creators and become the property of editors, reviewers, and readers. For a writer, the one truly valuable possession is the ongoing work—the writing habit, which may take some getting used to, but which soon becomes so natural as to be almost invisible.

What You Get for Good Writing

If you can only learn to write badly enough, you can make an awful lot of money.
—FLANNERY O'CONNOR
Mystery and Manners

G O O D   W R I T I N G is a calling. Whoever answers it should not do so naively. One of my first "mature" stories, "Poison Oak," went through around 25 drafts to reach its final draft of 28 pages. I composed it on a typewriter; so I typed approximately 700 pages of words to produce the story—at about fifteen minutes a page, or some 175 hours of typing labor. Back then, the going rate for typing was a dollar a page. So if I'd typed all those pages for somebody else, I'd have made $700. Or if I'd typed only the 28 pages of the final draft of the manuscript for somebody else, I'd have made $28. *The New England Review* paid me $25 for "Poison Oak." For all the writing I've published and that I count as "my own work"—eight books counting those forthcoming in 1992, forty stories, a couple hundred poems, and maybe a dozen essays—my pay probably works out to a little more than a dollar an hour. In spite of, or maybe even because of, the lousy pay, I've turned out to be a better writer than I first envisioned myself becoming. A commercial hack is what I first aspired to be.

My quick definition of an artist—someone whose primary aim is to produce original work of the highest quality—suggests high-mindedness, nobility, integrity by choice. But my experience has demonstrated to me that it's much more a matter of inclination than choice. When I encounter unlikely people who happen to be artists, I have to remind myself of what I know quite intimately, that the inclination toward artistry is common, human, and random. It's mostly a matter of dissatisfaction—of feeling vaguely askew with the universe and wanting to construct something—some magical object or talisman—that we hope will correct our cosmic alignment. Then it's a matter of being unable to leave that constructed something alone until we have pestered it into being exactly the way we want it to be. Choosing to be an artist won't help you become one if you're not inclined that way. Choosing not to be an artist may not save you from becoming one if you are inclined that way.

Around the age of nineteen, I was enormously impressed by Herman Wouk's *Youngblood Hawke*, a popular novel based loosely and sensationally on the life of Thomas Wolfe. That book was what set me thinking about trying to become a writer. My education since then has taught me to perceive the inaccuracies in its portrayal of the life of a writer, along with its esthetic failures; even so, I remember *Youngblood Hawke* with a kind of wistful pleasure.

I'd like to write books that lots of people would read and love. If I could write like Stephen King, I'd be sorely tempted to do it; whereas if I could write like Marcel Proust or James Joyce or William Gass or William Gaddis or Guy Davenport, I definitely wouldn't. Given a choice, I expect I'd take the low road.

But blessed or cursed—whichever, it all comes to the same thing— I have no choice but to write like myself.

I write the way I write because that's how the language and I work it out. The act of composition, for me, is a gradual working my way toward a certain way for my writing to be that seems to me *right*. That intuitively determined "certain way"—down to the length and the tone of my sentences, the number of conjunctions I'll allow myself in a given paragraph, and the way I use dashes—is the truth of things, as I am able to locate it in my stories, poems, or essays.

My personal inclination is to fuss with my writing over a period of time, to ask my writer pals to criticize it, to try one thing and another, to cut and add and change and combine and separate and move the parts around this way and that way, to revise the piece of writing many times in an effort to move it closer to that "certain way." To work in this tedious manner has also come to feel right to me. Fussing is the method that suits my abilities; I'm not good at fast thinking or off-the-top-of-my-head composing; I need to write a thing over and over again to be able to understand it and to get it right.

Along with fussing, what I write about—my subject matter—is

also a basic impulse of my personality. Given crayons and paper, my oldest daughter, at around the age of seven, used to draw elaborate bunny palaces. Given the same materials at the same age, my youngest daughter drew rows of ballerinas. Given language, there are certain patterns I am similarly inclined to pursue—for reasons deeply embedded in my brain and body cells.

From 23 years of commitment to the craft of writing, I've refined my methods of pursuing these patterns of my personality through composing narratives. I'm better able to recognize when I'm on the right track, and when a pattern is emerging in a piece of my writing, I've come to know how to use revision to go further with it, to get deeper into it. Once I have completely grasped it, a pattern loses its value to me, except insofar as it leads to the next one. I can't stay where I am and can't go backwards. Whether I want to or not, I have to keep on moving forward. What I call "my own writing" is what I'm producing when I am pursuing those patterns, seeking to write in that "certain way." Training and luck (a part of which is that I've never made a lot of money with my own writing) have allowed me to give this very personal activity a more and more important place in my daily life. Having done lots of other kinds of writing (some of which *has* paid me well), I've come to understand a clear distinction between that work and the kind that offers me a chance to pursue what W. S. Merwin's speaker in "Lemuel's Blessing" calls "what is essential to me." The difference is one of direction: "other writing" is aimed outward; its target is money, explanation, communication, persuasiveness, something other than the realization of those patterns of an author's personality.

When I'm working on "my own writing," though I rarely pay attention to it, I experience a sense of physical "rightness"—very much like eating when I'm hungry, drinking when I'm thirsty, sleeping when I'm tired: My body's signals are that I'm doing exactly what I ought to be doing. All my other activities of choice fail to give me such a sense of rightness, even the ones I enjoy (such as tennis, volleyball, or croquet), the ones I'm thought to be good at (such as teaching or reading aloud), or the ones that the world would judge to be "appropriate" (such as cooking dinner for my family, watering the houseplants, or writing letters to my distant family members and friends).

I'd even go so far as to say that my body gives signals of protest about all my other activities of choice. I can be playing my best tennis ever and become aware of my legs' yearning to carry me back to my room, my desk, my computer. I can be engaged in a spirited classroom debate when suddenly I'll feel this trickle of anxious sweat down my ribcage and hear a faint voice way down in some dark corridor of my brain whispering, "Phony! Show-off! Shit-Merchant!"

The most important aspects of "my own writing" are beyond (or beneath or above) my conscious will. I'm not a zombie—at least I hope I'm not, I suppose you never know—and I think I have a general idea about where I'm going when I begin a piece of writing. In terms of the piece I end up producing, that general idea may be entirely correct or all wrong. But the good stuff of my writing, the part that continues to interest me through the years, is what has come unexpectedly—during the actual act of composition—what my intuition rather than my planning has brought onto the page.

Autobiography may be the most direct approach to one's "own writing," but it does not guarantee realization of any pattern, let alone a deep one; sometimes autobiography is just autobiography, a sequence of facts about a life. Sometimes its author may realize a superficial or an imposed pattern. Sometimes the biggest problem with autobiography is that the author knows too much about the subject, so that the known crowds out the possibility of discovering the unknown.

Discovery is the spark that ignites the essential energy of a work of art. When I sit down to write, I don't have a thing to say, not even the beginning of a message, but I usually have a great deal that I have begun to feel the need to find out. When revelation begins to emerge from a poem or story or essay as I'm working on it, that's when I feel the thing taking on its own life.

What do I mean by "discovery" and "finding out something"? Usually the kind of discovery I make is a connection—or maybe an understanding of the connection—between or among certain elements that present themselves in my writing. "Poison Oak" is as good an example as any: it's a story about a young boy's partial understanding of a hired man's dangerous and harmful sexual obsession with his mother. The main insight I gained from writing that story is suggested in the following passage about the dangerous man's replacement:

I liked [the new hired man] because he was very nice to me, . . . but I was becoming less and less interested in him. The only time he seemed at all dangerous was when he went into the barn to pray . . .

Through writing "Poison Oak," I made a connection between my feelings toward two hired men I vividly remembered from my childhood, one diabolical and the other angelic; in the process of writing about characters based on them, I was able to think about these men and how they informed my personality. Therefore, I learned something—or I came to acknowledge something—about my own attraction to the dangerous, the forbidden, and the harmful.

Here are some basic principles I believe about writing and art:

· Essential to the making of literary art is the artist's pursuit through writing of the deepest patterns of his or her personality.

· The aim of this pursuit for the artist is a written work that embodies significant personal discovery. The artist may pursue those patterns, but if the artist doesn't find out anything in the writing, what he or she produces will lack the crucial energy of art.

· Revision is the refining of a piece of writing to such an extent that the discovered pattern yields an exact revelation. Revision is the artist's struggle to achieve a precise understanding of what has been generally discovered in drafting a piece of writing.

· Usually what the artist finds out is "hard knowledge," something perhaps unattractive or difficult to accept, such as the fact that one is attracted to what is dangerous and harmful.

· The discoveries made through writing are liberating to the artist. If they are "hard knowledge," these discoveries nevertheless grant the artist a permanent unburdening. Thus, personal liberation is the basic incentive for trying to write as well as one can. Through writing—the process itself must produce the discovery—the literary artist seeks to work through the confining forces of his or her life toward freedom.

My subscription to these principles has emerged from my writing life. They weren't the ideas I had in mind when I began my writing life. What I had in mind then was more in the line of *Youngblood Hawke*, both in terms of the kind of book I wanted to write and in terms of the kind of life I thought I wanted to live. I had in mind work that would come easy to me and for which I would receive a good deal of money and adoration. I did not have in mind typing 700 pages to get a 28-page story. I did not have in mind having to come to terms with unpleasant facts about myself. I had in mind quickly becoming a beloved genius. What I have gotten to be over almost a quarter of a century is a more or less respected writer.

I know that I'm lucky to have gotten what I have. I'm acquainted with more gifted people who've worked harder on their writing than I have and haven't gotten anything.

Here are some of the elements of my luck:

· Members of both sides of my family loved books. My parents read aloud to and with my brothers and me. My grandfather was a great story-teller.

· From both sides of my family I have inherited patience, powers of concentration, the inclination to work hard and to try to overcome discouragement.

· For eighth-grade, freshman, junior, and senior English, Mrs. Arraga Young was my teacher. She gave me a superior understanding of syntax.

· As a boy, I had a good deal of training in and experience with music.

· I couldn't really "cut it" as an English major at the University of Virginia. Thus I was fortunate enough to flunk out of Virginia and serve in the U.S. Army as an enlisted man in Germany and Vietnam.

· My readings of Faulkner, Hemingway, James Baldwin, and others were passionately accomplished outside the classroom. Thus I evaded a good deal of the conventional intellectualization of literature that occurs in the academy.

· My early writing teachers at the University of Virginia—John Coleman, James Kraft, and Peter Taylor—encouraged me. Taylor gave me a good look at a man with a writing life and served as a valuable role model of a respected story-writer. When it became evident that I wasn't a Hemingway, a Faulkner, or even a Herman Wouk, I took refuge in what I knew about Peter Taylor's life and his work.

· My wife was willing to work to support me and my efforts to write during the first years of our marriage. For almost twenty-four years she has continued to provide emotional support for my writing even though my writing is not always to her liking.

· My experience in Vietnam gave me something to write about that was of interest to some editors. Thus, my first two story-publications, in *The Georgia Review* in Fall 1969 and in *Esquire* in January 1971, were stories about Vietnam.

· My year of graduate study at Hollins College under the mentor-ship of George Garrett helped me begin thinking of myself as a writer.

· My two years of graduate study at Columbia University helped me to understand literary and publishing politics and to see how I could successfully compete with my aspiring-writer peers.

· My story in *Esquire* was on the newsstands when I interviewed for a teaching job at the MLA meeting in New York in December 1970. Thus I got a good job at the University of Vermont.

· As it turned out, after I got my teaching job (with no teaching ex-perience whatsoever), I did have some ability in the classroom. Thus I have been granted a way of supporting myself other than through what I can make with my writing alone.

Luck has everything to do with an artist's being able to take pos-session of his or her given work. For one thing, an artist needs a number of years to understand in personal terms how the process of making art works and to establish the working habits that will produce works of art. In my own case, flunking out of the University of Virginia and joining the army gave me three extra years of grow-ing up before I had to graduate; then I was granted an additional three years of graduate study in which writing had first claims on my time, energy, and attention. So I got six "free" years seriously to try to realize my dreams of becoming a writer, to discover my artistic inclinations, and to establish the habits that would enable me to be productive. I also had the benefit of advice and counsel from older writers who knew what I needed. Had I proceeded on track and on schedule, I would have taken my B.A. after four or five years, gone to law school or gotten a job, and forever after, I'd have been trying to squeeze out an hour or two to give my writing—or worse and more likely, when things got bad at the office, I'd have simply daydreamed about giving it all up and running away to become a writer.

If you wish to make art, an obvious necessity is that you give first priority to your artistic work—in spirit and in fact. Why is this the case? Because works of art only come out of the artist's wholehearted effort, out of the artist's being able to give the work everything—knowledge, feeling, energy, passion. The artist must be able to give him- or herself to the work again and again, day in and day out. If your family or your job makes first claims on you, you cannot give your whole self to your artistic work, and what you produce is not likely to be satisfactory to you or to others.

Please note that I do not say that the artist must forget or disregard his or her family. The artist builds his or her life on the belief that an hour of writing time is more important than grocery shopping, but in my view it's possible to write for a couple of hours and then do the grocery shopping, possible to try to write well *and* to keep more or less fresh produce in the refrigerator. You may have to pay for these luxuries with sleep or with a lousy social life, but they're nevertheless available.

So what do you get out of such labor and sacrifice? Mostly what you get is the privilege of doing something that makes extreme demands of you, that asks you for everything you've got. If you're lucky enough to be able to give art what it wants, even occasionally, you should bow your head and say thanks. But even though they are little discussed, there are some "social" rewards for good writing.

Aside and apart from matters of employment, I am a person who has chosen to define himself as a writer. If you're more than casually acquainted with me, you have to know that about me. If we're having a conversation, and you don't ask me what I do, I'm likely to tell you anyway. That's how I wish to live in the world, as a person whose main work in life is known to be writing.

That's the surface of my identity. The substance of it is my writing itself, which I have chosen to place out in the world. If you've read two or three of my books, the odds are that you know me better than you know your next-door neighbor. You may even know me better than you know your brother, your father, your husband, your wife, your son or your daughter. I don't mean *know* literally, because even the most autobiographical of my work is filled with so much made-up material that it will not yield a trustworthy factual account of my experience. But you'll know me—there isn't any other way to put this—spiritually: You'll know what is at the center of my personality; you'll know what I think about, what troubles me, what comforts me, what I'm afraid of, what I admire, what I care about, what I hate, what I notice about people, and so on.

Admittedly this is a controlled, an edited, maybe even a contrived, version of myself that my written work puts forth. Since I obviously have the power *not* to publish those works that reveal aspects of myself I don't want to reveal, it's accurate to say that whatever I *have* revealed in my published work has been a matter of deliberate choice. So far as I know, I haven't let anything slip.

Yet it seems to me that in pages any stranger or enemy can easily find and examine in a library, I have revealed everything there is to reveal about myself. I feel that in my published work all my weaknesses of character have been made so evident that balding, duck-footed, and pot-bellied, I stand naked before my reader.

Of course, in the same pages, what can be said in my favor has also been put forth. If my weaknesses are revealed, then so, too, are my strengths—straightforwardly there, not in the form of the self-promotion I might try to hand you if I were applying to you for a job.

In making my narratives, I have pitted these pros and cons of the self against each other. What I have come up with in the finished pieces are the ways I have weighed them out, the ways I have tried to make them balance. On the one hand, in every piece of my writing that I care about, I've engaged in some kind of spiritual struggle. On the other hand, I've simply tried to tell a good story. These two aspects of my writing process—the high-minded and the trashy—are inseparable.

Perhaps the basic discoveries of my writing life have been that in order to tell a good story, I have to carry out a spiritual struggle and that making narratives is my method of spiritual inquiry. If I'd had my choice years ago, I'd have picked another approach to writing—namely, the quick and easy. In this regard, I've taken comfort from these lines from Franz Kafka's "The Hunger Artist": ". . . I couldn't find the food I liked. If I had found it, believe me, I should have made no fuss and stuffed myself like you or anyone else."

A valuable by-product of the way I have been forced to write—or the one way that I have discovered it to be possible for me to write—is that I live in the world as a known person. I'm not talking about fame or reputation here; I'm talking about the fact that my spiritual checkbook is out there in the open for you or anybody else to have a look at. My work enables me to examine my life, and the struggles of that examination are a matter of public record. People who associate with me know the most important things there are to know about me. I can be "straight" with the world.

Difficulties go with making oneself so available. In the process of reckoning with oneself, one can hurt family members and friends, who might not wish to be revealed to the world or who might prefer to reveal themselves in their own terms. Instead of love and admiration, one can win anger and alienation. One can show oneself to be stupid, obtuse, insensitive, ignorant, treacherous, and generally despicable. And one can't take it back.

This ongoing nakedness, in my opinion, is one reason why some very fine writers get nervous, defensive, and sometimes pretty tricky about discussing their own work. We admire their writing so much we can't imagine why they'd feel weird talking about it. But it's one thing to walk around naked in a world where most people are very well dressed; most of the time, nobody says anything about it, and you can pretend that you're just like everybody else. It's something else when you're called upon to try to account for why you choose to live this way; that's when you begin to seem a little freakish to yourself.

In spite of these liabilities, it seems to me that living in the world as a known person is a privilege. It is perhaps the ultimate incentive for trying to practice an art form. The opposite circumstance, living within reticence or a permanent disguise, must be a severe form of suffering.

A teasing game sometimes played by German parents and their young children goes this way: Though the child may be in the immediate presence of the parent, the parent nevertheless calls out, *Wo bist du?*—Where are you?—and the child responds, *Ich bin hier!*—I am here! This ritual is repeated until the parent finally gives in to the child's insistence that it is in fact *hier.* The world constantly whispers this same question to us, "Where are you?" and our lives are our answers: "I am here." Lots of times my answer has had to be, "I don't know where the hell I am," or "Maybe I'm over here," or "I hope this is me here."

My best answer, though, is my written work, and it probably goes something like this: "It may not be much, but at least I'm here by the page and a half that I wrote this morning. I am here in this poem. I set down a word and then another beside it. I am here." By virtue of writing the way I write and therefore living in the world as a known person, I am granted above-average metaphysical certainty.

In less pretentious terms, if trying to write the best you can is what is most important to you, your pay may be lousy, your family may have disowned you, your enemies may be suing you, your agent may not be returning your calls, your editor may have been fired, your friends may be ready to do serious harm to you, and the lettuce in your refrigerator may be turning brown and mushy around the edges, but for better or for worse, you've taken possession of your life.

The Writer as Emotional Engineer

O N E afternoon, reading Eudora Welty's short story "The Wide Net," I encountered the phrase "the smell of the river cool and secret." Those seven ordinary words had a powerful effect on me, in some part informed by the circumstances of my having grown up about two hundred yards from the New River in rural Southwestern Virginia and that I read them in a Manhattan apartment where there was not the slightest possibility of my catching a whiff of a fragrance I had smelled only in my boyhood experience of walking along a sun-speckled path through the woods toward the muddy bank of the New River.

This was probably the first occasion when I took note of a way in which ordinary language could take hold of me, could affect me so strongly that I was wholly transported into the experience of the story I was reading. In this case it's that phrase *cool and secret* that holds the power to evoke so precisely the actual scent I knew from my boyhood, but it's also the syntax that unlocks the power of the phrase, the ordering of *cool and secret* after *the smell of the river* has instructed my brain to receive some olfactory data. And the ultimate magic, of course, is in the diction, the choice of those two special words *cool* and *secret* to name something as elusive as the smell of a river.

Though I wasn't particularly analytical about them, I began to be aware of the unusual powers that could be exercised through syntax and diction, the *engineering* of language. My dictionary tells me that the word *engineer* is derived from the Late Latin "*ingeniarius*, one who makes or uses an engine," from "*ingenium*, an engine or mechanical contrivance." Diction and syntax—words and the order in which one arranges words—may be used to construct "contrivances," or "engines" that have the power to transport—or move or affect—readers.

Such a contrivance is a sentence from another Eudora Welty story, "A Worn Path," a scene in which a white town lady gets down to the sidewalk to tie the shoes of an old Black country lady.

> "What do you want, Grandma?"
> "See my shoe," said Phoenix. "Do all right for out in the country, but wouldn't look right to go in a big building."
> "Stand still then, Grandma," said the lady. She put her packages down on the sidewalk beside her and laced and tied both shoes tightly.
> "Can't lace 'em with a cane," said Phoenix. "Thank you, missy. I don't mind asking a nice lady to tie up my shoe, when I gets out on the street."

The most efficient version of this shoe-lacing sentence would be *Putting her packages down, the lady tied Old Phoenix's shoes.* So with the language she chooses here, Welty means to accomplish more than merely conveying the information of what happened. She wants you to register the experience physiologically—with your body— and so she writes it in such a way that the language actually performs a version of the action: *She put her packages down on the sidewalk beside her and laced and tied both shoes tightly.* The sentence itself is an "engine" that causes you to experience a certain kind of physical exertion that is necessary for an accurate understanding of the subtle racial politics of this scene of Welty's story.

Another example is the following fragment from William Faulkner's "Barn Burning":

> . . . then the boy, deluged as though by a warm wave by a suave turn of carpeted stair and a pendant glitter of chandeliers and a mute gleam of gold frames, heard the swift feet and saw her too, a lady—perhaps he had never seen her like before either—in a gray, smooth gown with lace at the throat and an apron tied at the waist and the sleeves turned back, wiping cake or biscuit dough from her hands with a towel as she came up the hall . . .

The centerpiece of this paragraph is *a lady*, but Faulkner exercises his linguistic engineering to mythify this particular *lady*, so that we readers feel the shocking impact of the sight of her on the protagonist here, the illiterate tenant farmer's illiterate son, Sarty Snopes. The phrases *deluged as though by a warm wave by a suave turn of carpeted stair and a pendant glitter of chandeliers and a mute gleam of gold frames, heard the swift feet and saw her too* serve as a heralding flourish of trumpets—Ta-ta-ta-ta, etc.—for the appearance of the lady. The clause *perhaps he had never seen her like before either* serves as drum-roll to inform us that we are in the presence of someone of consequence. The descriptive phrasing *in a gray, smooth gown with lace at the throat and an apron tied at the waist and the sleeves turned back, wiping cake or biscuit dough from her hands with a towel as she came up the hall* . . . makes us witness the appearance of *the lady* in cinematic terms; its syntax and diction and rhythm place us right there just inside the front door with Sarty Snopes watching this person moving through the hallway toward us.

The object of such engineering is to transport the reader into the story, to transform the reader from a spectator into a participant. A story that merely informs us of what happened, no matter how exotically plotted or stylishly written, makes very little difference to us; the beautiful story is the one that makes us feel that we are *there*. We experience the story as if we were living it. The beautiful story is the one that possesses us. Linguistic engineering is the means by which the literary artist empowers his or her work to take hold of its readers.

So far I've been discussing the elementary business of involving the reader by way of the five senses, using words to make the reader intensely see, hear, taste, smell, or touch something in a story. The most advanced form of linguistic engineering, however, is *emotional engineering*—using diction and syntax to make the reader experience the deeper emotional current of a human circumstance.

To convey strong emotion in fiction or poetry, the author must do something other than merely finding the words to name or express that emotion. For example, the sentence *I feel joyful today* registers very little joy with a reader.

If I wanted you to send me apples from your orchard, I could write you a note, *Please send me some of your Red Delicious apples*, and you would know exactly what I meant. With apples, communication is simple; with joy (sadness, fear, anxiety, despair, hatred, love and so on), communication is complicated.

This perversity of language—that when it comes to articulating the emotional life, words won't do what we think they're supposed to do—baffles many a young poet and fiction writer and presents a subtle problem to a writing teacher. For more than twenty years I've been frustrated by my students' failed attempts to write about emotional experience. When their stories or poems included sentences like *I feel joyful today*, I saw the failure of their writing as a failure of their artistic souls. Only recently have I understood that such writing has nothing to do with esthetic depth or shallowness.

Writing about emotion is a practical issue. Apprentice writers need to consider *methods*, but too many of us writing teachers have fallen into the habit of hauling out that old, dull workshop saw of *showing* instead of *telling*. Though it sounds sensible (and to those who practice the principle, it is), *show, don't tell* can be the general advice a lazy teacher offers to a lazy student that enables both of them to avoid getting down to specifics. However, it is possible to encourage writing students to try to locate the methods that are available to someone who wishes to write well about strong emotion. It is possible for a teacher to offer specific advice that demystifies the writing process in ways that are healthy and helpful:

1. Locate the *particulars*. The literal circumstances that produce joy have their rightful place in a text that asserts the joy. We do not experience emotion in a vacuum. Maybe one morning a character just wakes up feeling exuberant—for no good reason. Nevertheless, the writer can provide us readers with the particulars of the room in which our character awakes, the light at the window, the whiteness of the wall, the softness of the yellow blanket, the scent of coffee wafting up from downstairs. Like the weird ingredients of a love potion (lizard's tongue, fur of a rat, bird beak, crushed rose petal, etc.), these worldly particulars hold powers that may be combined to conjure up invisible textures of emotion.

2. *Empathize.* As completely and intensely as possible, project into the moment, into the situation, into the character. Discover emotional truth by living it imaginatively. The writer who wishes a reader to experience emotion must first experience it him- or herself. If there is any mystery to writing about emotion, this is the territory in which it resides, but even here the task has its practical dimension. Locating the particulars helps induce an empathetic trance. The assignment is something like what an actor takes on in playing a role, like what a kid carries out in pretending to be a soldier, princess, or rock star. For a grown-up writer the trick is in taking your own imagination seriously, and looking for the right words is the best way to go about doing that.

3. Choose appropriate *diction*. Individual words convey infor-

mation, but they have connotative lives of their own that skilled writers use to support the overall effect of a scene. For instance, *A slice of light split the room in half* is probably not an effective sentence for a scene in which a character is feeling joyful—because the words *slice* and *split* have abrasive connotations. *Sunlight beamed across the floor, then ribboned one bright yellow stripe up the white wall* contains diction that might better serve the joyful mood of our character.

4. Use *sentence rhythm* to contribute to emotional effect. *Heat. Light. Coffee smell. Got to get up*: Such a choppy rhythm might better convey anxiety than joy. To render a sense of a joyful awakening, try a gentle cadence: *With the smooth side of the blanket warming my cheek and sunlight beaming across my bed, my eyes fluttered open to a morning of such ineffable sweetness . . .*

5. Use *stylistic variation* to convey emotional dynamics. For instance, a character may awake in a state of joy but then encounter an experience that produces anxiety. A writer's stylistic choices should enhance such a change in mood: *With the smooth side of the blanket warming my cheek and sunlight softly beaming across my bed, my eyes fluttered open to a morning of such ineffable sweetness that I quickly arose and opened my window.*

Heat. Car Horns. Carbon monoxide. A fire truck shrieking down the street. Angry shouts.

Quickly I closed the window and jumped back into bed, pulling the blanket up tightly over my shoulders and brushing it across my cheek to try to regain the joy that had seemed to fly away from me at the window.

My own awakening to the emotional engineering of imaginative writing came intuitively through my reading of literature as a young man. I began to know what to do before I knew what I was doing. I understood how to achieve emotionally affecting language long before I understood the nature of the achievement. From the last lines of Theodore Roethke's short poem "Child on Top of a Greenhouse," I saw how an accelerating syncopated rhythm of language can produce a sense of wild excitement even in a reader sitting alone and reading silently:

> a few white elms plunging and tossing like horses
> and everyone everyone pointing up and shouting.

From the long looping rhythms of William Faulkner's prose in "The Bear," I learned how repetition combined with narrative pacing can build the suspense and intensity that produce the thrill of revelation. From Hemingway I learned editing. From Cheever, I saw ambivalence transformed into vision. From Reynolds Price, I saw how sweetness and generosity can take writer and reader deeper into a character's personality than cool cynicism. From Peter Taylor I discovered the pleasures of using a first-person narrator with a discernibly small soul. From Eudora Welty, Leonard Michaels, and Toni Cade Bambara, I learned how to heighten prose energy. From Jayne Anne Phillips, I learned how sexual explicitness may become a method of spiritual inquiry. From John Casey I learned to appreciate the texture of worldly objects in prose.

Such schooling is constantly being carried out by writers and writing teachers in the privacy of the thousands of hours they spend reading. I'm grateful to have learned what I've learned from the authors of the stories and poems I've read, who learned it from the stories and poems they read. What seems to me to need correcting is the notion too many of us writers take to our summer conferences and too many of us college writing teachers carry into our classrooms, that our reading has somehow enlarged our souls, deepened our essential humanity, and therefore turned us into good writers. Reading literature may very well have enlarged our souls—just as it may have enlarged the souls of many politicians, accountants, attorneys, insurance salesmen, and oil-company executives—but what it actually has given us that enables us to write well is a great deal of practical instruction in the curriculum of emotional engineering. Perhaps even without knowing that we were doing it, we have learned the technical skill of manipulating language in such a way as to make our readers actually experience emotion through the act of reading. We have learned skills that are immensely teachable—skills that, in my opinion, may be learned with surprising ease.

What I have been discussing throughout this essay is writing technique; what I have been arguing is the paradox that the deepest emotional sense of a narrative is a matter of the author's adroit use of syntax and diction. Now I want to reverse myself: In spite of what I have argued here about technique, I believe that finally for the author the real secret of writing about emotion is to feel it him- or herself.

In the immortal words of Conway Twitty, "You can't sing it if you don't feel it."

There are such powers in the language that you *can* fake it to a certain extent—you *can* persuade your reader to feel something that you the writer in fact don't feel. But even the least sophisticated readers have built-in retrospective flapdoodle detectors: The highest success rate yet achieved on any reader through literary fakery is about 74 percent. The reader that you have fooled into feeling something on page 12 looks back at the experience from page 17 and knows he or she was fooled by you, That reader resents what you did.

But what matters more than what your reader thinks of you is the thing you have made. It is out there in the world, out there in the world when whatever money you were paid for it has long been spent and whatever praise you received for it has long faded from your memory. The text that you made is out there. It is undying testimony to your fakery or to your sincerity, whichever it was that went into the making of it. Probably your readers know which it was, but more importantly, *you know*.

So the real aim is not reader manipulation. Emotional engineering is the method we writers use to approach the experience itself. It is how we feel what we feel when we feel what we're writing about. To find exactly the right language to make a reader feel, we writers have to enter and explore and live that feeling. The way we writers approach and discover the feelings we want to convey is through the technique of emotional engineering. We take hold of emotion through syntax and diction; through language we both think *and feel*.

This isn't necessarily good news. I've had to face up to the fact that in regular human situations I'm an emotional oaf. My daughter Bess, who's a fine writer herself, says that I ought to have the words carved into my forehead: CAN'T DEAL. Usually it is only in retrospect that I discover my true emotional response to a difficult situation. All too often I find out what I felt too late to be able to act appropriately. I carry out a huge portion of my emotional life sitting down in front of my computer. What can I tell you? There are at least 842 better ways than mine for living your life. I'm grateful that I do in fact have an emotional life, even if mine is tinged by the green light of my computer screen.

But when I read a story, I want the same thing any reader wants. I want to feel the truth of lived experience—difficult truth maybe, ugly truth maybe, disturbing truth maybe, but I want the writer to be there, feeling it right along with me. When I write a story, that's what I'm aiming for, too, to feel what I feel—*with* the characters and *in* the world of my story—and to have you readers right there with us in the words on the page. Emotional oaf though I may be in my life, I want to be a good engineer in my writing.

Do You Wanna Dance?

Never trust a god who doesn't dance.
—NIETZSCHE

I N A couple of months, I would be thirteen years old, I had just reached my adult height of six feet one and a quarter inch, and I hadn't ever done anything like this before. Miss Jackson was out of our classroom, leaving behind one of those boxy old school phonographs; somebody put a record on that thing, and a bunch of us kids started dancing. The windows were open to a spring day pretty enough to inspire a roomful of seventh-grade non-dancers to get up and dance. I don't remember what the music was—maybe Rosemary Clooney singing "This Old House"—it seems to me the tune had to be pre-rock & roll, because even though the year was 1955, this wasn't a true rock & roll experience. This was in Ivanhoe, Virginia, population around nine hundred, and seventy miles from any place that even claimed to be a city. Cultural forces didn't reach us Ivanhoians until they had already swept over the rest of the nation. So far as I know, not one of us in that room knew the first step of any kind of dance. We didn't dance with each other, and we didn't dance like each other. We just moved our bodies according to how the music provoked us. Given the logistical confusion of my body, it amazes me that I had the nerve to try it and furthermore that I didn't break something or hurt somebody as a result of my efforts. I fell into a leg-swinging, arm-flapping calisthenic kind of movement that brought with it a spiritual ecstasy worthy of an Aztec priest celebrating a spectacular maize harvest.

Nineteen hundred fifty-five holds another memory of consequence for me, one of both glory and ignominy: Early in the fall of my eighth grade year, I was invited to Kay Barnett's birthday party in the basement of the Washington Restaurant in Wytheville, Virginia. When I walked down the steps into that room, Elvis Presley was singing "Heartbreak Hotel." In that one moment I lost my spiritual virginity, I became a man, and my basic world view was formed. Until then, I had been the kind of kid who enjoyed watching Lawrence Welk with his parents. Until then, my ultimate musical experience had been listening to Frankie Layne sing "Rose, Rose, I Love You" on the car radio on the way to Hester's Drive-in. Nothing in my thirteen years of life had prepared me for hearing "Heartbreak Hotel."

Elvis is the glorious part of that experience. The ignominous part is that when Susan Puckett whispered to Sarah Parsons, who passed it on to Mary Sawyers, who came up to me and told me directly that Becky Hampton would like to dance with me, I didn't have the gumption to ask her. I don't really blame myself for this failure. All the lights were on down in that boxcar of a room; the only ones dancing were T. W. Alley and Judy Grubb and Pete Sadler and Judy Allison, the coolest ones of the Wytheville kids. But the heat that came to my forehead and the back of my neck when I realized the impossibility of walking across that floor and asking Becky to dance was my introduction to the humiliation of not dancing when you ought to be.

Two elements from Kay Barnett's thirteenth birthday party remained with me and became fused with each other in my adolescent psyche: 1) a specific girl sent a specific invitation to me, and 2) such a human being as Elvis Presley existed. Girls plus Elvis equals an exciting invitation was the crude equation that began thumping at the base of my cortex.

In no time at all, Becky Hampton was my official girlfriend, and I was cruising the hallways of George Wythe High School in black pegged pants slung low on the hips, white-buck shoes with pink socks, a half-buttoned-up pink shirt with the collar turned up, and hair on the sides of my head heavily butch-waxed to aim back toward what I hoped would soon become a duck-tail.

If I had stopped to take inventory that fall of 1955, I'd have been crushed by the weight of all I had going against me—the acne; the lack of hygienic sophistication (I'd just started taking baths more regularly than once a week, I was trying to remember to use deodorant every morning, and I hadn't really learned how to shave properly); the limited wardrobe (so far, I had only the one cool outfit); the lousy manners (my mother, my chauffeur for my first date, had to tell me to get out of the car and walk Becky up to her front porch); the sexual ignorance (my education consisted of all the nasty talk I'd heard from my pals through seven and a half years of school, plus the book my parents had left on my bedside table, *What Every Boy Should Know*, of which I had read only selected parts); the lack of a driver's license or a car; and the overwhelmingly inescapable fact that I couldn't dance.

Well, actually, with Becky's kind insistence and patient instruction, I did learn to slow-dance—testimony to her kindness, to the inspiring pedagogy of her slender forearm rising to my shoulder, and to the instructive skills of her hand at the base of my neck. It's not surprising that she quickly stopped trying to teach me to jitterbug. My brothers and my parents didn't dance. I was rural and self-conscious; my motor skills were lousy. In my brief efforts to duplicate Becky's footwork, I think I must have appeared to her as something like an epileptic stork.

Jitterbugging is still the coolest form of fast-dancing with which I am familiar, and not learning to do it is still high on the list of things I hold against my youthful self. I denied myself my rightful cultural heritage as somebody who grew up in the age of Elvis, Chuck Berry, Bill Haley, and Little Richard. Girls other than Becky Hampton tried to teach me. Melva Stevens and Susan Crockett were both young women of formidable powers in 1956, '57, and '58. Either one of them could have requested that I go out and lie down in the street, and I'd have tried to figure out how to do it without getting myself killed. But neither Melva nor Susan could successfully command my feet to land in the right place on the right beat. I just had to accept it that for my entire high school career, I was forever consigned to sit out the fast ones.

At our school dances, making the record selections off in a secret little room, must have been some teacher or parent with a concern for teenage pregnancy. In spite of the fact that only about a third as many dancers took the floor for the fast ones, the ratio was about four fast to one slow. Body contact had to be the reason. Kids nowadays wouldn't stand for it. More people dance to the slow ones (*Oh,*

49

my love, my darling, I've hungered for your touch); therefore, play more slow ones (*They asked me how I knew . . . my true love was true*) would have been an obvious argument. But so far as I know, nobody ever raised it. Like farmers taking the weather, we accepted the tunes that came down to us from the rafters of the gym.

Lots of girls danced with each other through the fast ones, but most of us boys sat in the bleachers or stood hands-in-our-pockets up against the wall or went out to the hallway for a smoke, all the while huddling up with each other, keeping at least one eye on the girls, now and then remarking Sue Himmelman's ass or Janet Hale's titties or making claims to have seen Linda Umberger naked one time. ("You didn't, you lying bastard!" "I did, I did, I swear I did!") Dignity among us bystanding males was hard to come by, and we forgave each other for even the lowest-minded strategies. Either you were a dancer, like T.W. and Pete and Billy Kincer (even though Billy was overweight), or you were a spectator. Among us spectating high school boys, life between the slow numbers was nothing but squalor, and sexual validity was a constant struggle. But if you could get out there and dance with Annie B. Crockett or Joyce Eversole to "Rave On" or "Hail, Hail Rock & Roll," your power was immense.

College was another story. When we departed our old hometowns, we were granted new lives. In Charlottesville, Virginia, the hand of destiny shoved me in the direction of a fraternity house. The hands of my fraternity brothers shoved me out onto the floor when my first date in the house expressed a desire to dance. Like a boy flung into a river for his first swimming lesson, I found that I could do it! Or I could do something—nobody ever quite defined exactly what it was I did out there on the floor in the general vicinity of my Mary Washington and Sweet Briar and Mary Baldwin dates. What other people did was the U.T., the Twist, or the Bird. I sort of stomped around and sometimes gyrated my hips.

In the early sixties my body had begun working out the kinks of its engineering, but what moves it made on the dance floor didn't matter. Fraternity house dancing was just how you passed the time while you consumed (or pretended to consume) large quantities of alcohol and/or plotted how to get your hands into your date's underwear.

Those were the final years of dating in America—they were followed by the era of hanging out—and from 1960 to 1964, I went through a lot of dates at the University of Virginia. There are two ways to account for that behavior, the first being that in one date almost any girl could plainly see that I was a vain, zit-faced hick with lousy coordination, little ability to handle my liquor, and an obtuse determination to unhook her bra. I prefer the second view, which was that a charming young Virginia gentleman such as myself was bound to keep meeting attractive young women.

From those years I mostly remember a blur of endings, Beverly and Judy and Jayne and Andrea and Joyce and Pat and a fair number of others sweetly explaining to me why they didn't want to have any more dates with me. The grounds of U.Va. hold many romantic settings, in most of which some young woman shot me down. However, the experience I choose to remember in detail from that part of my life is one of bold conquest.

The drummer of a band that came down from Washington to play at our fraternity house brought with him a young woman of startling appearance. She had elaborately done-up red hair; she wore orange lipstick, a tight sweater, and a tight skirt. The college girls my fraternity brothers and I were dating wore their hair short and free; they wore kilts and cardigan sweaters and blouses with Peter Pan collars and circle pins; they wore knee socks and Weejuns. Though this stranger sat in a chair discreetly placed behind the drums, every brother and every date in the house was acutely aware of her. My date for the weekend hadn't shown up, so that I was forced to hang around the party, drink a lot of keg beer, and do my bystander routines from high school. Noting the red-haired young woman nodding her head and moving her shoulders in time to the music, I walked over and made gestures to her to signal my desire for her to come out from behind the band and dance.

Dancing with Sally Stratton was one of the significant developments of my undergraduate education. She liked to dance so much that at the moment I asked her, she'd have accepted anyone's invitation, and she was such a superior dancer that as we carried out our moves, she couldn't help instructing me. She didn't say anything, and she didn't touch me. But her body conveyed to my body what my body ought to do to stay in sync with her body. This was new for me. New for me also was my body's response: It actually accepted Sally's body's instruction. This was the first evidence in its twenty-one years of tenure in life that my body was teachable. This was a body that held a negative record of discus-throwing at George Wythe

High School because it hadn't been able to learn how to spin and release the discus in the right direction and so had sent it skimming over the heads of my phys. ed. classmates standing behind me. This was a body so duck-footed that I'd seen perfect strangers grin at the sight of me walking to class in the morning. But now this body was demonstrating something resembling physical intelligence.

Now that I have experienced it, I understand that our culture constantly celebrates the not uncommon phenomenon of accord between one human body and another: Ballet's duets tell us about it; Ginger and Fred tell us about it; even square-dance callers tell us about it in their laconic way. But if I hadn't encountered Sally Stratton at that Teke House party in October 1963, I could have passed through my lifetime without receiving the message: *your moves are exactly right / for a few things in this world,* James Dickey's poem "Encounter in the Cage Country" says, and even now, without Sally's instruction, I wouldn't truly understand those lines. What does it mean when on exactly the same beat she puts her foot there, turns that way, and you put your foot here, turn this way, and at the end of your separate turns, you're touching fingertips and moving together with the music in a completely new and perfectly, mutually understood direction? It means that our bodies remember how we once shared paradise.

Sally and I weren't a successful couple in any other way than on the dance floor. Though at the time I thought I was hot stuff, my guess now is that I was probably one of her least capable dance partners. Sally was a genius of party dancing. With a few hours of effort, she transformed me from a true oaf of the dance floor to a beginning-level student. But there were moves in that woman's body that only a Baryshnikov of rock & roll could have properly complemented.

Sally Stratton lived in her body more completely than most people. She had what Prince refers to as "That Look," which is to say a powerful and unabashed sexual charisma. The very sight of her caused my fraternity brothers to cavort around, fidget, wink at me, blush at her, and make grade-school remarks to each other. But neither Sally nor I seemed to understand how ill-suited we were for each other.

In November 1963, hitchhiking from Charlottesville up to D.C. to see Sally, I heard the news of President Kennedy's shooting over a car radio. That night in her car, Sally and I drove around Washington in the rain, more or less aimlessly, for a long while. Then we took a motel room somewhere around Culpepper and drank a bottle of scotch and watched TV and had minimally competent sex. If dancing with Sally was the closest I'd been to Heaven, then being with her that night of Kennedy's death was as weirdly hellish an experience as I've ever had. Like most Americans in those hours, Sally and I were hurting, but we were using the wrong resources to try to make ourselves feel better. The fact that we'd achieved angelic accord on the dance floor made it all the more cruel that when we really needed comfort, all we could do was grind our bodies against each other, get distracted by the TV, get up, walk around the room, fix another drink, stare at the black and white screen. In the morning, in almost complete silence and in the continuing rain, Sally drove me back to my apartment in Charlottesville, let me out in the parking lot, and headed straight back to D.C. Waiting for me inside was a letter from the Dean of the College informing me that I had been put on probation for having cut too many classes. Sally and I never saw each other again.

Of the many sad variations of human experience, one of the saddest is that those people who influence us most significantly—for example, first friends, first loves, first great teachers—usually disappear from our lives without due ceremony. I let Sally Stratton drive away from me in that rainy parking lot, when I had hardly been able to look her in the eye long enough to say, "See you later," much less to embrace her, kiss her tenderly, and tell her that she had immeasurably deepened my sense of human possibility and that I could never adequately thank her for it. With me registering only about ten percent of what was important in it, my life was relentlessly proceeding. I was so absorbed in the project of flunking out of the University of Virginia that I couldn't even realize how a remarkable woman had just escorted me through heaven and hell.

In the summer of 1964, by enlisting in the U.S. Army, I officially began a three-year sequence of non-dancing experiences, a period of drastic soul-diminishment. Only on fast-forward am I able to view this phase of my life:

—Home for a few days after basic training, I am out with Melissa Williams, a pretty girl whom I dated intermittently in high school and when I was home on vacation from U.Va. Always before, within certain definite boundaries, Melissa and I have enjoyed physical affection. Always before, Melissa has sat right up beside me as I drove my parents' car around town. Tonight, when I pick her up and she comes out onto her parents' front porch, I see her seeing me, sunbaked, short-haired, sex-starved, and oddly wrong-looking in my civilian clothes. Tonight Melissa's only physical relationship is with the passenger-side car door. Tonight I begin to understand how the army has disassembled and reconstructed me so as to spook even the friendly girls with whom I used to slow-dance in the George Wythe High School gym.

—In Germany, in Airborne training at Wiesbaden Air Base, we devote hours to specific forms of pummeling our bodies: forward, backward, and sideways, we jump and fall into sawdust pits; we strap ourselves into various harnesses that snap at our bodies when we jump from the 34-foot tower; climbing one parachute riser and then another, we hang in our harnesses that bind our crotches like ingenious torture devices. At night in my barracks room, I know that if a woman caressed my body, I would suffer brain-damage. Going through Airborne training and getting my convict-style hair trimmed every three days, I suddenly understand that I love my pretty little barber. She speaks minimal English; my German isn't even up to a preschool conversation. So with a German-English dictionary and a grammar book, I labor at composing a letter to her proposing a Saturday noontime rendezvous at the small bakery shop by the main train station. I mail the letter to her, then become too embarrassed to face her in person, and so have to change barbershops. Of course she doesn't show up. Brooding over the next couple of days, I remember that my letter didn't say *which* Saturday she was to meet me. So for the next three Saturdays in a row, long after I have finished airborne training, I drive to Wiesbaden around noontime and sit by myself in the small bakery shop by the train station, having a lemon pastry.

—At the 25th Infantry Division's garbage dump, near Bac Ha Hamlet, near Cu Chi, Vietnam, my buddy Gary Reynolds and I, in our sunglasses and tailored fatigues, drive our jeep up to a crowd of peasants surrounding two girls who look to be around eight and ten years old and who have been shot in the legs for entering the dump. Both children are conscious. They are being attended by a South Vietnamese Army Medic.

—In the Crystal Gardens Nightclub of Bangkok, the all-Thai band plays "Mustang Sally" three or four times a night for twenty minutes at a stretch. The only clearly audible lyrics are the title phrase. Each time "Mustang Sally" begins, forty or fifty of us GIs stand up to cheer and scream as if it were our national anthem, and more than a hundred Thai whores run out onto the dance floor, some with a GI in tow, most to dance with each other, a few to dance alone, and one or two simply to prance around the floor, tossing shimmering black hip-length pony-tails behind them. Though powerfully moved, I do not wish to dance. In this circumstance, the barrage of audio-visual experience that is "Mustang Sally" is of a spiritual nature; I could no more dance to it than to "Amazing Grace" or "The Old Rugged Cross."

Release from military service did not immediately put me back on the dance floor. I returned to Charlottesville and gained readmission to the University of Virginia, but I couldn't shake that army look. I had dates, but they were uneasy occasions. I hadn't shot anybody in Vietnam—hadn't even shot *at* anybody—but young women treated me as if I might have machine-gunned infants. There was something in me, too, some cauterization of feeling that made it so that I was never on the same frequency with anybody I was with. Then I met Jannie Timm.

Jannie was from Richmond, mildly pretty and a little overweight and doing time, God knows why, waiting tables in the Charlottes-ville HoJo's, working the late night shift, because those were the only hours she liked to work. About ninety percent of the time, Jannie gave the appearance of being on automatic pilot. She smoked a little pot—she'd have had to do something to stand that job for very long—but she couldn't have been all that stoned because her boss kept an eye on her and wouldn't let her smoke when she was on duty.

For about a month, before she quit HoJo's, Jannie was more or less my girl. When I was around her, I felt neither connected nor disconnected. Sometimes she sat in a trance with her mind drifting, but then she'd come awake and grin and touch one finger to my temple and ask me how I was doing. "Great, Jannie," I'd always say on such occasions. "I'm doing great." For me in those days, she was absolutely the best company for riding around town listening to the car radio, driving up to the skyline drive to make out on a blanket under the stars, or passing an afternoon in a bar, drinking beer and smoking and plugging quarters into the jukebox. A few years back, Jannie had gone up to Eastman on a scholarship to study the viola, but you couldn't tell it from her musical taste, which ran heavily toward soul music.

On one rare occasion of her having a Saturday night off, Jannie got a sudden notion and insisted that we drive to Richmond. I didn't know the city, but she gave me clear directions. Around eleven that night, we walked into an all-Black nightclub called Doctor Yes's, with Jannie getting helloed and hi-honeyed and hugged, and me getting hostile once-overs from every direction. This was a place she used to spend a lot of time in, she explained to me, and I didn't know whether or not she noticed the sweat broken out across my brow. The bartender-owner was her special pal. He cleared a couple of seats so that we could sit up at the bar.

Jannie chatted with the bartender and this person and that. After a while I got used to being there enough so that I could breathe normally. Then I noticed that people had stopped looking at me. I was a ghost among the living. I could relax and take a look around. The place was packed; the music was records being played over a serious sound system; the tunes weren't what I usually heard, but they were what I wished I'd been hearing. The dance floor was wall-to-wall dancers, and their movement was of a sort I'd never seen before. Restrained but intricate precision was the dominant characteristic; couples executed these polished moves, but effortlessly and with neutral facial expressions. During the slow numbers, the movements couples made were almost imperceptible. If the beginning of my dancing life was the savage separate cavorting of some boys and girls in my seventh grade classroom, this was the most civilized version of social dancing I had ever witnessed.

A song Jannie liked came on, a slow one called "The Sea of Love," a version of it that I hadn't heard before and haven't heard since. The bartender grinned at me and said that if Jannie wanted to dance, I'd better oblige her. I knew he meant to be kidding Jannie about being willful, but I couldn't help taking it as a threat that I'd get my white ass kicked if I didn't get out there with her on the floor.

To dance that one dance with Jannie was to feel both imperiled and enraptured. Couples were dancing with each other as usual, and there was certainly nothing organized about it, but about halfway through "The Sea of Love," I had a sense of Jannie and me being among many people moving massively together. I knew I didn't really belong in that place; I knew there were young men around me who would have liked an excuse to harm me. But Jannie and the music and the dance and all the subtly moving people conspired to make me feel impossibly connected to them and to everything outside myself.

When it was over, Jannie and I walked back to our seats at the bar, where for a while, both of us seemed to drop into separate trances. Suddenly, as she was given to doing, Jannie sort of jerked her head around and took note of me, which gesture also pulled me out of my coma. When Jannie had said her farewells, we got out of there and drove back to Charlottesville. Not too long afterward, Jannie quit her job, told me goodbye in a distracted kind of way, and moved back to Richmond. She and I parted amiably enough, but once again, I hadn't properly understood someone's gift to me, which in this case was reconnecting me with the world and its citizens.

One of the blessings of my recent years has been to teach in a graduate summer program, the Bread Loaf School of English, where there are dances almost every weekend. They take place in a barn whose floor one day will collapse and drop a hundred and seventy-five of us dancing fools down into what used to be milking stalls and pig pens. But meanwhile I am able to keep on receiving dancing illuminations on a regular basis. I heave and puff, I sweat, I run keg-beer through my system, and the next morning I feel as if I'm an athlete of some unknown sport who stayed out too late celebrating a victory. Dancing, man, I won at dancing last night, I have to tell myself.

So what am I discovering with my dancing nowadays? Hoofing it out on the barn floor one night with one of my best young writing students to The Talking Heads' "Burning Down the House," I discovered something essential about her generation and mine. I was striving to match at least some of my moves to some of hers when I suddenly realized that her aim was the opposite of mine: she flung her body most admirably this way and that, but pattern wasn't what she sought; chaos of movement was her guiding principle. If there had been any synchronizing of her body and mine, we wouldn't have been burning down the house. This was a young woman whose mind and talent I admired, and so her decision to stop making sense on the dance floor was most disturbing to me. The values of Western Civilization are deeply corrupt, I was willing to grant her that, but did that mean that we could never dance *with* each other again? Had I been thrown back dancewise to my seventh-grade classroom?

It is that *with* that has been the guiding principle of my dancing curriculum. To dance *with* someone is to celebrate the fact that there are two of us, is to demonstrate how two of us can make a particular kind of beauty that can't be made by just one, is to assert that the connection between self and other is meaningful, is to defy spiritual isolation. In this mature phase of my dancing life, I think that certain people are suited to dance with each other and certain others are not. It doesn't have anything to do with common background or liking or intellectual capacity or hobbies or anything else. It's the same as somebody else's smell, either you like it or you don't: Either you can dance with somebody or you can't. There's a woman I've come to be friends with through our attending for the Bread Loaf Writers' Conference for the past eight or nine years. She likes the Writers' Conference dances just as much as I do; she stands on the edge of the dance floor and nods and sways to the music. Whenever I see her doing that, I ask her to dance, and she always says no. She hurts my feelings a little bit, but I respect her choice in this matter. What I hope she thinks is that if we danced and our moves weren't right for each other, we might ruin our friendship. But as a former sweaty-palmed bystander, I say it's worth taking a chance. When your moves are right for someone else, it is wholly rewarding in and of itself: You don't need to talk with, go to bed with, or for that matter, even dance again with that person. Like few other experiences available to modern men and women, dancing with somebody can be a nonprofit activity that is utterly satisfying.

At the Bread Loaf School of English, in the summer of 1979, I asked someone to dance whom I had seen around but whose name hadn't stayed with me. She was a small, quiet, modestly dressed young woman. From our first steps, she and I knew we were perfectly suited for each other. The song was Marvin Gaye's "Sexual Healing," which always pleasantly embarrasses me. I blushed from the words of it, but I kept on blushing for the pleasure of our dance, blushing, grinning, and going on and on with it. It felt as if she and I gradually levitated above the crowd of dancers and became a vision they imagined of The Heavenly Dancers. When Marvin (may he rest in peace) started winding down, she and I gently descended to the floor. We thanked each other and went our separate ways and didn't ever dance again, though at later dances I looked for her.

At the graduation ceremony this past summer of 1988, I was the faculty member selected as the Class Hooder; when each graduate had received a diploma and had shaken hands with the president, my job was to drape the hood of the school's colors over his or her head. Throughout the ceremony, we faculty members sat on a stage, from which we could look down and see all the candidates for graduation. I knew most of them by name, but a few from previous years, having completed their final requirements off campus, had shown up just for this ceremony. A young woman in a cap and gown seemed very familiar to me, but I didn't place her until she walked, smiling, up to the platform to receive her diploma from the president. In the middle of this dignified ceremony, I almost shouted, "Hey, aren't you the one I danced with to 'Sexual Healing' nine years ago?"

That I have sometimes attempted with another of my species to construct some beauty of movement with our bodies is among the small, fragile, saving graces of my life. I'm afraid that too much of my history has been relentlessly proceeding toward the making of this Age of Personal Betrayal in which we now live. I vote for public officials who lie and who know and don't care that I know they are lying. I consume ravenously while my spiritual life is in disarray. I can't stop destroying the planet, I can't stop killing its magnificent creatures. I rarely resist my culture's basic teaching point, which is that manipulating people through false offers of friendship, trust-worthiness, and loyalty is not only o.k., it's admirable. More and more I understand my witting and unwitting participation in this Age of Personal Betrayal, in which by so simple an act as taking my kids to their favorite place to eat, I'm contributing to the destruction of the rain forests and the ozone layer, in which my driving to the post office to mail a manuscript makes me a small stock-holder—maybe half a sea otter's worth—in the Valdez disaster. More and more I am confronted with the logical conclusion of this Age, which is that nothing really matters in all of human intercourse: You and I may choose to take a meal together, to talk, to exchange gifts, to write letters to each other, to love each other, or we may choose to fight, imprison, contaminate, rape, torture, maim, or murder each other, and *it doesn't matter which choice we make*, it is, in this Age, all the same, of no consequence whatsoever. Robert Frost's worrying the issue of Fire or Ice, which once seemed such a witty and courageous facing of the dark future, has become an almost comforting nursery rhyme: Fire or ice would be easy; the greater likelihood is that we human beings are going to poison ourselves and each other and all the living creatures of the planet, are going to choose the slowest and most ignominious of all possible deaths.

The unspeakable sadness I feel in thinking about this Age is exactly what I deserve for having done my part to make it what it is. I deeply wish it and us to be otherwise. In the Pike Street Marketplace of Seattle I have cried for the beauty of music and the dignity of ordinary men when a burnt-out old hippy couple sang "Teach Your Children" with an open guitar case before them to catch thrown pocket change. The common making of beauty is what I would wish to be remembered about poor humankind: old long-hairs raising their voices together into the damp air of Seattle, Washington; my first-grade daughter singing the elephant song—"they had such enormous fun"—in the car on the way home from school; a high school band playing a transcendent rendition of "King Cotton March" at the Bristol, Virginia, Band Festival; Fred Bonnie and Ellen Sullivan composing a country song that was never recorded and never remembered by them or by anyone else; and Laura Wilson and I dancing in perfect accord in the Bread Loaf Barn near Ripton, Vermont: These are instances of beauty being made and instantly dissolving into time. Such small matters won't save us, but they will go on ricocheting out into the twelve million billion light years of frozen space that is our immediate future. For a moment, my body moved to music with your body, and you and I made a small matter.

Ingrained Reflexes

I N 1970, the University of Virginia was forced by a legal decision to open its doors to women, but when I enrolled in Mr. Jefferson's University in 1960, its undergraduate college was still an all male institution. To spend time in the company of the opposite sex of our own social class, we Virginia Gentlemen went "down the road" to Sweet Briar, Hollins, Mary Washington, Mary Baldwin, Randolph Macon, those Virginia Women's Colleges where our coed counterparts were sent for finishing. Or else we imported girls from those schools to Charlottesville, by inviting them up for a big weekend. (Regardless of where the girl was coming from, the preposition was always "up.")

By joining a fraternity, officially I became a brother to the thirty or forty other active fraternity members of my house. But I had no sisters. During my entire undergraduate education I had no friendships with women. Either I went with a woman or I had nothing to do with her. During one particularly unhappy semester I was pinned, in rapid sequence, to half a dozen young women. I was too much of a coward to break up face to face with these girls on whose blouses dangled the little gold doo-dad that was my fraternity pin. Usually after I'd escorted them to the bus or train station on a Sunday afternoon, I'd walk back to the fraternity house in the company of some of my brothers and go upstairs for a few minutes alone in my room to type a letter telling the girl of that afternoon that I realized I didn't love her after all. Reprehensible as I knew this behavior to be, expensive as it was having to buy all those fraternity pins, I nevertheless was driven to it, and I was encouraged in it when I discovered that, instead of being condemned, I gained stature with my brothers with each episode.

Not much of the way we behaved in those days was gentlemanly.

Because my fraternity had a high grade-point average, it was considered one of the least animal-like houses on the grounds, but much of our big weekend behavior was overtly hostile to women. Brothers would "drop trou" while standing and talking to another brother's date, especially if it was the first time that girl had been "brought up," especially if she was a freshman, especially if she was "a nice girl." Brothers walked through parties with "roots out," which they must have considered a sort of sociable form of flashing, and became heroes for it. For some months all over the grounds there was a phase of "ass-biting," a phase that ended at my house the night a brother who'd sneaked up behind a dancing young woman and tried to sink his teeth into her buttock found himself being backed up into a corner and slugged severely by that Sweet Briar "honey."

Looking back at those days tempts me to be smug. In 1986 it's all too easy to remark the greatly improved sexual-political atmosphere at the University of Virginia, now that it has been coeducational for more than 15 years, righteously to condemn the woman-hating rituals of my fraternity, and to see the undergraduate pig that I was as a tiny figure steadily receding into my past.

Nowadays I'm a new man. My wife has an extremely demanding career, and so I am the cook of my family's household, I tend the plants, I do most of the cleaning and the laundry. I take some pride in my house-husbanding, and I also understand some of the practical advantages of the role: household tasks serve me very well as a change of pace from the desk work that my job requires of me. Instead of resenting meals to be prepared or vacuuming to be done, I'm often grateful for a chance to do a little manual labor while I'm thinking about an issue with my writing or my teaching.

But at a deeper level than these arrangements of women's work and men's work I feel myself to be incorrigibly unreconstructed, irreparably sexist. I know that I am permanently "down the road" from women, permanently distant. When I meet an attractive woman, I automatically rely on the flirtatious manners that I polished up standing around my fraternity house fireplace with my "brothers" and their dates. I do have friendships with women, but I don't quite trust these friendships: I suspect myself of being capable at any moment of propositioning my woman friends or of typing letters to tell them I realize I don't love them.

However many meals I cook, dishes I wash, floors I vacuum, or drying racks of scrubbed-out lingerie I hang up, I understand that I still carry within me a sexually oppressed and oppressive self. In spite of the rising consciousness of contemporary American culture, the toughest battles remain to be fought in the inner lives of those of us who imagine we have freed ourselves from so much of past "education."

In the days of ass-biting, I lacked the nerve actually to do such a thing myself; I was a spectator, an egger-on-er, a guffawer. But I cannot yet throw off my understanding of the gesture: Part of what ass-biting signaled was that those young men, my brothers, whose daily lives were spent only in the company of other men, didn't know what to make of those young women, our weekend visitors. In their bafflement, under the influence of alcohol, loud music, and tribal dancing, they reverted to bestial communication.

I know I'm even less likely now than I was then to carry out such an act, but I still experience deeply recidivistic moments.

Walking on 56th street one afternoon, I noticed the young woman beside me, a stranger whom I perceived to be dressed in high fashion, wore her blouse unbuttoned in such a way that one of her breasts was wholly visible. I walked beside her long enough to decide she wasn't a prostitute. Finally I couldn't stop myself from asking her, "Excuse me, but why is your blouse unbuttoned like that?" and she delivered me a look like a hard right to the solar plexus. In such moments I am so baffled by women that my teeth ache.

Just Looking, Thank You

' ' Y O U ' R E trying to look up her skirt."

"What did you say?

"I said, 'You're trying to look up Susan's skirt.' "

"I am not! I most certainly am not!"

This exchange took place when I was in first grade. As I remember it, we were putting up Halloween decorations, with Susan Sharp standing on a chair and Betty Umberger and me handing crepe paper and thumbtacks up to her, when Betty made the accusation. I was acutely embarrassed. I was outraged by the injustice of Betty's remark; I didn't think I had been trying to look up Susan's skirt. My memory is still so bruised by the event that it insists I wanted to say something like "Don't you know I'm a nice boy, and I haven't even begun thinking thoughts like that?"

Forty years later I have to confess that I possess this distinct memory of Susan Sharp's legs in a plaid dress that I liked a lot. And as I recall Betty Umberger, she was a sensible and amiable girl, not a finger-pointing sort of person. It now seems to me likely that I was guilty as charged. The accuracy of the accusation was probably what made it sting so much.

That episode marks the beginning of my awareness of an inclination to look at women "that way." It doesn't have to be looking up skirts or looking down blouses to be looking with an erotic content, to be, in short, *ogling*.

But the last few years, I've had some disturbing insights into my ogling inclination. It suddenly came to me one day that if a young woman smiled at me, it did not necessarily mean she might be willing to go to bed with me. I don't even remember the occasion of that

Originally appeared in *Playboy* magazine.

lightning bolt, but when it struck, it was a disillusionment of a high order. And with that flash of truth came the understanding that for years I had assumed that if a woman presented me with a pleasant expression, it meant that sexual negotiation with her was possible. So at least some of what was involved in my ogling was a shopping process, a sorting out of the ones who would from the ones who wouldn't. This had little to do with anybody's actually going to bed with anybody else; gathering the data was usually rewarding for its own sake—that one wouldn't, that one would, that one wouldn't, and ah yes, that one would. But that I held such an assumption and behaved in such a way, even if entirely in the privacy of my own brain, seems to me both comical and shameful; it also seems to me simply a characteristic of the species; male and female *Homo sapiens* are constructed to begin exploring mating suitability through eye contact and facial expression. So though I may disapprove of my ogling inclination and rightly term it *primitive*, its origins are the ordinary working out of biological destiny.

Another insight that came to me along this line of inquiry was that my recognizing beauty in a woman drew me toward wanting to possess her—and here I mean *possess*. The impulse seems to me connected to my earliest sexual fantasies, which had to do with *having* individual females the way I *had* my toys, holding them exclusively for myself, playing with them, controlling their every action, and doing with them as I pleased. This childish impulse to possess the beautiful seems to me to account for why many of us men are so powerfully drawn to pictures of women—we don't want a human relationship, we want toys.

Still more disturbing was my realization that merely witnessing a woman's beauty made me feel that I had some actual claim to possessing her. Just to see a pretty woman was, to some extent, to feel that she belonged to me. Yes, I know that versions of this feeling can lead to kidnaping, murderous jealousy, obsession, fixation. But my guess is that at least the shadow of this impulse is present in the psyches of most heterosexual males. It is the license claimed by those men who pinch a girl's ass on the street or who lean out of a car window to shout at her, "Hey, baby, want to f———?" How else can we account for such overwhelmingly negative sexual strategies? If a man, even a crude man, really meant to initiate a sexual relationship, would he do it with a pinch or a shout from a car window?

So why does he act this way? He acts out of the powerful illusion of possession; he behaves this way because a circuit of his brain tells him he has a right to do it. And interestingly enough, he acts this way because he knows it *won't* work, because he can be sexually aggressive without having to risk sexual performance.

A final late-arriving insight about my ogling is that when I see a woman's breast or see up her skirt, I am pulled toward an even deeper and more irrational illusion, the fancy that something intimate has been exchanged, that carnal knowledge has passed between the woman and myself. Maybe an exchange has taken place if the woman has willingly offered the view, but it's more often the case that I've stolen the sight. I can't really say that I know what to make of this phenomenon, except that it has immense potential for misunderstanding between the seer and the seen. Such a misunderstanding might provoke a violent response from some men, though in my own case, I must say that I find the experience oddly pacifying: If I see a woman's breast, I'm likely to feel tender toward her, possessively tender, yes, but at least not violently inclined toward her.

Once, coming up a set of subway steps in midtown Manhattan, I looked up to see a woman standing with her back to the staircase railing, a woman a couple of yards away from me wearing a mini-skirt and no underpants. I didn't stop in my tracks to continue looking, but I did slow my pace considerably, and when I got to the street, I examined the woman with some care, a bottle-blonde, around thirty, with a hard, heavily made-up face. Her buttocks had expressed a greater innocence and deeper humanity than her face. For almost twenty years I've remembered her as a stranger toward whose backside I felt a baffling surge of tenderness.

In a published essay, I once confessed as follows:

Walking on 56th Street one afternoon, I noticed that the young woman beside me, a stranger whom I perceived to be dressed in high fashion, wore her blouse unbuttoned in such a way that one of her breasts was wholly visible to me. I walked beside her long enough to decide she wasn't a prostitute; finally I couldn't stop myself from asking her, "Excuse me, but why is your blouse unbuttoned like that?" and she delivered me a look like a hard right to the solar plexus. In such moments I am so baffled by women that my teeth ache.

Several female friends of mine found my behavior and my writing about it offensive. They took pains to share their thoughts with me, but the most rewarding response to my confession came in a letter from a gentleman from Stony Brook, New York:

Your last paragraph beggars belief: You were "baffled" by her response? You "walked beside her long enough to decide she wasn't a prostitute" (doubtless peering fervently at her exposed breast!)? What alternative reasons did you conjecture to explain her unbuttoned blouse, so that you had to ask which was correct? And did it really not occur to you that, in asking, you were being an offensive ass?

This was a chastising that I found so deeply satisfying that I almost wrote the gentleman to thank him for it. But I also felt oddly righteous.

Mike, a character suffering no ogling-confusion in Irwin Shaw's "The Girls in Their Summer Dresses," makes a case for looking at women as a healthy-minded activity:

I look at everything. God gave me eyes and I look at women and men in subway excavations and moving pictures and the little flowers of the field. I casually inspect the universe. . . . I look at women. . . . Correct. I don't say it's wrong or right. . . . I love the way women look. One of the things I like best about New York is the battalions of women. When I first came to New York from Ohio that was the first thing I noticed, the million wonderful women all over the city. I walked around with my heart in my throat . . . . I still love to walk along Fifth Avenue at three o'clock on the east side of the street between Fiftieth and Fifty-seventh Streets. They're all out then, shopping in their furs and their crazy hats, everything all concentrated from all over the world into seven blocks—the best furs, the best clothes, the handsomest women, out to spend money and feeling good about it. . . . I like the girls in the offices. Neat, with their eyeglasses, smart, chipper, knowing what everything is about. I like the girls on Forty-fourth Street at lunchtime, the actresses, all dressed up on nothing a week. I like the salesgirls in the stores, paying attention to you first because you're a man, leaving lady customers waiting . . . . I feel as though I'm at a picnic in this city. I like to sit near the women in the theaters, the famous beauties who've taken six hours to get ready and look it. And the young girls at football games, with the red cheeks, and when the warm weather comes, the girls in their summer dresses. . . . That's the story.

I want to identify with Mike. I want to look at women, and I want women to take my looking as a sign that I appreciate them more deeply than the men who don't. But I lack Mike's clear feelings on the matter.

Of course, much of what we're talking about here is manners. When you're about to go out to dinner to celebrate your wedding anniversary and your wife comes downstairs in her pretty new dress and you give her a whistle and a look and tell her, "Lady, I can hardly wait to help you take that dress off," who can say you're not the admirable diplomat of that occasion? And if you notice, as she comes into your office to discuss the grant proposal she's writing with you, that your female co-worker has just gotten her hair done, is it not appropriate to remark, "Hey, Genevieve, you look terrific today"? The social code encourages such acceptable "looking." But if your female co-worker comes into your office in her pretty new dress and you give her a whistle and a look and tell her, "Genevieve, I can hardly wait to help you take that dress off," nowadays you're likely to find yourself quoting Irwin Shaw at a sexual harassment hearing.

Father of a teenaged daughter, I've come to understand that the matter of a young girl's getting dressed to leave the house is enormously complex. Her choice of what to wear is her choice of what signals she means to convey to the people who will see her. As she prepares to go out, she has a "look" for herself in mind. The range of possibilities available to her is staggering: If she chooses her baggy army pants and her father's old stretched-out Irish fisherman's sweater to wear downtown, then she's going to be almost invisible. But if she chooses her pink mini-skirt with her white tank-top, then she's going to get a lot of attention, with only a small portion of it coming from the people she'd like to receive it from or being the kind of attention she'd like to get from them.

These are matters in which very early in her life, with a collection of nineteen Barbies and one Ken, my daughter began carrying out an apprenticeship. To choose what to wear is to exercise a power, the technology of which young women master by the time they are in their mid-teens. It is of course a power that exacts a considerable penalty from its holders; as John Berger remarks in *Ways of Seeing*,

. . . how she appears to others, and ultimately how she appears to men, is of crucial importance for what is normally thought of as the success of her life. Her own sense of being in herself is supplanted by a sense of being appreciated as herself by another.

In warm weather young women and men gather outside my office building at the University of Vermont, and the level of hormonal energy often runs so high out there that it renders completely invisible a professorial type like myself. But it's an ideal anthropological circumstance for observing the preliminary mating rituals of *Studentus Americanus Universitatus*. Spoken language may be essential for the male of the tribe, but in this setting, the female could get along very well on body language and wardrobe signals alone. But mainstream species survival-selection loses its mystery after a very little bit of observing. It's the drop-outs who merit real scrutiny, the young women who for one reason or another have said good-bye to all that and have chosen to dress plainly. While their fashionably dressed sisters are standing, sitting, or strolling in conversation with young men, the drop-outs in their drab, loose-fitting clothes move through the crowd, alone and apparently purposeful. They are literally out of it, the *it* being the sexual fray.

Since they are so much in the minority—say, one for approximately every thirty or forty consciously adorned coeds—one can hardly help wondering why they've made such a choice. Do they hate their bodies? Are they lesbians? Religious fanatics? Victims of rape or child molesting? The fact is that they may simply not want to be looked at "that way." And it is remarkably easy for them to choose not to be.

But is this what I really want, women to stop constructing their appearances so that I will stop ogling them? The truth is that I'd hate it if women stopped putting on "their summer dresses." It does seem to me comfortingly evident that we two genders are collaborators in this ogling business and that we'll all feel a lot better about it if we understand both the fact and the nature of our collaboration.

Maybe we do all understand it, maybe I'm just one of a few men who don't know how to swim with the flow of contemporary sexual politics. Standing in a grocery store check-out line recently, I can't help remarking a *Mademoiselle* cover with a provocatively dressed young woman on it and the caption, "Say Yes to Sexy." Checking out other magazine covers, I am intensely reminded of how "Sexy" is a way of life in a culture whose dominant force is advertising. "Sexy" is mainstream American ideology. But I can't help noticing, too, that not one person around me has "said yes to sexy," that the forty or fifty of us there in the check-out area are your basic, drably dressed mid-Saturday morning grocery-shoppers.

If I follow a young woman who has "said yes to sexy" all over town, it may be that I've simply received some positive signals that weren't intended for me. Or else I've chosen to ignore any negative signals she has transmitted and allowed my actions to be determined by testosterone alone. In either case, faulty technology is the issue, and the end result won't be fun for anybody.

On the other hand, if in walking behind her toward the English Department's main office, I take note of my colleague Professor Ann Fisher's pretty legs, am I not simply registering once again the refreshing fact that I am a living creature? Out of my usual guilt, I may lightly slap my cheek and swear not to be affected by Professor Fisher's high heel shoes, subtly shaded hose, and smoothly shaved legs. (I still have that instinct to whine about what a nice boy I am.)

I think now of Ellen Bryant Voigt's poem "The Wide and Varied World," which entertains the question of its epigraph, "Women, women what do they want?" and ends with this dark answer:

> We want what you want, only
> we have to want it more.

Perhaps included in this *it* is our mutual desire for more freedom from sexual oppression. I find it painfully humiliating to be inappropriately provoked to desire a woman. With me, as with everyone, it goes back a long way: I remember attending a high school dance around the age of fourteen and walking across about forty acres of open floor to ask Teresa Robinson to dance, only to have her glance up briefly and say, "No thanks." Am I talking about mere social embarrassment? Obviously that's part of it, but I'm also talking about self-worth, about feeling so diminished in value that you want to shrivel up and die. Manners may be the surface of this topic, but at its center are crucial issues of dignity and debasement. I know it's reasonable for a woman to want to be desired by invitation only. I also think it's reasonable of a man to want the invitation to desire to be as precisely transmitted as possible.

Nobody's talking about putting an end to ogling. I've had occasion to remind myself of how healthy a pleasure looking at women can be. Professor Ann Fisher and I are long-time friends, each of us married for the long haul. But by God, I like the sight of that woman, and if her face and manners are any sign at all, she doesn't half mind the sight of me. Professor Fisher and I have an ongoing regard for each other. Professor Fisher wears dresses I like, maybe a little old fashioned in style and conservative in cut, but they give her a cheerful, dressed-up look. She keeps her hair a decently generous length. In my professional opinion, Professor Ann Fisher has a smile that'd make an angel gain altitude.

But this is easy, right? Looking at an old pal isn't ogling, except maybe by Muslim standards. Let's try something tough, a healthy case of ogling a stranger. O.k.: I am about to pull out of the P&C parking lot when a car pulls over beside me and before I even look over that way I know the driver is a woman. You know how when your car is sitting beside another car, you can't help but let your eyes shift over that way, but you don't want to do it when the other person is looking at you? Well, this time when it happens, she and I lock eyeballs before we know what we're doing. It's warm weather; we have our windows rolled down; my radio is playing some aching, mid-afternoon hillbilly ballad; and all of a sudden, five yards away from each other, this woman and I are looking deeply into each other's eyes. Nothing for it but to smile a bit and look back straight ahead; we both do that. But I've liked what I've seen. This is a lady of my own generation, and her face is both lively and showing some wear. The history of her love-life is more than one chapter long, I'd bet on that. I like her smile which has a rueful discipline to it, a wry turn at the corners of her mouth. Just as the light changes, she and I turn back toward each other and exchange another one, and this is the old heart-squeezer, the look that says, stranger, you've got your life and I've got mine, and we're not ever going to see each other again, but given a chance, we'd know how to spend some hours together, now wouldn't we? She pulls out, I follow, and a block later, I turn right to go up to the gym, and she keeps going. I'm still feeling the buzz from exchanging that last look with her, and so when I turn off, I lift a hand to wave to her. I don't expect her even to see it, though she could if she glanced in her rearview mirror. Sure enough, she does, she lifts a hand and waves back. I drive on up to the gym, squinting little tears out of the corners of my eyes.

All right, so maybe within speaking three sentences aloud, the woman and I would have hated each other. Maybe if we'd gotten out of our cars, we'd have been horrified at seeing what the rest of us looked like. That's at least part of the point: The lady and I didn't see a whole lot—and maybe that's the essence of looking, that you never get to see it all—but we liked what we saw. I liked remembering the sight of her so much that in the gym before I changed clothes for racquetball, I went to the big mirror in the men's locker room and checked myself out, a dangerous act for a man my age and my weight. But I wanted to see what that lady might have seen in me that earned me a smile like hers. And you know, I didn't think I looked so bad.

AFTERWORD

Here is a selection of newspaper responses to "Just Looking, Thank You," which appeared under the title "Here's Looking at You" in the September 1991 issue of *Playboy*:

From *The Roanoke* [Virginia] *Times* [A Commentary by Monty S. Leitch], August 12, 1991:

... Here's what I admire most about Huddle's work—a quality evident in this article as well as in his short fiction: his willingness to risk opprobrium.

Huddle grew up in Ivanhoe and now lives and teaches in Vermont. He's published at least five volumes of poetry and fiction and has held appointments on many prestigious faculties, including those of the Bread Loaf School of English and Bread Loaf Writers' Conference. These accomplishments indicate his full membership in the "literary establishment," which is almost universally liberal and certainly, consciously, "politically correct."

Huddle's also been a featured speaker at Wytheville's Chautauqua and has taught several times at Radford University's Highland Summer Conference—both locations that, like his hometown Ivanhoe, value Southern gentlemanliness and mannerliness above raw honesty.

Yet, right there in black and white, Huddle has outright celebrated girlwatching—an *outre* activity in 1991 if there ever was one. And he's done it in a publication that many consider at least a little bit shady, if not downright degrading. This is not PC behavior, especially in a Southern gentleman.

But it seems to me that it's courageous and admirable behavior; behavior critical to freedom and human progress.

The scourge of "political correctness" has been getting a lot of press lately, mostly for its effects in academia. It's stylish now to pooh-pooh PC, to the point that even pooh-poohing PC has become a PC pressure. But style robs this important issue of its substance. The effects of PC pressures have gone beyond freedom of speech; freedom of thought is also everywhere threatened.

On any issue, the freedom to imagine angles that go beyond "acceptable" stances is critical to creative advancement. This is what Huddle has done: He's set aside all the PC stances on girl-watching (including the liberal, feminist, conservative, ageist and polite) and he's considered the reality. He's wrangled with empirical evidence and concluded, "It seems comfortably evident that we two genders are collaborators in this ogling business and we'll both feel a lot better about it if we understand both the fact and the nature of our collaboration."

Good heavens, yes! Let's try to understand something for a change. Let's look at something honestly without worrying what others will think. Let's even, for heavens sake, look a bit at each other.

From *The Vermont Times*, "Clips," by Dwight Garner, August 29, 1991:

HUBBA HUBBA 101: Ever wonder why so many female UVM students tend to dress in shapeless, asexual and discreetly torn clothing? Could be they're hiding from the prying eyes of college English professor David Huddle, who in September's issue of *Playboy* magazine holds forth on the agonies and ecstasies of ogling women. The teeming grounds outside his UVM office building provide Huddle "the ideal anthropological circumstance for observing the preliminary mating rituals of *Studentus americanus universitatus*." Gratefully drinking in the view, Huddle can't get a handle on this dressing down thing. "Do they hate their bodies? Are they lesbians? Religious fanatics? Victims of rape or child molestation?" Are women, he then wonders, "constructing their appearances so that I will stop ogling them?" Bingo.

SKIRTING THE ISSUE: To be fair, Huddle's essay, despite its position directly preceding a centerfold model whose "turn-ons" include animals and sunsets, isn't merely the overheated confessions of a horny geezer in the grandstands. Huddle, who's married, has some Portnoyesque, tragicomic things to say about the sexual politics of eyeballing the opposite sex, the PC Police be damned. "Homo sapiens," he concludes, "are constructed to begin exploring mating suitability through eye contact and facial expression." That's fair enough. But in one or two other places, his frankness and naivete are borderline way scary. A mere few years ago, writes this gifted late-fortysomething novelist [sic], did he realize "that if a young woman smiled at me, it did not necessarily mean she might be willing to go to bed with me." That lightning bolt tends to singe other menfolk before middle age (and tenure) sets in.

PEER REVIEW: Huddle's calibrated eye doesn't merely register coeds. "I take note of my colleague Professor Ann Fisher's pretty legs," he writes, and her "high heels, subtly shaded hose and smoothly shaved legs." A few paragraphs later, warming to his subject, he adds, "[B]y God, I like the sight of that woman, and if her face and manners are any sign at all, she doesn't half mind the sight of me . . . she has a smile that would make an angel gain altitude." Fisher and Huddle, longtime friends, are both married "for the long haul." Too bad they're not American Lit profs, though. The pair could co-teach a course on *To Have and Have Not*.

From *The Burlington* [Vermont] *Free Press*, August 29, 1991:

. . . Huddle writes that the most interesting women on campus are those who choose not to dress for the mating ritual. He wondered why these women dress in drab and loose-fitting clothes.

"Do they hate their bodies? Are they lesbians? Religious fanatics? Victims of rape or child molestation? The fact is that they may simply not want to be looked at 'that way,' " he writes.

Elaine McCrate, an assistant professor of economics, said she thinks women may choose to dress in sneakers or loose-fitting clothes to be comfortable. She and another female professor were read portions of the article.

"I think what he's afraid of is women just might be indifferent to men. These women who are so unconscious to style—rather than being victims of incest or rape or maybe lesbians—what he's reacting to is that they are simply showing disregard for his opinion of them," McCrate said.

The former chairwoman of the UVM English department, professor Virginia Clark, said: "We all know sex is a very powerful drive. We also all know that there are places where sex does not belong . . ."

Huddle said, "The climate of political correctness is such that people are very reluctant to talk about (sex)." He said it is much healthier to admit that sexual looking exists than to banish it as inappropriate behavior.

"My writing the article is to understand that line, to try to figure out what is healthy looking at the other sex and what is not healthy. I would attribute the feminist movement with providing some insight in that area."

From (page 1 of) *The Rutland* [Vermont] *Herald*, August 30, 1991:

BURLINGTON—University of Vermont English professor David Huddle went to classes Thursday prepared for battle. Ready for discourse on political correctness. Intent on defending his honor.

. . . When a UVM public relations person called him at home two nights ago, following a phone call from a reporter, Huddle grew nervous.

"I got no sleep . . . I thought I would be crucified," recalled Huddle, a UVM professor since 1971. "I went to class with my tie unusually tight."

Visions of unemployment flashed through his mind.

But despite his preparedness, Huddle has yet to find the battle. He asked his students if they cared to discuss it. They didn't. And while fellow faculty have engaged in talk, Huddle's right of free expression appears to have won out—so far.

"I've had a few friends of mine who have spoken with me crisply about several parts," Huddle conceded. "I've appreciated it. I think they were certainly within their boundaries."

Here at UVM, in an atmosphere where political correctness appears very much alive, Huddle's *Playboy* piece might be read with furrowed brow. After all, he does seem to have an uncanny memory for the strangers he has ogled in the past. And in his account of the mating rituals of UVM coeds, his references to women who choose to wear loose-fitting clothing could be construed as sexist.

. . . One UVM faculty member with the women's studies department suggested that the only controversy stemming from Huddle's piece is being stirred by the media.

"It seems to me that third parties are trying to pick fights," said the woman, who did not want her name used. She has not read Huddle's piece, and has no immediate plans to do so. And, she noted, not one of the students in her women's studies classes said they had read the piece.

. . . Nicola Marro, director of public relations at UVM, shunned the suggestion that the *Playboy* piece may cause embarrassment for the college.

"In this day and age, it doesn't take much to offend somebody," said Marro, who referred to any ensuing controversy as "much ado about nothing."

. . . Huddle, who generally publishes fiction and poetry, said he wrote the piece somewhat tongue-in-cheek with the hope of sparking "spirited discussion," but with no intention of being antagonistic.

. . . So what does English professor Ann Fisher think of his reference to her "pretty legs" on the pages of *Playboy*?

We may never know. The UVM directory lists no Professor Ann Fisher at the college. She is, Huddle admitted, "a composite," a twist of fiction.

"I confess to using some of that."

From *The Vermont Times* [an unsigned editorial], September 5, 1991:

HOORAY FOR DAVID HUDDLE

University of Vermont English professor David Huddle's latest essay in *Playboy* magazine, "The Art of Ogling Women [*sic*]," may well stand out as a minor literary landmark. It earns landmark status not so much for what it says—that eying the opposite sex is an underappreciated art form—as for what was said, or rather not said, about it.

The essay languished unnoticed for weeks inside *Playboy*'s September issue (a testament to how few members of Vermont's press corps actually read the magazine; surely plenty of them peruse it for other items of interest). And then, last week, this paper first pounced on the revelations of possible politically incorrect pronouncements from the academy. With that, the feeding frenzy began, as daily papers picked up the story, one even putting it on the front page. You could almost hear the scribes rubbing their dry hands together in anticipation: "This guy is gonna get creamed." The press managed to dredge up a few mild rebukes from fellow UVM profs, but then, wonder of wonders, *nothing happened.*

It wasn't too long ago that the advancement of infantile leftism had ruled out all but the most guarded assessments on controversial subjects like race, sex and class. Take the case earlier this year of Bennington College professor Edward Hoagland, who was nearly ridden off campus on a rail after he made rather vague remarks about homosexuality. These developments had a good many deeply concerned observers of all political persuasions worried that the national discourse would be reduced to inoffensive platitudes as commentators hid from the PC police.

But here, in the middle of PC land, David Huddle can hold forth on his contradictory feelings about ogling and nobody much cares. The import of Huddle's essay was that he took some chances, revealed his loutish past and subsequent conversion—several passages of which could easily brand him as unenlightened, to say the least—and got away with it.

All this is not to say we agree with Huddle or subscribe to his philosophy of ogling. But we appreciate hearing his thoughts, if only because it gives us opportunity to disagree. It's this exchange of ideas, agreements and disagreements, that enriches the public discourse and advances us. That's why we're glad to see September's *Playboy*.

From *The Vermont Times* [Letters to the Editor], September 12, 1991:

When the mall was installed on Church Street we watched the deployment of the cobblestones, the teak benches, the planters, the rocks, the trees, the snow-awnings, the street-lights, the sculptures, and the banners. When the workmen went away we felt that there was still something missing but we couldn't figure out what.

Years passed and then we read Dwight Garner's excoriation of David Huddle (Clips, Aug. 29) and it came to us: *stocks*! No small town square is complete without them, and although we recognize that there is something borderline way scary about stocks, we feel that stocks are the answer to the question of what to do with those ungovernable citizens who insist on exposing their thoughts.

Elaine Segal

Fire in the House

THE DREADFUL, high pinging of the smoke alarm in the hallway stops me from shaving and sends me running down the hall toward the steps, the downstairs hallway, the kitchen. Smoke thickens as I go, and when I reach the kitchen, I see flames rising around the teakettle on the stove burner, black smoke billowing up. I flip the burner switch to off, run back upstairs for the fire extinguisher, snapping light switches on as I go. My wife appears in the hallway as I am digging the extinguisher out of the linen drawer where I keep it. "Fire in the kitchen," I tell her while I am pulling the pin from the extinguisher, then I run back downstairs to the kitchen and spray the flames. My wife is behind me. When they spring up again, I squirt them again, and this time the fire is out.

My wife and I both are almost gagging from the poisonous-tasting fumes. We turn on the ventilator fans. We open doors to the outside, where the temperature is well below zero. Cold air sweeps in; the smoke begins to depart. We stand in the doorway looking into the kitchen as if it is a display of how much damage a small fire can do to somebody's home, as if we shouldn't really enter the display area. A coating of yellowish chemical powder covers the stove floor, the counters, and the floor. Another coating of blackish ash-like stuff covers everything else.

Somewhere in these moments I lose the intense fear that at the first ping of the alarm replaced intelligence and moved me through the experience. Still coughing and choking on some terrible taste in my throat, I begin a whining, thin-voiced cursing. This ruined kitchen and the work it will take to put it back in order seem to me outrageously unfair.

Last night when my wife wiped off the stove-top, she set the plastic slab we use as a spoon holder on one of the burners. I always get up around four or five to work on my writing, and I always go downstairs, fill the teakettle, set it on a burner, and turn it on so that I will have hot water for coffee when I finish my shower. Because when I first wake up I can't immediately face bright lights I always carry out the ritual in the dark. This morning I simply set the full teakettle on top of the plastic slab and turned the burner on under it.

These quirky circumstances of the fire's cause are maddeningly ambiguous, but my first response is entirely to blame my wife. After all, I have been a good citizen, gotten up early to do my work, efficiently carried out my routine as I always carry it out. Only good things have I done this morning, and yet I am being punished with this fire and ruination. Instead of fine-tuning my novel manuscript as I intended, I will have to spend these hard-won writing hours washing, wiping, scrubbing, and mopping. At 4:30 a.m. as we begin the overwhelming cleaning job, I explain to my wife what caused the fire and then rasp out to her through clenched teeth, "Don't you know I always put the water on in the dark?"

Some part of my consciousness knows how absurdly I am responding to what has occurred. My two daughters, twelve and three years old, have slept through this entire drama. My wife and I are unharmed. The damage is mostly confined to the kitchen. We didn't even have to call the fire department and embarrass ourselves in front of the neighbors. I am not a religious man, but some part of my consciousness knows that the appropriate behavior at this moment would be to get down on my knees on the floor and say a prayer of thanks. Yet here I am barely speaking to my wife while we work and seething inwardly at the fact that I have lost a day of writing.

My wife goes back to bed to try to catch another hour of sleep before she has to go to work. By the time my daughter comes downstairs for her breakfast around 7:45, the kitchen's appearance has been improved by about ninety percent. Still, this daughter is deliciously horrified at the mess here and amazed at the story I tell her of the fire. "You mean I slept through that?" she asks me, and I say I guess she did. She dawdles in her eating and getting ready for school; I tell her she's going to be late, and she tells me not to worry, she'll simply tell her teacher there was a fire at her house this morning. I shake my head at her.

Hearing my daughter's plan to use the fire as an excuse for tardiness sets me searching earnestly for the right track in my own thinking. I keep working on the mess, both in the kitchen and in my mind. By two o'clock in the afternoon, I've gotten it through my thick skull that the fire was my fault at least as much as it was my wife's. I call her at work and chat. I don't directly tell her that I'm sorry—after all we're not talking about a complete change of character here—but I think she understands that I mean to be apologizing. Our conversation takes on a tone of joking affection: My wife tells me that the thing she thinks she'll remember most clearly is the sight of me naked running down the hall with the fire extinguisher.

Still later in the afternoon, when I am out picking up odds and ends at the corner grocery store, I decide to buy a bottle of wine. My wife is pleased with me for doing that, and at dinner I lift my glass and propose a toast to our all still being alive. My wife lifts her glass, and our daughters raise their milkglasses, too. The ritual is funny and appropriate for settling this most unsettling issue of the fire in our minds, for assuring us that our lives will go on as usual and that tragedies are what we will read about in the newspapers.

POEMS

The Brown Snake Poem

A small, tame
but exquisitely poisonous
snake adores you
and wins your heart.
You feed the snake
yogurt and pecans.
You give it a box
to sleep in.
Soon you become bored
with the snake.
You tell it, "Snake,
love is not peaches,"
and you begin
the mistreatment.
You make the snake
eat grits.
At night you put
needles into its box.
You push the snake
around, but still
it adores you.
One day you are drunk.
You insult the snake
and kick at it.
You throw the snake
out the window.
Sorrowfully the snake
sneaks back into your house
and bites you.
In seventeen minutes
you are dead.
The snake nestles
beside your body
for the last warmth.

My friends, we get drunk
sometimes and sometimes
we leave our vomit
in the houses of ones we love.

We wince in the morning light
and know they've cleaned up
after us, but it's no use
denying our treachery.

Not that we ought to celebrate it.
Mostly we act decent,
we are kind, we do not inflict
ourselves too much on each other.

What makes us cringe is knowing
we have to live knowing
tomorrow night we might
spit in a friend's face,

call him a name, deny
we ever loved him, and then again
have to lurch home, hanging
our flesh around the neck

of a wife, a friend, whoever
will help us. It doesn't matter
at that point; we stink
beyond caring who smells us.

My friends, no wonder we commit
ourselves to poems. What's good
about us has got to be spun off
apart from this flesh.

Something has to hold
when the light snaps out,
the bed begins whirling,
and the darkness careens around us.

Curmudgeon's Song

From a distance I hear something soft, sung
as though someone knew half the words, was shy.
I want a song this spring against hate. The young

go out to loll in the grass, their coats flung
aside, forgotten as winter, and I
go walking toward what's so softly sung.

I almost lose it. I hurry among
crowds of laughers, dazed gazers at the sky.
This spring I want a song against hate. The young

get in my way, their bright colored packs slung
across their backs, careless of passers-by,
and far ahead I can barely hear it, sung

so sweetly words shape themselves on my tongue.
Wait! I know that song. I can tell you why
in spring you sing against hate. Oh, the young

don't know this. Did I tell you that I've rung
bells in May, that I've known I wouldn't die?
But why this distance, this thing softly sung
so far away? In spring I hate the young.

From *Paper Boy* (1979)

Gregory's House

It was a testimony
to something that
could make my daddy
mad even talking about
it, how when one side
of the house collapsed
they just stopped using
those rooms, and when
the front porch dropped
off Gregory was upset
because he had to do
his drinking in the
kitchen with the kids
whining all around him
and the TV turned up so
loud he couldn't half
concentrate. And they
say when the outhouse
folded over one January
Gregory cut a hole in
the floor and was happy
not to have to make that
trip in cold weather.
But every Saturday
morning they sent out
one dirty-fisted child
to pay me for the paper.
Until that Sunday I
threw a heavy, rolled-up
one too high and up onto
the roof, and it fell
right on through, and
the next Saturday Gregory
himself came out to the

fence and cussed me and
said I owed him damages
for knocking a hole in
his house.

Miss Florence Jackson

Mother said thirty years ago
Miss Jackson had been a handsome
soft-haired girl getting
her certificate from Radford
and coming back home
to teach high-school math.
But I had trouble seeing back
past that loose flesh
that flapped on her arm
when she wrote staccato
on the blackboard.
They moved the high school
20 miles away to the county seat,
but she stayed there
taught sixth grade
like a kind of basic training,
and got the boys
to make her new paddles
every time she broke an old one.
James Newman,
drawing pictures of her,
called her "old goose bosom,"
and Bernard Burchett said
she had a voice
like a good sharp hatchet.
Grimmer than God one morning
she told us there would be no more
wrestling matches
between the boys and the girls
during recess,
and that put a permanent
stop to it.
In class I told a joke
my grandaddy had told Peaks
and I hadn't understood
about a cow and a bull
and a preacher,

and she sent me to Mr. Whitt's office.
He made me go back
and tell her I was sorry,
to which she replied
she was too.
Angry in Geography she told
us the explanation for birth control:
"People have a choice
about whether or not
to have children."
They say Miss Jackson
mellowed out
just before she died,
but I was always afraid of her,
everybody was.

Jeep Alley, Emperor of Baseball

Jeep stayed a senior
3 years to pitch ball
because Mr. Whitt was
coach and principal,
but the baseball team
disappeared along with
the high school, and Jeep
was left stranded, just
hanging around the diamond
in warm weather waiting
for us sixth and seventh grade
boys to come play a pick-
up game, cussing us out
for missing grounders or
dropping easy pop-ups.
It flattered us he was
interested because Jeep
weighed better than 200
pounds, always wore his old
blue Yankee cap, and could
fire without even trying
a fastball none of us could
catch. Miss Jackson tried
running him off, but Jeep
treated her like he would
a little thunder shower
that had to be politely
waited out, and we lied for
him because baseball was
the only game any of us
knew how to play, and God
it was good to hear him holler,
"Christ Almighty, Burchett,
getcha glove down ina dirt
and keepya god damn eyes
ona ball."

Janie Swecker and Me
and Gone With the Wind

Janie Swecker had to act
like she wasn't half
as smart as she was
because if she rattled off
the facts fast as she could
think of them, Miss Jackson
would sniff and say, "Well,
Janie, if you're that bored
with the history of your state,
why don't you go back
in the corner and sit
by yourself?" and Janie
hated that because back
there she couldn't get by
with sneaking to read those
library books she loved
while Miss Jackson drilled
the rest of us. So she made
herself talk slow and give
a wrong answer now and then,
and we stopped teasing her
after we understood that
if we hadn't got it done
she'd do our homework
for us even though she did
C. H. King's and Leo Spraker's
on a regular basis. Janie
let me borrow her mother's
copy of Gone with the Wind,
got impatient with me
to finish it but finally
I did and after that in class
sometimes we'd look at each
other and know what we knew.
One night I even dreamed

Miss Jackson was marching
through Georgia,
Atlanta was burning,
and I was riding hard
to pull Janie
out of the flames.

Mrs. Green

At the screen door
a pretty woman just
married and in shorts
on a Saturday in May,
she was sweet to me
when I came up to collect,
offered me something cold
to drink,
        which I refused
for the sake of dreaming
the whole summer I was
twelve about what it
would be like some
morning to walk
softly into
that lady's
kitchen.

My Brother Flies Over Low

Nobody could believe
my brother ever got through
that pilot school in Texas
because it was well known
in town he couldn't drive
a car worth a damn. So he'd
made a point of wearing his
uniform whenever he came
home and telling people
to watch out for him, he
was going to fly over low
one of these days. Which
he did, he and a buddy also
stationed down in Goldsboro,
made 2 passes, each one sounding
like 14 freight trains
falling off a cliff, waggled
their wings and headed on back
down to North Carolina,
gaining altitude as they went.
Mother was hanging out a wash,
and Mary King was coming up
the hill to help her with
spring cleaning, and they say
Miss Ossie Price came running
out of her store to see what
was the matter. And nobody
sees my brother now but what
they grin at him, shake their
heads and say something like,
"Great God Almighty, Bill."
Mother won't talk about it
in public, claims to be
embarrassed about the whole
thing, but she doesn't fool
anybody.

Theory

Everybody dug a hole and lived in it
when Division first cleared the land near Cu Chi.
Snipers kept the men low a while, but then tents
went up, then big tents. Later, frames of wood, screen
wire siding, and plywood floors rose under those tents
and that was called a hooch. Time I got there,
base camp was five square miles of hooches, not
a sniper round was fired in daylight, and good posture

was common. What we wanted was a tin roof.
I was there the day we got the tin to do it with,
blistering hot even that morning we stripped off
the old canvas, took hammers and climbed the rafters
to nail down sheets of tin. Drinking beer afterwards,
we were the sweaty survivors, we were the fit.

Bac Ha

As G-5 put it, Bac Ha hamlet was a good
neighbor in 25th Infantry Division's
eyes. Neighbor was a fact, eyes was a lie, and good
was a joke for a fool. Holes in the fence,
paths to the guard shacks, were for Bac Ha whores,
famous for clap, who maybe last year'd worn white
ao dais and ribboned hats to walk the warm
mornings to school, lessons from French-taught priests.

Division's garbage dump was three acres
fenced off from that hamlet's former front yard.
Black-toothed women, children, former farmers
squatted in the shade all day, smiled at the guards,
watched what the trucks dumped out. Walking nights
out there, you'd be under somebody's rifle sights.

Words

What did those girls say when you walked the strip
of tin shack bars, gewgaw stores, barber shops,
laundries and restaurants, most all of which
had beds in back, those girls who had to get up
in Saigon before dawn to catch their rides to Cu Chi,
packed ten to a Lambretta, chattering, happy
in their own lovely tongue, on the dusty
circus road to work, but then what did they say?

Come here, talk to me, you handsome, GI,
I miss you, I love you too much, you want
short time, go in back, I don't care, I want
your baby, sorry about that, GI,
you number ten. A history away
I translate dumbly what those girls would say.

Them

Sergeant Dieu, frail Vietnamese man,
once sat down with me, shirtless, on my bunk
and most astonishingly in my opinion
(not his) squeezed a pimple on my back.
My first trip to the field, I saw Vietnamese
infantry troops, loaded with combat gear,
walking the paddy dikes and holding hands.
I was new then. I thought they were queer.

Co Ngoc at the California Laundry
wouldn't say any of our words, but she
explained anyway a Vietnamese treatment
for sore throat: over where it's sore inside
you rub outside until that hurts too. That
way won't work for American pain. I've tried.

Cousin

I grew up staring at the picture of him:
oak leaves on his shoulders, crossed rifles
on his lapels, and down his chest so many medals
the camera lost them. He wore gold-rimmed
glasses, smiled, joked about fear. He told true
stories that were like movies on our front porch:
he'd fought a German hand to hand. The word
courage meant Uncle Jack in World War Two.

Ten years from my war, thirty from his, we
hit a summer visit together; again
the stories came. He remembered names of his men,
little French towns, a line of trees. I could see
his better than mine. He'd known Hemingway!
I tried hard but couldn't find a thing to say.

for John H. Kent, Jr., 1919–1982

Vermont

I'm forty-six. I was twenty-three then.
I'm here with what I've dreamed or remembered.
In the Grand Hotel in Vung Tau one weekend
I spent some time with the most delicate
sixteen-year-old girl who ever delivered
casual heartbreak to a moon-eyed GI.
I am trying to make it balance, but I
can't. Believe me, I've weighed it out:

rising that morning up to the cool air where
the green land moved in its own dream down there,
and I was seeing, the whole flight back to Cu Chi,
a girl turning her elegant face away
after I'd said all I had to say.
This was in Vietnam. Who didn't love me.

Music

Their white duck trousers, their dark coats, their grave
faces give us out here in the future
to understand such dignity was no
small matter. They surround two demure
women in long dresses, the best piano
players in town. The men hold instruments they've
just started making payments on, their large hands
cradling the horns. Most players of this band,
formally seated here, are carbide men who might
in two hours be shoveling grey dust: trumpet,
trombone, clarinet, tenor saxophone.
The one standing, holding his alto like that,
is my jaunty father, whose music I've known
all my life from this silent black-and-white.

The Field

The breeze stops, the afternoon heat rises,
and she hears his back porch screen door slap shut.
She sits still, lets her mind follow him through
the swinging gate into the field, his shirt
and white flannel pants freshly pressed, his new
racquet held so loosely that it balances
exactly in his hand. Now my father
takes the stile in two steps. And now my mother
turns in the lawn chair, allows herself the sight
of him lifting the racquet as if to
keep it dry. This instant, before he comes
to where she sits under the trees, these two
can choose whatever lives they want, but from
the next it is fixed in shadow and light.

The School

On one side the high school, on the other
grades one through seven, the purple-curtained
auditorium shrank and grew shabbier
each August we came back. Mr. Whitt one year
decided Charles Tomlinson, Slick King, Dwayne
Burchett, Bobby Peaks, and Big Face Cather
could be a basketball team. They practiced
on a rocky, red-dirt court with a basket
and some boards on a post. They drove to games—
always at the other school—in Slick's Ford.
Uniforms were jeans and T-shirts. Big Face
and Bobby played barefoot. They lost by scores
like ten to ninety-three, unaccustomed to such space,
wooden floors, lights, adults calling them names.

Croquet

This decorous, nineteenth-century
entertainment my Newbern grandmother
and great aunts come down from front porch rocking chairs
to play an afternoon hot enough to smother
Methodist ladies who say their prayers
at night but who roquet in quiet fury:
Gran gathers her concentration, pauses,
then lets her red mallet fly forth, causes
her skirt to follow her follow-through, then sweeps
it down and follows her red ball. Two wicked
split shots Aunt Iva fires. Aunt Stella, bones
skewed by childhood polio, makes wicket
after wicket, strikes the post, and in dining room tones
says, "Keep your manners but play for keeps."

Icicle

I smacked you in the mouth for no good reason
except that the icicle had broken off
so easily and that it felt like a club
in my hand, and so I swung it, the soft
pad of your lower lip sprouting a drop,
then gushing a trail onto the snow even
though we both squeezed the place with our fingers.
I'd give a lot not to be the swinger
of that icicle. I'd like another
morning just like that, cold, windy, and bright
as Russia, your glasses fogging up, your face
turning to me again. I tell you I might
help both our lives by changing that act to this,
by handing you the ice, a gift, my brother.

Sunday Dinner

If the whole length of the white tableclothed
table my grandparents called each other
Old Devil, Battle Ax, Bastard, and Bitch,
if having stopped smoking for Lent, Mother
was in a pout, if New Deal politics
had my father telling us how much he loathed
Roosevelt, if Grandma Lawson's notion
that we boys needed a dose of worm potion
had Charles trying hard not to look amused
and Bill whining for dessert even though
he hadn't finished his beets, if all this
and Uncle Lawrence's thick White Owl smoke,
Aunt Elrica's hoots, and Inez's craziness
weren't my one truth, I'd ask to be excused.

Stopping by Home

Five times since July my father
has been hospitalized. He's home
today, sitting up at his desk
in bathrobe, pajamas, slippers.
I am embarrassed, I want him
fat again, in khakis that smell
like sweat, cigarette smoke, carbide,

ignoring me because he'd rather
work the crossword puzzle, alone
or pretending to be, than risk
in those minutes before supper
finding out what meanness I'd been
up to. He's thin now. And pale.
Waiting to hear what's on my mind.

                    ·

In the summer in the hospital
he sat on the bed's edge clutching
that Formica table they crank up
and put your food tray on. He coughed
up white mucus, took oxygen
from a thin green tube, couldn't sleep,
couldn't lie back and breathe. He

and my mother thought it was all
finished the day he got medicine
to make him relax, make him sleep,
then couldn't sit up because he'd lost
his strength but couldn't breathe lying
back. They rang for the nurse, but he
passed through something you couldn't see.

                    ·

They say his hair turned white. It's true,
it's grayer than it was, almost
white. He can't read much now, has no
power of concentration, mind
strays. Today he talks about friends
who've died, relatives long gone.
In a photograph he points out

which ones are dead now. "But you
and Lester Waller and Tom Pope
and George Schreiber and James Payne—so
many still alive," I remind
him. He seems not to hear and bends
to put the picture away. "Some
still around," he says. "Yes, no doubt."

.

My mother wants us to talk. This
is what she always wants, her sons
sitting around with their dad, talk
being evidence of love, she
thinks. My evenings home from school,
the army, New York, or Vermont,
she'd leave the room for us to do it.

We always argued politics.
Didn't intend to, but reasons
came to us. Once he said I ought
to go to Russia and see
how what I'd just said was pure bull,
and I walked out. Words are too hard
for us now. We'll just have to sit.

.

Their lives in that house before he got too sick must have been
    so filled with silence that even when a truck would pass
    on the highway down the hill they would listen. Those
    clear sunny days of May and June she sat with him
    on the front porch where sometimes the soft wind
    rustled in that hack-berry that's grown
    so high now. I hold an infant

                    recollection of the sun
                warming the three of us,
                    their holding me so
                    close between them
                        I knew then
                        what home
                        meant.

                        So
                        if I
                    care so much
                    about them I
                have to sit up here
            a thousand miles away
        and write myself back home, why

                not look for a job down there, try
            to find some town close enough to say,
            "I'm going to see them," drive over there
        and walk in the door and not even surprise
    them, sit down with them and talk, maybe stay for lunch,
        say an easy good-bye and leave without feeling like
    I betrayed them, and I will never find my way back home.

                        •

Night comes down, the winter sky
momentarily ecstatic,
then stunned, bruised, ruined with pain, dark . . .

Coal on the fire, our old habits
keep us still, without lights, sitting
until the study's bay window
yields maybe one moving tree branch.

Then Mother rises, breathes a sigh
for all three of us when she flicks
on the overhead light. The dog barks
lightly in its sleep. We blink. It's
not late. His fingers shake setting
his watch. Before us are the slow
hours, each breath he takes a chance.

.

At six we move from the study
to the living room for the news,
the weather report our excuse.
The man draws snow over the whole
Northeast, freely uses the word
blizzard, and I stand up before
he's finished and say I think I

better keep driving north, maybe
I can beat that storm. "But Son, you
just got here." Mother's hurt. He's used
to my skedaddling ways, and so
makes himself grin, offers his hand
for me to shake and at the door
we say our word for love. Good-bye.

.

I scuttle out into the dark
and drive three hundred miles north, numb,
knowing that I hurt but not able
to register it, a busted

speedometer on a car that
hurtles forward. In the morning
I get what's coming to me. Snow

starts in Pennsylvania, slick
stuff on those mountains south of Scranton,
the interstate a long white table
of ice, everything blasted
white. Wind and drifts in those high flat
stretches near nowhere. Endless dream
of losing control, moving through snow.

.

Tell me whose parents don't get old.
Your father's sick, and you can't stand
to be around him and help him
die or get well, whichever it
turns out he's going to do. Well,
son, you deserve to drive through snow,
wind and freezing cold, past Hometown,

Port Jervis, Newburgh, Kingston. No
decent motel would have you, can't
stop, can't give your old man an arm
to help him walk into the next
room. Albany says go to hell,
keep driving, boy, get your ass home
where you've got children of your own.

From *The Nature of Yearning* (1992)

Local Metaphysics

Finally the mother had to pack up the kids
in the car and take them to see her, Miss
Ossie Price, who had tended Prices' Store
six days a week for the lifetimes of both
generations, though the mother found it hard,
after she'd knocked on the door of the house
and Miss Ossie was standing there, so tired
and still not finished crying but polite
as always, to speak: "Ossie, I'm sorry
to ask this, but the children can't believe you
weren't in the fire. They never saw you
anywhere but in the store. Could you just
come out to the car and let them see you?"
The great burnt corpse that had been Prices' Store
lay just across the street, and it stung her
eyes even to glance that way, but she walked down
there and talked to them through the car window,
three little girls. The youngest, a tow-head,
a runny-nosed pretty one named Christine,
sat frozen and wide-eyed until Miss Ossie
opened the door, pulled the child into her
arms and hugged her close. Finally Christine
cried. Then they thanked Miss Ossie and drove home.
This was in Ivanhoe, Virginia,
a Blue Ridge Mountain town so small there's no
store there at all now that Prices' has burnt.
My mother, who lives there and who heard it
from somebody, told me this, but I've filled
in such details as I need to live with it,
as did my mother and her reliable
source, and as will those children, forgetting
it and holding on to it through the years
until one day that little one, who smelled
to Miss Ossie like a country child in need
of a bath, whose cheek left a smear of tears

and mucus on her dress, will be telling it
to her friend over lunch in some city
restaurant, the story will be spilling
out with such passion that they will both laugh,
and this well-dressed woman with a mountain
twang in her voice will find herself saying,
"This actually happened to me, I
remember it clearly," as in amazement
she asks herself, "Why am I making this up?"

Inside the Hummingbird Aviary

Thumb-sized birds in gaudy greens,
iridescent vermilions, stop
on invisible floating dimes
intricately to pivot and kiss

sugar-water bottles or desert
blossoms. Within easy snatching
distance, a Broad-billed perches,
preens, pisses in a quick squirt,

darts out a tongue half
its body length. Suddenly
suspended at breast level,
a Calliope confronts a man,

marking its possession of that
quadrant of space, the sheer force
of its watch-part heart stopping
the giant, making him laugh.

These wings are the furious
energy of perfect stillness
to make him forget kestrels
and red-masked vultures.

Here in this airy cage
he has seen five whole
hummingbirds fit
into the chambers

of his hog-sized heart.
What the man wants now
is to be desert soil
beneath a thorny bush,

the black tongues of hummers
engineering sweetness
from blossoms that once
were his body.

The Snow Monkey Argues With God

Four days the mother
Snow Monkey carries
her still-born baby
before she leaves it

by a rocky stream. Then
she finds a high place
where she can brood alone
and still see her sisters

with their babies.
Four days she groomed
what should have been
as lively as these others.

If the Snow Monkey hurts
this way, can she not
also know what death is?
Or at least what it is not.

The thing she left downstream,
is not like these babies,
tugging and pulling
at their mothers, trying

to focus four-day-old
eyes on falling water
and sunlight skittering
under moving tree-branches.

While she watches her sisters
tenderly nursing
their young, she must feel
the wordless

old quarrel: better
that this paradise be burnt

to a clean white ash
than for any living

creature to have to lay down
on streamside rocks
what has been loved, what
stinks to high heaven.

Love and Art

At the Chagall Exhibit
the woman moves slowly
from picture to picture.

The man hardly pauses.
He eats the pictures,
wishing he could have
them all for himself.

Bella with a White Collar
surrounds the woman, as God
must cradle the universe.

The man strides past The Wedding,
Bride and Groom of the Eiffel Tower,
all of Daphnis and Chloe.
He is eager to buy postcards.

At the Magic Flute costumes,
the woman suddenly hears Chagall
and Mozart telling jokes, filling
the museum with their laughter.

The man buys a Fall of Icarus
T-shirt and a Milking the Cow poster
for the kids and sits down to wait.

Bella Writing is where she stops,
knowing the moment the painter
found her like that and took up
what was handy, a page of notepaper,

and that is where he finds her,
standing with strangers, brushing
her eyes, and smiling into the light.

Upstairs Hallway, 5 A.M.

My daughter's voice
wafts into the dark
through which, freshly
showered and shaved,
I am feeling my way.
I stop and listen
but hear only the house
hum, click, and groan.

A friend says a voice
on the phone instantly
reveals sex, age, ethnic
background, education
and intelligence.

But from this sentence
spoken out of her
dreams by my child,
I discern no words,
only a tone: quiet,
serious, friendly,
somewhat formal.

The dead must hear
their living speak
just this way: *Yes,
you are there forever
running your fingers
along the cool wall
of darkness, while I
so deeply dream this
world of sunlit shapes.
Soon enough I shall be
moving behind you.
Please, let me sleep
a little longer.*

Thinking About My Father

I have to go back
past the way he was
at the end, panting
for breath, begging
for medicine, crazy
from medicine taken
for years. This is
hard because in his
dying, he was vivid,
excruciatingly slow,
and profoundly self-
absorbed, as if his
death required more
energy and devotion
than we could ever
bring to his bedside.

But then there he is
at home, at his desk
in the den, where he
was able to be most
truly himself, paying
bills—he was happy
doing that—reading
the paper, then best
of all, beautifully
solving its crossword
puzzle. My father was
the absolute master
of crossword puzzles
in the Roanoke Times.

I do not mean to say
that he shut himself
off from us. It was
just that we learned
to approach his desk

for quiet attention.
He breathed a light
whistle between his
teeth while he helped
me balance my paper
route money, coat my
model airplane's silk
wing with banana oil,
hinge a new Brazilian
stamp into my album.

My father did things
with a care that was
more important to him
than the thing itself.
For example, painting
by the numbers: no one
ever number-painted so
gravely and precisely.
His Saint Bernards hang
over his desk, his blue
jays over the toilet so
that every peeing male
must witness the craft
of his terrible picture.

His pleasures were fresh
things, mail just pulled
from his post office box,
unthumbed newspapers, new
model airplane kits, sets
of mint-condition stamps
in glassine envelopes.
With his hands he savored
a new harmonica so that I
still see as sacred those
little Hohner boxes with

pictures on them of old-
time German concert bands.

I don't have any fresh
insight into my father
or his life. Thinking
about him like this, I
miss him, and I forget
how horrible his death
was. Some mornings I
wake up feeling bad for
no reason I can think of,
and then all day he'll be
on my mind, dying again.

I have no memory of his
holding me as an infant,
but we have an old home
movie in which my twenty-
two year old mother walks
out onto the front porch
and hands a baby to this
thin young man. Some days
I wake up limp and happy
as that child, smiled at
and lifted up to the sun
by someone who wanted me
right here in this world.

Poem at Fifty, Mostly in Long Lines

At night in a blizzard in 1959 I stood
halfway up the drifted bank of Route 94 a hundred yards down
from Samps Blair's service station and watched
a drunk driving too fast and hitting his brakes too late
and so sliding his truck into the back fender of the stuck car
of another drunk and bamming that thing right out of the drift
and twenty yards up the road. *Hoooeeee!*
hollered the struck one who'd been standing out with me
higher up in the drift to discuss his plight of being stuck.
I guess she ain't stuck no more! he hollered,
and he ran—or he rather quickly plodded—down to the road to
    confer
with the driver, who'd gotten out to examine
the damage to his truck's front end. I don't know
what those two said, or if they knew each other, but I heard some
    laughter,
before they both got into their still-idling vehicles and drove,
truck following car, down toward Ivanhoe and left me standing
in the dark to be further snowed upon. I don't know
why I happened to be standing in that particular snow drift
at that late hour, *Coming back from a date in Wytheville,* I guess
—at least that's what my dad would say, if he were alive.
Why, Dave, to see a girl in Wytheville, he'd tell me,
you'd have driven through the fires of hell!
But anyway I remember I hadn't been able to get his car up
either slick side of the hill to our house. I can't remember
now where I'd parked it—that green Dodge of his
with the push-button drive—or what I figured
I was going to do after I'd finished talking to the stuck drunk.
It doesn't matter. Somehow, I got home,
and in my seventeenth year, I had it in my possession that I
    had stood

beside a grown man who'd hollered up into the swirling night sky,
 Hoooeee!
I guess she ain't stuck no more!
I'm not at all sure
I'll be able
to hold on
to this story
for thirty-three
more years.

This Poem Is the End of a Long Story

Muncie Webb and Doctor Santiago and I
are riding to Ivanhoe in Muncie's jeep
at 7:30 the morning after a blizzard.
The air is sharp, cold, clear, still.
There's very little traffic on Route 11;
the fields are a dazzling whiteness.
We notice someone hanging onto the side
of a stopped eighteen-wheeler, someone
banging now on the driver's window.
Muncie pulls over in front of the truck,
we get out and walk back to where the guy
banging on the window hollers down to us:
the truck must have been running all night,
the door is locked, and the driver is slumped
over the wheel. Muncie pushes Dr. Santiago
forward and says, "This man's a doctor."
A state trooper arrives and jimmies the door.
We make way for Dr. Santiago who with his black
doctor's bag steps up to the cab, to the gray-faced
driver. Quickly he gives this man a shot,
and the driver begins making the slow movements
of a stunned monster. With Dr. Santiago's help,
he turns toward the door to step down, then pukes
rather fabulously all down his pants. The day
is uncommon in its cold clarity; the driver,
trucking through our part of Virginia in 1958,
is a light-skinned Negro; Doctor Santiago,
recently come to us from the Philipines,
speaks very little English. Muncie talks
all the way to Ivanhoe about how proud he is:
of himself for knowing to stop, of the little doc
for his good work with the needle, and of me—
though I'm just fifteen—for not flinching
at the sight of a dead man coming back to life.

Mother Encounters Monkey
at the Post Office

And because I have written so much about Monkey,
she brings him home with her to talk with me.

I don't like to talk at 8:30 in the morning,
I write on my laptop computer until well after nine.

It was as a boy that I had so much to say to Monkey,
who is eighty-two years old and *Deaf now*, he shouts

at me, *Can't hear a thing, honey, but that's how
the Lord meant things to be, I guess. We don't always*

*understand, now do we, honey? You know about Jonah
and the whale, don't you? I know you do. I went to school*

*with your mother, did you know that? First I went
to school with your daddy, then I went to school*

*with your mother; they went on ahead, and I stayed
right there till they told me I could quit,*

*and then I went to work for your grandaddy. I guess
you remember that time Charles fell off the threshing*

*machine and I caught him? Well, the Bible tells us
we can't always understand. I've still got my health,*

and I've still got my Bible—Monkey pats his overalls
chest pocket. His simian eyes take on this abstracted

look as if an inner voice is giving him instructions,
to which he must listen carefully before deciding

what to do next. I hear stirring upstairs that means
Lindsey, Bess, and Molly have wakened to Monkey's and my

conversation. You're looking good, Monkey, I tell him
quietly. You look just like you did forty years ago.

Monkey doesn't hear my fatuous remarks. He smiles and rises.
Well, I better be getting down the hill, he says,

and when I offer him a ride, he sweetly refuses. *Next time*
you come home for a visit, I hope I'll see you. We're all

real proud of you, he says. When I was a boy,
he never did this, but he does now, gives me a good-bye hug,

which I stiffly try my best to return. Then Monkey walks
down through the field of high wet grass toward Ivanhoe, leaving

my mother and me to explain to each other, and a little later
to Lindsey and Bess and Molly, when they come downstairs

looking quizzical, what has transpired that required
such a lot of shouting in the living room this morning.

STORIES

From *Only the Little Bone* (1986)

Summer of the Magic Show

O N E   O C T O B E R   night in his second year at the University of Virginia, my brother persuaded a young woman to drive him to a scenic overlook at the top of Afton Mountain. They sat in the dark car a few moments, but they didn't talk. The young woman lit a cigarette just before they both climbed out. There were no stars, no moon, no street or house or car lights.

And they stayed quiet. The woman leaned against her car's front fender, crossed one arm in front of her, held the cigarette near her face, and kept her eyes on Duncan.

It was so dark, Duncan says, he could step away from her only a pace and a half and still see her face and her blond hair. He took a white handkerchief from his jacket pocket—U. Va. students wore coats and ties then—shook the folds out, and held it at arm's length from himself.

A rifle-shot went off not ten yards from them, so loud that Duncan, who knew it was coming, says he couldn't help flinching. The young woman yelped, crouched, dropped her cigarette, crossed her arms in front of her face to protect herself. Duncan had been too startled to notice if the handkerchief had flapped or not, but it had the bullet hole through it, and he carried it over to show to the young woman. He made the desired impression on her: that night so frightened her that she moved away from Charlottesville, where she'd lived most of her life.

Duncan says he regrets what he did. He had arranged for his friend Bobby Langston to wait with his squirrel-rifle up there on the Skyline Drive, and he was lucky Bobby had his night vision and was such an accurate shot as to be able to hit that handkerchief, dark as it was. With the shot, Duncan stopped wanting to harm the woman, but by then, of course, he had already done it. I regret knowing the story and what it tells about him.

Back when he was fourteen, Duncan was taller than anybody in our town—six-five—and thin, but very strong. No matter how much needling he took from the coaches over at Madison High School, he wouldn't play basketball or football for them. Duncan was an intellectual, and he was an innocent boy. He was pale and hairy, wore glasses, was not what anybody'd call handsome. He never really had a date until his senior year of high school.

He was the smartest one ever to come out of our town. No one begrudged him his brains, though my father often shook his head over what he called "the ways Duncan chooses to put his intelligence to use." Duncan's passion was magic. When he was thirteen he found an old *Tarbell Correspondence Course for the Apprentice Magician* in my grandparents' attic, and he read through the year's worth of lessons in about a week.

He put on his first magic show, in our living room, for Uncle Jack and Aunt Mary Alice. I remember that he messed up the Mystical Multiplying Balls, dropped one of the hollow shells right in the middle of his audience and had to stoop, humiliatingly, and pick it up. But he went on, and when he finished the show my parents and aunt and uncle applauded. What else could they do? They didn't know it was going to have a permanent effect on him.

Duncan went on doing tricks for the kids on the bus, who thought he was a freak, and for the kids in his homeroom, who were happy to have him pass the time for them, and so on, until finally Mrs. Pug Jones promised him five dollars if he'd come to Buntsy's birthday party and keep the kids from tearing her house apart. When he came back from Buntsy's party, Duncan showed me the five-dollar bill and said that now he was a professional.

The time I was closest to Duncan was the summer between his first and second years in engineering school at the University of Virginia. He was a National Merit Scholar, the only one we'd had from our whole county. He'd gotten a summer job running the scales for Pendleton over at the rock quarry, and he'd decided to put on a magic show for the town of Rosemary. He told us his plans and started working on us at the supper Mother fixed to celebrate his homecoming from Charlottesville. He wanted my mother to get the Ladies' Aid to sponsor him and my father to talk to the Superintendent of Schools to get him the use of the auditorium. My mother was still a little intoxicated from seeing the Lawn and the Rotunda at the University of Virginia when she drove up there to get him. My father gave Duncan his old slow shake of the head, but he didn't say no. It was a supper where Duncan did all the talking anyway, which was his right, having managed not to flunk out of school like everybody else from Rosemary who went away to college. The plans he told us about for the show were modest ones, a lot of card tricks and sleight-of-hand stuff he'd been practicing for his roommate, Will Greenwood. My father and I packed in the steak and mashed potatoes and peas that were Duncan's celebration supper, and my mother listened to his newly sophisticated talk, hardly touching what was on her plate.

Duncan just assumed I'd help him with the magic show, but that didn't bother me. I had nothing else to do that summer except mow yards for the three or four people in town who wanted them mowed. Rosemary probably had more houses in it that were surrounded by packed-down dirt, with chickens pecking in the dust and dogs under the porch, than it had houses with grass around them. Even the people who were willing to pay me to cut their grass were doing me a favor. So was Duncan, who pronounced me his "stage manager and first assistant."

The more Duncan thought about it—mostly while he was wearing a hard hat and making check-marks on a clipboard over at the rock quarry—the more he realized card tricks and sleight-of-hand wouldn't be good enough for his show. We had to have more illusions, a Chinese Disappearing Cabinet, a Flaming Omelet Bowl that changed the fire into dozens of silk scarves and then changed them into two white doves, a Guillotined Girl, and a Floating Lady. He talked my grandfather into helping him weld together an elaborate device of heavy pipes that he needed for the Floating Lady. He set me to work building, according to diagrams he drew, the Chinese Cabinet. He saw Toots Polk down at the post office one morning, and he persuaded her to be his Guillotined Girl. While he was at it, he asked her if she wouldn't mind doing a few of her dance numbers.

He decided I'd do a couple of trumpet solos, too, just to balance out Toots's tap-dancing. I'd gotten to be pretty good at "It's Cherry

Pink and Apple Blossom White." Duncan said I could do that one and one more. I chose "Tammy," which in my opinion I played with a great deal of feeling.

On weekends when Duncan didn't have to work for Pendleton, he and I spent most of the day in the empty schoolhouse, building and painting flats for the set, working on the lighting, blocking out the show. There was a battered upright school piano in there, below and to the right of the stage. I plunked around on that when things got slow. Duncan always asked me to play one of the two songs he liked to sing, "Old Man River" and "Unchained Melody." He stood at center stage and bellowed out the words at the top of his voice, but he held himself formally, as if he had on white tie and tails. At least once every time he and I were in there alone, he had a go at "Unchained Melody."

Duncan had been getting letters from Charlottesville, and he'd mentioned a woman's name in connection with the theater group for which he had done some lighting work. So it wasn't quite a surprise when he announced that Susan O'Meara would be visiting us for a week at the beginning of July.

Susan was twenty-two. Duncan was eighteen. She smoked and wore jeans, men's shirts untucked, and no makeup; what her blond hair looked like didn't seem to matter to her. She drove up to our house one afternoon in a beat-up white Ford. She got there before Duncan had come home from the rock quarry, and right off she told Mother that it was so damn hot in that car, could she please take a bath? I couldn't remember when a woman had ever said *damn* in front of my mother; it startled me to have a strange woman come into our house and go straight upstairs to take a bath. I waited for a sign from Mother, but she remained calm. I was dumbfounded at supper that evening, halfway through my first piece of fried chicken, when I looked and saw, first, that Susan O'Meara was cutting hers with a knife and fork, and then that Mother and Duncan were doing the same with theirs. My father and I stuck to our usual method, but neither of us went beyond our second piece.

Susan talked about the heat in Charlottesville, about her father, who was a doctor, about her mother, who taught biology at St. Ann's. Susan said *damn* again during the meal; then during dessert she laughed and said she had recently told David Weiss of the Virginia Players to go to hell.

I figured my mother was bound to correct that kind of talk at her supper table, but they all went on eating their berry pie, and I was the only one who drowned his in sugar and milk—my mother had given my father a look when he reached for the cream pitcher.

Duncan, for once, wasn't saying much, but he sure was listening to every word Susan spoke. Finally the two of them excused themselves and left the house to go to the drive-in. When I stepped to the window to see which one of them was going to drive, Mother snapped at me to stop spying on them. I saw Duncan open the door of her Ford and Susan climb in on the driver's side.

I waited around the table hoping to hear some interesting opinions of Susan from one or the other of my parents, but they offered nothing. My father did have seconds on the berry pie, and this time he treated himself to plenty of sugar and milk. I asked them straight out, "What do you think of her?"

It was one of the most reasonable questions I'd ever asked them, but I didn't get an answer. What I did get was a look from each of them, neither of which I understood. Then they gave each other another look, and I didn't understand that either.

On the weekend Susan, in her jeans and a sweatshirt, worked over at the schoolhouse with Duncan and me. Mostly she sat in the second row, dangling her feet over the wooden back of the seat in front of her, smoking, and offering suggestions to Duncan. Anything I had to say he had always only half-listened to, but he took notes when Susan told him something. Once she climbed up on a ladder to examine some of the lights above the stage. For a long while she shouted down remarks for Duncan, who stood holding the ladder and gazing up at her.

She wasn't rude to me or to my father, but she dealt with us as if we were photographs of Duncan's cute little brother and his old codger of a father. She never asked us questions the way she sometimes did Mother.

On the last evening she spent with us, Susan wore this little diamond ring Duncan had bought her with his Pendleton money. It couldn't have been anything but the smallest stone they had at Smith's Jewelers, but it probably cost Duncan every cent he had in his savings account at the time. I wouldn't have noticed it if I hadn't caught Mother with her eye on it during the meal.

Obviously Duncan and Susan meant for the rest of us to understand that they were engaged, but for some reason neither of them said anything aloud about it. My father and I weren't about to say anything on our own, and so it was up to my mother to mention it if anybody was going to, and she chose not to. It was as if since nobody gave voice to it, the engagement hadn't really come about. There was the ring on Susan's finger—she chewed her nails, by the way—but without any words being spoken there was no engagement. That last night I did notice a way Susan had of widening her eyes when she talked that made me understand just for an instant what Duncan saw in her, "one of the most brilliant minds in Albemarle County," as he put it.

Next morning, to see her leave, I snuck out of bed and knelt by the window. It was early because Duncan had to go to work at the quarry. My mother and Duncan and Susan all came out to the car together. Mother gave Susan a sort of official kiss on the cheek, so measured that I imagined she must have thought about it all through their breakfast, and Susan had to hold her cigarette away from Mother with her free hand. Then Mother went back inside, Susan stamped out her cigarette in our driveway, and she and Duncan went into this farewell embrace and kiss. I was surprised at how embarrassed I felt to be seeing it, though I confess it was exactly what I had come to the window to see. Maybe I thought it was going to be funny or sexy, but it was neither of those, and I can't really say what it was. When Susan climbed in behind the steering wheel, Duncan leaned in to kiss her goodbye again. And when she was gone, with the dust from her car still hanging above the driveway, Duncan stood out there alone with his hands in his pockets, toeing at something on the ground. I noticed then how skinny he was, how the sun had burnt his neck and arms.

This was the same morning my mother decided, as she put it, "to inaugurate a custom for the good of our family." She meant to correct the social behavior of my father and me, who had not gracefully carried off Susan O'Meara's visit. Mother didn't ask us what we thought about it, and we knew from her tone of voice not to argue. She commissioned me to ask a girl to our house for my birthday supper. Every birthday, she said, a girl should be invited.

To put it in straightforward terms, girls made my father uncomfortable. Susan O'Meara had come close to paralyzing him. He was a courtly man. When we sat in the dining room, which was when we had company, he stood and held my mother's chair for her until she came in to sit down. He spoke with elaborate courtesy to all the women on my mother's side of the family and said *yes ma'am* and *no ma'am* to most of them. In fact, I felt that in the presence of women, my mother excepted, my father was never himself. He limited his conversation to expressing agreement with the people around him or to asking questions of them. If questioned himself, he phrased his replies in such a way as to generalize or abstract whatever he was telling, so that his opinions in this voice were dull, his experiences hardly worth mentioning. My father was a man who had faced an old toolshed full of rattlesnakes, had been shot at by union strikers, had taken a knife away from Bernard Seeger at a high-school dance, but around women who came to our house as company, and especially around Susan O'Meara that past week, my father took on the personality of somebody who'd stayed indoors all his life and eaten nothing but cheese sandwiches.

I didn't resent my mother's decision, as perhaps I might have any other summer. I had noticed that my parents treated Duncan like a grownup while Susan was in the house; I knew a girl who was almost as formidable as Susan: Jean Sharp. She was from Palm Beach, Florida. Even though she was only thirteen, I'd heard her say things that showed she thought Rosemary, Virginia, was far back in the wilderness.

I was Jean's grandmother's yard-boy. When I finished mowing her yard, old Mrs. Sharp had me come inside for lemonade before she paid me. While I stood there, sweating in her kitchen, she coaxed some conversation out of me, then some out of Jean standing in the kitchen doorway. Jean had very fine dark hair, a small nose and mouth, a lanky frame. When Jean and I gave the appearance of being able to talk with each other, Mrs. Sharp handed me the money and suggested that we go into the living room and play cards. Jean taught me cribbage while sitting forward on the sofa with her back very straight, her knees bent and together, her ankles crossed. All that summer Jean had worn sundresses; they emphasized her flat-chestedness, but there was something about her in those dresses, her thin shoulders maybe, that was sexy. Her fingers playing the cards or moving the pegs on the cribbage board held my attention. Her soft voice, her precise diction, made me feel I was learning something every time she spoke to me.

My father had seen Jean only a few times in all her summers of visiting her grandmother in Rosemary, but he knew about her. When my mother and I talked it through to the conclusion that Jean was the one I would ask to my fourteenth-birthday supper, my father's face showed that he dreaded it. I dreaded it, too, a little bit.

Duncan, of course, when he heard about it, got a bright idea. His turn of mind that summer was one where everything that came to his attention had to be connected in some way to his magic show. He would ask Jean to be his Floating Lady. He was so excited about the notion that he drove me up to old Mrs. Sharp's house that Saturday so I could ask Jean to the supper and so he could get a fresh look at her to see how she'd work on stage. He didn't get out of the car, but while I was talking to Jean on her grandmother's front porch I could feel Duncan staring at us from the car window. Then, driving up to the schoolhouse, Duncan chattered away about Jean, how it was great she was so thin and wouldn't be likely to break down the Floating Lady apparatus, as we'd both joked that Toots might have done, and how Jean's "ethereal face," as he put it, would appeal to the audience. He'd stopped thinking about a Rosemary audience, which would be made up mostly of a bunch of antsy, loud-mouthed, bad-smelling, runny-nosed kids, Jeep Alley, Big-Face Limeberry, Thelma Darby and all her freckle-faced family, Mr. and Mrs..Pug Jones and Buntsy, people like that. Duncan was thinking about *audience* in the way they probably thought about it in Charlottesville.

He had this hyperbolic way of talking about everybody: Will Greenwood was the greatest drum major in the history of his high school, Bobby Langston was a fearless and diabolical genius, and so on. About Jean Sharp, I heard him telling our mother in the kitchen, "She's truly beautiful, don't you think?" This was on my birthday, just before Jean's grandmother drove her up to our house, and my father and I, in the living room, exchanged glances when we heard Duncan talking like that. We knew Jean wasn't "truly beautiful." She was just a girl who was visiting in our town. Duncan didn't have to exaggerate what she was just because he wanted her to be in his show. But my father and I were used to his ways that summer. We were grateful to him for doing most of the talking when Jean first walked into our house.

She had on another sundress, this one white with a sort of primly high front to it. It set off her tanned shoulders and face, her dark hair. Something about the way that dress fit her at the arms bothered me, though. It made a loose place where, I knew, if I looked at the right angle, I'd see her breast, or what should have been her breast.

There were girls in my classes at school whose breasts or bras I'd strained my neck trying to get a peek at, but they weren't like Jean. I didn't want to see into her dress, but sitting beside her at the table, I could hardly help noticing that opening every time I cast my eyes in her direction. To make things worse, I became aware of the sounds my father was making as he ate.

Courtly man though he was, his table manners, or rather the things that went on between him and the food on his plate, were pretty crude. He took large bites of things, and there was a kind of liquid inhaling noise that went with each bite. Often he chewed with his mouth open, so that you could hear it, and he liked to roll the food around in his mouth so that he made sloshing noises. It bothered me even though I knew why he did it. It was the result of his courtliness: his way of signaling to my mother that he liked the food was to make eating noises that expressed his pleasure, his gratitude to her for cooking the food for him. The noises had to be loud enough for her to hear him at the opposite end of the table, and I expect they were that evening, even though I knew he was holding back on Jean's account.

I was thinking about asking to be excused when suddenly Duncan asked Jean if she would be his Floating Lady, and she choked on a sip of iced tea.

She was all right, of course. Nobody ever died of iced tea going down the wrong way, at least not that I know of, and you would think the incident—Jean gasping and coughing into her napkin, my father and brother and I rising and coming around behind her chair, ready to pound on her back (though not one of us was going to touch those elegant shoulders unless she got really serious about her choking), my mother coming around the table, too, carrying her napkin for some reason and saying, "Oh, you poor dear, you poor thing"—you'd think the incident would have humanized us all. It didn't. There was a short moment after Jean recovered and we'd all gone back to our places when nobody made a sound, one of those embarrassing lulls in the conversation that are usually broken by somebody's polite giggle. In this case my mother managed a feeble "Well . . . ," and then we had more silence before we fell back to eating, and my father's mouth noises recommenced.

After a while Jean managed to squeak out to Duncan that, yes, she would be happy to be his Floating Lady, and he was released from responsibility for her condition. He went on with his inflated jabbering about the show. But because she had made such a red-faced, watery-eyed, spluttering spectacle of herself, she who was as serene as a piece of sculpture in every other circumstance of my seeing her, Jean now was repulsive to me. Sitting beside her, I lost my appetite.

My mother must also have experienced some kind of pivotal moment that summer evening when Jean Sharp choked in our dining room. That was the last angel food cake with pink icing she ever made for my birthday, though I have never stopped thinking of it as the only legitimate kind of birthday cake.

Next morning, as usual, Duncan and I walked down to the post office where I waited with him while he waited for his ride to Pendleton's quarry. It was an occasion for talking about the magic show. He'd glance at his letter from Susan, if he got one. Then, when he left, I'd take my parents' mail back up the hill to our house.

That morning, though, Duncan had to sign for a little package from Susan. He opened it while he and I were discussing what we were going to do about the kids who'd go around behind the schoolhouse to try to peek in the windows and cracks in the doors to see how the tricks worked. All of a sudden he was holding the diamond ring in his fingers, and I was looking at it, and it was registering on both of us what that meant.

"Aw God, Duncan," I said, "that's a shame." I didn't know what else to say. I wanted to put my arm around his shoulder, but we weren't that kind of a family, and this was in the post office anyway. So I just got out of there as quick as I could and left him standing there staring at the ring with no expression on his face.

I guess he went to work, though I don't know how he got through the day. He came home at the regular time, and he sat with us at the table in the kitchen where we ate supper. But he just dangled his fork over his food and wouldn't eat, wouldn't talk. We'd gotten used to all his jabber-jabber, as my father called it, and the three of us had a hard time filling up the silence. We'd have understood if he'd called off the show. We'd have even understood if he'd taken the car out, gotten drunk, and run it up the side of a tree—there was a tradition of that kind of behavior in our county.

But Duncan was his own man. He worked harder than ever on the magic show, and he said what was necessary to make me work harder on it, too. We'd begun rehearsing in earnest. It wasn't fun for us anymore, what with him losing his temper and going off to sulk when one of us made a mistake. "There is no margin for error in magic," he spat at me once when I lost my balance on the tiny little platform of the Chinese Disappearing Cabinet and put a foot down where the whole audience would have seen it.

Toots asked him to leave the auditorium while she ran through her tap numbers. She said they weren't magic, and she didn't want to know what he thought if she made a mistake. I was surprised when he agreed to leave, and I found that my pleasure in watching the little shimmering of her thighs increased with Duncan out of the room. When I went outside to tell him Toots was finished, I saw him walking over at the far end of the red-dirt elementary-school playground. He had his head down, and I first thought maybe he was crying and then that maybe he was thinking real hard about something. But then I could see little puffs of red dust coming up from his footsteps, and I knew he was stomping the ground, was raging to himself. I went back inside and waited for him to come back in on his own.

I had become a good deal more objective about Jean Sharp by that time. I didn't like to be around her, but I continued to think that I ought to be attracted to her. She was prettier in the face than Toots Polk, and I knew I ought to like looking at her just as much as I liked looking at Toots. But I didn't. The *didn't* and the *ought to* canceled each other out, and I felt nothing.

One night Herky Thompson and Toots took Jean and me out with them on a double date to the drive-in. (Toots's mother made them do it, I expect, because she didn't trust Herky, who was from Piney.) After dark, Jean and I sat in the back seat doing our best to concentrate on *Miss Tatlock's Millions* while Herky and Toots coiled around each other in Toots's corner of the front seat.

I snuck my arm around Jean—she was wearing a sweater—and though I knew she was aware of my arm, I felt no loosening of her good posture, no impulse on her part to lean my way. At the time I resented her for that coldness, but later I decided that she was in the right: She felt no real affection or desire in that arm behind her, those fingers lightly touching her shoulder. She didn't respond because I didn't offer her any part of myself to which she could respond.

All through the final rehearsals Duncan growled at us and cursed under his breath and once put his fist through one of the flats so that we had to repair it. Jean and Toots and I had grown frightened of him. Jean, who rarely said much, told Toots and me that she thought he was going to scare the audience right out of their seats. Toots nodded. I thought about telling them how it had been, earlier in the summer, when Duncan and I had performed "Unchained Melody" to the empty auditorium, but I didn't.

I opened the show out in front of the curtain, ignoring the giggles that Thelma Darby started in the audience when I stepped into the spotlight. I couldn't see past the first row anyway, though my father had passed back the word that we had a full house. I lifted my trumpet and silenced everybody with "It's Cherry Pink and Apple Blossom White."

I finished, the curtain opened, and there was "Duncan the Great" standing in his tuxedo at center stage with Toots a step or two to the side holding the top hat out of which shortly Duncan would yank the three-pound white rabbit I'd bought from Gilmer Hyatt two weeks ago. But he had time for small talk, or "patter," as magicians call it, before the trick. In the most lighthearted tone I'd ever heard him use, he paid me a compliment: "That's Reed Bryant, my brother, ladies and gentlemen, and isn't he some musician?" I got another feeble little round of applause, along with a couple of jeers that I ignored.

Jean really didn't have many duties for the show. She assisted Duncan for a couple of little tricks, but she didn't have any talents that we really needed; so she spent a lot of time standing around near me when I was offstage. Sometimes it was pitch dark back there when Duncan was doing one of the tricks with flames or working with a deck of cards in the spotlight out front. I could feel Jean standing there with me and reminding me of how much I dreaded the Floating Lady trick.

Toots and I were both assistants for that one. We were to pull the chairs out from each end of the Floating Lady's little platform. Toots was at Jean's head, and I was at her feet. I'd bargained with Toots to trade sides, but Duncan hadn't allowed it. I had to get back to the lighting board immediately after the trick to douse the lights, and so

it had to be the feet side for me. I had been anxious all through the
rehearsals when Jean had worn shorts or slacks, because I knew that
in the performance she was to wear a dress. There was a good chance
I'd have to see all the way to the north pole, whether I wanted to or
not, and in front of half the town of Rosemary. In any circumstance
Jean was a girl up whose dress I did not want to see.

The apparatus for the Floating Lady was heavy and elaborate, because of course it had to hold the lady up, but it had to be so cleverly
arranged and concealed that the audience couldn't see it or imagine
how it might be set up. Duncan had to brace himself against part of it
and stand so that he hid one huge black pipe from the audience. Even
then there had to be a four-by-four post holding that thing down behind the rear curtain and braced against the top of a window well. In
rehearsal, Toots and I had laughed because all those pipes looked so
crude to us that we couldn't believe anybody would ever be fooled.
Duncan assured us that the trick would work.

In the performance Duncan and Toots and I were sweating out
there under the lights. When Jean in her yellow sundress walked out
on stage, she was loudly and somewhat lewdly cheered, but then
something about her appearance quieted the audience right down.
She really did appear to fall under Duncan's hypnotic spell when he
had her sit and then lie down on the platform. Toots fixed Jean's
dark hair to lie prettily at the side of her head, and Jean's face and
body became waxen, spiritless.

A hush came down over the audience when Toots removed the first
chair. Duncan, standing directly behind her, kept his hands held high
over Jean while she lay there, and he looked like a crazy preacher
held in a spell himself. I looked up at his face then, just before I was
to pull my chair. Duncan was charged with some kind of emotion
I'd never seen in anybody. I knew that part of it must have had to do
with Susan O'Meara, but another part of it was willing that illusion
into being: Jean Sharp was by God going to float in the air on the
stage of Rosemary Elementary School!

With exaggerated wariness, I removed my chair. Jean wobbled
a little bit. Then she held steady. A noise came from the audience,
as if everyone had inhaled at once. Clarence Shinault, who'd gone
through seventh grade with Duncan, said clearly from way in the
back, "Gah-odd *damn*, Duncan."

Gravely, Duncan passed the hoop, with agonizing slowness, from

Jean's feet to her head and then back again from her head to her feet. Then he held the hoop up for everyone to see. The applause came just when it should have, Toots and I put our chairs back under the platform, Jean awoke from her spell, smiled, and began climbing down while I skipped back to the lighting board. The trick was over, and I couldn't remember whether or not I'd seen up Jean's dress.

In the week or two before he went back to Charlottesville, thanks to his success with the show, Duncan recovered some of his good spirits. Once he even asked me why I wasn't trying to see more of "The Exquisite Miss Sharp," as he had taken to calling her. I wouldn't have been inclined to explain it to him even if I had understood my feelings about her and even if he had been free enough of his own troubles to be more than halfway interested.

It was my father who gave me the most comfort in that time. Even earlier in the summer he'd started helping me, at the end of the terrible birthday supper when my mother had herded us all into the living room to chat with Jean before she went home. We sat there for an excruciating length of time. I found myself copying my father's manner. I agreed with things Duncan said, things my mother said, and especially with any slight remark of Jean's. Once, the rhythm of conversation demanded that I say something, and so I asked Jean a question about Palm Beach, then pretended to listen while she, with much graceful gesturing of her slender arms and hands, tried to make us understand where in the city she lived and how far that was from the actual beach.

When my father stood up to signal that he wished the occasion to be over, I was the first one to rise and second his motion. Duncan wanted to ride with us on the way over to Jean's grandmother's house so that he could tell her more about the magic show. I'd have been glad to have him along, but my mother put a hand on his sleeve, and he said that, well, now he remembered he had a letter he had to write before he went to sleep.

Outside, standing by the car, my father instructed Jean and me to ride in the back seat. By that time the fireflies were out, the bats were swooping over our heads, it was warm, and there was the scent of honeysuckle over the whole yard, but Jean seemed glad to be climbing into the car. When my father saw that she and I weren't going to have much to say to each other on the drive across the ridge and around the town, he turned on the radio. I've always been grateful to him for that, because I know for a fact that he hated the car radio, especially the hillbilly and rhythm & blues stations that were all we could get at night in our part of the country.

In the cool air I walked Jean up onto her grandmother's front porch, said a quickly retreating goodnight, and scuttled back to sit in the front seat with my father. In his kindness he neither asked me anything nor said a word to me. He'd turned off the radio, and he took his time driving back home. The two of us were quiet, except once when we came to a place where we could see a light way up on the hill at our house.

I said, "I'll bet that's the light in Duncan's room," and my father chuckled and said yes, he guessed Duncan was writing that letter to Charlottesville. That was the night before Duncan got the ring back in the mail from Susan O'Meara, and it was several months before the night he sent Bobby Langston with his squirrel-rifle up on Afton Mountain to wait for him and Susan. It was almost a full year before Duncan flunked out of the University of Virginia. That night, sitting at his bedside table to write that letter to Susan, all Duncan knew that was coming to him was his magic show. My father and I kept driving slowly around the ridge, both he and I watching the road in the headlights and occasionally glancing out our side windows at the dark. Then, at almost exactly the same moment, though our tunes were different, we each began whistling through our teeth.

The Undesirable

I G O T over to the side of the road as far as I could, into the grass and the weeds, but my father steered the car over that way, too. Through the windshield I could see his work hat, the shadow of his face and shoulders, the specks of light that were his glasses. I pushed right up against the fence, squeezed into the honeysuckle vines. In a bright haze of sunlight I watched him come at me, the green hood of the Ford growing huge as it came close enough for me to see the waves of heat rising from it. Then he swerved the car over to the middle of the driveway and stopped it beside me. I could see him, in his khaki work clothes, shifting to neutral, pulling the emergency brake, sliding over to the passenger side of the front seat, picking up his dinner-bucket to hold in his lap. He waited for me while I scuffled in the vines and trash beside the fence to reach my glasses.

"You weren't scared, were you?" he asked when I opened the door. There was that sharp smell in the car with him. Sometimes I imagined, when he came home from work, that there was a coating of gray dust all over him. I got in behind the steering wheel and slammed the door. Every day now I met him at the head of our driveway and drove the car the quarter of a mile in to our house. I was practice-driving with him.

"I knew you wouldn't hit me," I said. When I said it, I knew it was true, sitting there beside him with the sunlight coming down through the trees onto the gravel road in front of us. My father scooted down to rest his head against the back of the seat. He took off his glasses and rubbed the two spots they had dented into the bridge of his nose. He wasn't going to hit me with the car. He'd never even hit me with his hand except once, when I was eight and I'd splashed bathwater on him. I said it again, "I knew you wouldn't hit me." I put the car into low and started it moving, concentrating on easing the clutch out. Then the car jerked. I said "Damn car." My father chuckled to himself, his hat down over his eyes.

I was soon going to be fifteen, which was how old you had to be to get a driver's license. My father might have made me wait until I was older. "You're like a stick of dynamite just waiting for somebody to come along and light your fuse. That somebody isn't going to be me," he said. I thought he understood a little of what it was like to live in Rosemary but go to high school in Madison, twenty miles away. Sometimes, when I was especially restless and jittering my foot or twirling my glasses around in my hand, I would see him looking at me.

Though he was what my grandfather called a fair-sized man, six feet tall and 190 pounds, my father had delicate features. In our hallway was a picture of him and my mother when they were first married, when my mother was fifteen and my father was twenty-one; my mother looked beautiful and much older than fifteen, but my father was even more boyish-looking than I was, I thought. He had a quick temper. He'd raise his voice to yell at Duncan or me. I had heard him yell into the phone at some man who had called him up from the carbide plant at suppertime. "Hell's bells!" my father would say; Duncan and I thought that was hilarious, always giggled when he said it. The skin of my father's body was pale; he wore a hat to keep the sun off his face and kept his shirtsleeves rolled down even on the hottest days. Whenever I saw the muscles of his arms or his legs, they looked to me stringy and slight. But when I'd been smaller, he had sometimes taken my shoulder or my elbow or my knee and squeezed, saying that he was testing my bones. Then his hands had felt powerful to me. I'd tried to imagine my father fist-fighting with some of the workmen at the carbide plant, but I couldn't really see it.

I never had reason to fear my father. But my brother and I did speculate about him. One morning a couple of years ago, Duncan had told me a story while we were standing down on the highway waiting for the school bus. It wasn't a story so much as it was a fact. In the full-length mirror of my grandmother's wardrobe were two bullet holes. They had been put there by my father, who'd used the .22 pistol my grandfather kept in the drawer of his bedside table. Duncan had worried that information out of my grandmother, and I admired him for it. I had seen the holes myself, I had had some curiosity about them, but I had never thought to ask anyone about them. Duncan said, "Now what do you suppose could have made him shoot into a mirror that way?" I didn't know. I didn't dare even venture a guess.

Driving the car home wasn't difficult after I got it started rolling. I could put it into second and high gears easily because the way was downhill, along the ridge of our hill where we could look down and see most of the houses in Rosemary in the valley below us. It looked like pictures I'd seen of villages where they made wine in Europe, except their hillsides were lined with vineyards and ours were mostly fields of broomsage and scrub cedars, cow pastures, cornfields, trash piles, gatherings of junked cars, and back behind us the smoke of the carbide plant rising up from the two tall stacks.

When we got home, the hardest thing of all was getting into the garage. That involved making the turn just exactly right, judging the straightening precisely, getting the rear wheels up over the hump without killing the engine, and then getting the car stopped before it plowed through the far wall. My father had started letting me do it. Today he didn't even watch me; he kept his head resting on the seat, his hat over his eyes. Then, when I turned off the ignition, he asked me, "Did you get it in all right, Son?"

He'd started using that tone of voice with me when he taught me to play his alto saxophone. When I'd just turned thirteen, he said I needed something to occupy my mind. We walked over to my grandfather's house, to the parlor, where he lifted the black leather carrying case out from behind the piano. He let me open it and hold it in my lap while he told me about it. The case was lined with dark purple velvet, and the horn, in two pieces, lay in exactly fitted compartments. There was a smell in there of age, of something valuable. The saxophone was still shiny, undented, a burnished silver with fancy engraving and a gold-plated inside of the bell. My father had sent it to the factory in Elkhart, Indiana, and had it put in perfect condition before he had packed it away. He taught me how to assemble the neck and the mouthpiece, to wet the reed and fasten it on. He showed me how the fingering worked to close the pads or open them. Then he put it in his mouth and played "Little Brown Jug." He handed it to me, and I made it squawk.

But in a month I could play "Little Brown Jug," "The Darktown Strutters' Ball," "The St. Louis Blues," and "Lullabye and Goodnight." My father had stacks of old sheet music and a box of arrangements he'd made for his own band. He said I was the fastest learner he'd ever encountered. He arranged an appointment with the Madison High School Band Director, Mr. Oliver, and took me to Madison to audition. While Mrs. Oliver fried chicken in the kitchen, my father and Mr. Oliver sat on the living-room sofa and listened to me play through "I Dream of Jeannie with the Light Brown Hair."

My father had packed that saxophone away at his parents' house when he began working at the carbide plant, just after he married my mother. He'd begun work there as a construction foreman. He became Personnel Manager, then Assistant Engineer, then Plant Engineer, and finally, a few years ago, Works Manager, supervisor of the whole thing. Most of the people in Rosemary had felt it was inevitable that my father would become the boss of the carbide plant, but he didn't like for anybody to say anything that suggested he hadn't earned every one of his promotions. All my life he'd smelled of carbide, a sharp, nose-pinching odor that wasn't unpleasant after you got used to it. I could remember, from when I was a little boy being carried in his arms, the smooth starched surface of his khaki workshirts, the roughness of his bearded cheek, the smell of his sweat, cigarettes, carbide. Once he brought home a small can of carbide, the kind miners use in their headlamps, he said. He took Duncan and me out on the back porch, poured some of the gray, crumbly stuff out of the can into a bucket of water. The lumps of carbide fizzed and bubbled like dry ice, made a kind of steam. Then he struck a match, and there was a flame over the water. "It stinks," Duncan said. We were both impressed by my father's demonstration. We asked him to do it for us again the next day when he came home from work, and he did, but he wouldn't anymore after that.

He complained, getting out of the car, that he didn't have enough room between the door and the side of the garage, but I noticed that he was managing it anyway. I knew he was trying to josh me into a good mood. We went in then. My mother was in the kitchen, fixing supper. She had flour on her hands and held them away from my father while they kissed. While he was washing his hands and rinsing out his thermos bottle, he told her what he'd done, scaring me by driving the car at me. He said he wanted to see how I handled myself in an emergency. I knew he was telling her about it because he was uncomfortable with it. He wanted to see if telling my mother about it would bring back the joke he'd intended. I wanted to tell him not to worry. When he stood in the kitchen like that, after work, talking with my mother, as if by talking he could change himself from how he had to be at work to how he had to be at home, I was always pleased with him. But I didn't say anything. And by my mother's silence, I knew she didn't approve of his joke. She would tell him what she thought when I wasn't around.

While he was talking, she cleaned her own hands off, got him a beer and a glass and handed them to him. He made his usual offer to help her in the kitchen. She made her usual refusal, telling him to go on and get out of her way. I followed him into his study where he went to sit at his desk and read the paper. For several years my father had complained that his living-room chair wasn't comfortable. One Christmas my mother had gotten him a new easy chair, but, even though he hadn't complained, he'd squirmed and fidgeted in it. Finally he'd taken to sitting at his desk in the study to relax after work. He turned on the desk light and spread out the paper. I took a seat behind him and waited for him to offer me some of his beer. I breathed on my glasses, loudly, and wiped them with my handkerchief. Finally he did make the offer, and I took a gulp. I stood beside him with my hand on his shoulder while he read. I wanted him to know I didn't hold it against him, the joke with the car. I wanted to stay on his good side until I had my driver's license. He asked me what I'd done that day, and I started telling him about mowing old Mrs. Oakes's yard. While I was talking to him, he took out his pen and started working the crossword puzzle. I stopped halfway through a sentence and waited to see what would happen.

"Dad?" I said.

He grunted.

"Dad, are you listening?" I asked him.

"What?" he said, still in that preoccupied tone of voice.

"Why'd you ask me if you didn't want to hear?" I shouted at him. I went upstairs to my room, stomped on the steps and shut the door hard. I knew my mother would probably hold it against him that he'd provoked me. Upstairs I got out the saxophone and started practicing scales on the high notes. Then I worked on the saxophone breaks to "Burn That Candle" and "Blue Monday," two of my father's least favorite songs. Then Mother called me down for supper, and I came to the table. My father, with his face somewhat drawn, said grace.

Dinner was spaghetti with my mother's homemade bread. I ate rudely, slurping my noodles into my mouth and splashing sauce until my mother got enough of me and told me to behave at the table. My father chopped his spaghetti into small bites and told us about hiring a new secretary. Mrs. Millgram, the blue-haired lady who my mother said had lovely posture and who had worked at the carbide plant since before my father had come there, had finally retired. He had to find a replacement for her. The other secretary at the carbide plant, dumpy-looking, sour-tempered Mrs. Sharitz, would be there another twenty years before she retired. Of her my father had said, "I don't believe that if Mrs. Sharitz had all day to work on it, she could manage to stick her finger in her eye." Before he went off to the university, Duncan and I had laughed for a couple of days over that, and I still chuckled whenever I saw her. The new secretary my father said he had decided to hire was named Darcy Webster. He looked at my mother and me to see if we knew her.

He said that Darcy Webster was the daughter of Preacher Webster, the Mercy Circuit Methodist minister. That was why we couldn't have known her, because she was from Mercy County, had gone to high school over in Gantley. After that she'd taken a one-year course at Roanoke Business College, then had come home to look for a job. Of the five applicants my father interviewed for the job, Darcy had been by far the best. She typed seventy words per minute, made no errors. She took shorthand. She knew grammar and spelling. She was pleasant, cheerful, and pretty.

"What are you worried about?" my mother asked him.

My father smiled across the table at her. He hadn't said he was worried, but both of us had known that he was.

"That last," he said. "That she's pretty."

Mother raised her eyebrows at him, asking him four or five questions all at once without saying a word aloud.

"There are two hundred and eighty-five men who work at that plant," my father said. "To my certain knowledge, there have been, in the whole time that the plant has been in operation, only three women who have worked there. There's never been a young one. There's never been one who wasn't married. There's never been a pretty one." He took off his glasses, rubbed his eyes and the bridge of his nose, and looked mournfully at the shards of spaghetti on his plate.

"I'll look forward to seeing her," said my mother.

The first time my mother did see Darcy, I was with her. She'd needed the car for shopping, and so she'd taken my father to work that morning. At quitting time, I went with her to meet him. From our house, or from anywhere within ten miles of Rosemary, the smoke from the carbide plant was visible, a thick column of billowing white stuff. On a clear, sunny day, it looked beautiful, like the beginning of a cloud, white the way clouds are sometimes white in the sunlight. If the sky was overcast or if it was raining, then the smoke was gray, ugly stuff, a kind of soupy fog. But this was a clear day in June. My mother and I were both in a jolly mood, turning off the highway onto the carbide road, pulling slowly along past the lines of railroad cars, past the warehouses, over the siding of railroad tracks that went inside the plant fence, past the office buildings and then to the gatehouse where we turned around and parked so as to be able to see my father when he came out. I wanted her to stop the car between the buildings so that I could watch the men working the furnace, walking back and forth around the huge area of electrical fire. She wouldn't do it. Even that far away, sitting in the car, you could feel the heat of the furnace when they were tapping, when there was a great tub of molten stuff suspended in the air above the furnace that the men tipped and poured into containers that were hauled away by other men. My mother hated the heat, said she'd been seeing carbide furnaces long enough to suit her and didn't need to see any more. I liked to watch the men who shoved limestone and coke from up above, who my father said had to take salt tablets every couple of hours and had to wear sheepskin-lined jackets and winter underwear even in summer to hold in the sweat, to be able to stand the heat. I got out and stood behind the car to watch for a while. But then the tapping stopped. The men were about to change shifts. The shrill whistle blew for four-thirty quitting time.

The eight-to-four-thirty shift came out of the gatehouse, men in crumpled and sweated-through work hats, blue jeans or baggy-seated overalls, dark-blue or khaki or gray workshirts, and heavy steel-toed shoes or boots. Many of them nodded to my mother, touched their fingers to their hat brims: Tommy Alley who straightened his shoulders and smiled, Old Man Buck Weatherman whose chin was tucked down into his neck, and Bert Lawson who strutted, even after he'd put in a full day's work. The men came out of the gatehouse in twos and threes and fours, some of them not speaking a word, some joking and laughing, hitching up their pants, clapping each other on the back, dangling their dinner-buckets at the ends of their fingers. Then, in a fresh pink dress with a full skirt, in high-heeled shoes, with her chin up and her shoulders squared, with a ponytail of hair the color of wheat, came Darcy Webster. I'd never seen her before.

There were girls that pretty in my high school, but they were older than me, they didn't know who I was, and I never thought of speaking to them. Darcy gave me a smile and said "Hi!" I tried fixing my face in what I thought was approximately a smile.

She walked to the car window where my mother sat, leaned down, holding her white purse in both hands in front of her, and said, "Hi, are you Mrs. Bryant? I thought so. I'm Darcy Webster." I couldn't hear what my mother said just then. I stood with my hand on the car door for a moment before I got into the back seat. When I did get in and get the door shut, Darcy and my mother were saying their goodbyes. Then Darcy was walking down the road away from us. Men were walking along that way, too; they made way for her, a few of them smiling, speaking, reaching up to touch their hat brims to her. Then she came to her own car and got in it. My mother and I watched her with an attention that demanded silence. We were quiet. My father came to the door on the passenger side and climbed into the front seat.

"What do you think of my poster?" my father asked us while my mother got the car going, driving slowly through the crowd of men, stopping to let cars pull out ahead of her. My father had begun a safety campaign at the carbide plant a couple of years before. The most recent step he'd taken was to install a billboard-sized frame on the side of the main furnace building. The new poster showed a cartoon man, his mouth open as if to shout, his arms gesturing frantically, being pulled into the gears of an evil-looking machine while other cartoon men kept their backs turned to him. The motto of the poster was SAFETY IS EVERYBODY'S BUSINESS.

"That's real nice, Dad," I said. I was just learning the pleasures of sarcasm and ambiguity. He turned around to look at me, but I hid the grin sneaking onto my mouth by pushing my glasses up farther onto my nose.

"If I were you, I'd save my smartness for school," he said, but he wasn't really angry. As long as we were in *If-I-were-you* territory, I was safe.

"We met Darcy," my mother said when she'd gotten the car out of the carbide area, onto the highway. I appreciated her getting the conversation steered that way. I was hungry to hear them talk about Darcy. I was even eager to put in my own opinions. I'd decided that what I thought was prettiest about her was how her light-brown skin looked with that pink dress. I wondered if I would say that aloud. From the tone of my mother's voice, I thought she thought well of Darcy, at least so far. When we talked, in our family, about pretty women, my mother was the final judge, the authority none of us questioned.

"Oh, you did?" My father let the silence hang in the air. I could tell he wanted to know what my mother thought as much as I did.

"A lot of women couldn't get by with wearing that dress," my mother said.

"Let's see now, what . . ."

"The pink one," I said. It was possible that Darcy's dress had gone unnoticed by my father; on the other hand, it was more likely that he was acting as if he'd not paid any attention to it. At any rate, I wanted the conversation to move on.

"Yes, the sleeveless pink dress," my mother said. "She looks striking in it."

"Bad color, huh?" my father asked.

"No, not bad at all. Exactly right, as a matter of fact."

"Too sexy?" he asked. I was glad he brought it up like that. I wanted to see what my mother would say. She was the family authority on matters of sexiness, too.

"No, certainly not," she said. "She could wear that dress to go hear her father preach."

"Well, what?" my father asked.

"Well, nothing," she said. "I said that a lot of women couldn't get by with wearing that dress. I didn't say there was anything wrong with it."

"No, I guess you didn't."

"She handles herself with a great deal of poise, too," my mother said. "She came right up to the car and introduced herself. I'd be happy if I thought any child of mine"—I got a flick of her eyes from the rear-view mirror—"would have manners enough to know how to do that." Manners and poise were high on my mother's list of virtues, especially since Duncan and I didn't have much of either. She seemed to be taking inventory of Darcy's good points, as if she were determined to cover every one of them.

"Good for her," my father said.

"She spoke to me too," I piped up, leaning forward over the front seat between them. That put an end to our discussion of Darcy. I could tell they were saving what else they had to say for some time when I wasn't around to hear them. I was tired of being treated like someone who just wasn't mature enough to hear really important matters of conversation. I wanted to say more, to say something brilliant and stunning, but I wasn't about to let myself blurt out a stupid remark for them to hold against me.

My birthday was a hot July day. That morning my father drove me to the Madison courthouse to take the test for my driver's license. The windshields of the cars we passed glared so brightly that I had to squint my eyes. When we stopped in the courthouse parking lot, the pavement was soft and gummy under our feet. It felt good to go inside the cool stone and the vaulted ceiling of the courthouse. I knew I would pass the written part of the test; in school I enjoyed taking tests more than listening to the teachers. This one was easy. I got them all correct except for one, and the testing lady bragged on me for my high score. A large blond state trooper walked back outside with me. We both nodded at my father, sitting out there on the steps, fanning himself with his hat. Neither the policeman nor I spoke out loud to him; he might have been somebody we knew or didn't know. But I could see him giving me his solemn look meant to inspire confidence. I kept wondering what that state trooper, with his perfect uniform and his kind, official voice, was thinking about me. I put the car in gear, all right. I drove it around the block, stopping for lights, giving the correct hand-signals. Then I drove back to the parking lot where a yellow rectangle was painted on the concrete, and I parallel-parked. The trooper climbed out, saying over his shoulder, "Come on in, Son, and we'll write out your license." I was grinning like a fool when we passed my father that second time.

My father and I went home, with me driving the highway from Madison to Rosemary for the first time. When we got to our house, Mother sent me back in the car by myself to drive down to Elkins's store to buy eggs, cream, sugar, and rock salt for an ice-cream celebration. Down there, trying to park, I hit the back of Mrs. Peacock's old battered Plymouth; it made a loud bang, both cars rocked up and down, and people trotted outside the store to have a look. There were dents in both cars, but Mrs. Peacock folded her arms over the top of her bosom and said, "Lord, Reed, don't worry about it, Honey. One more dent in my car won't hurt a thing." I was grateful to her and felt a little guilty about always having thought of her as a fat, pig-eyed old woman. I didn't report that incident to my father, but the next day, first thing when I saw him before suppertime, he caught my eye and said, "Dent in the right front fender."

"Yes sir," I said. "That's mine."

"Yours?"

"Yes sir. I mean, I put it there."

He shook his head at me and didn't ask any more questions.

Back before I was born, Rosemary had been an iron-smelting town. In the other direction from the carbide plant were acres and acres of ripped-up, rocky land that had been surface-mined for low-grade iron ore. Almost all of the town had once been owned by the Pittsburgh Industrial Metals Corporation, which went out of business before it finished what it had in mind for Rosemary. On our side of the carbide plant, the Pittsburgh company had built large houses for its managers and engineers; we lived in one of those houses, my grandparents in another. The company had made plans for where other different sorts of people were going to live. Pittsburgh Industrial Metals had planned for Rosemary to grow. Streets were laid out, named, constructed, and paved, but no houses were ever built on them. There was a stone foundation of a huge building on a large plot of land near our house; my grandfather said that was to have become the Rosemary Hotel. He laughed when he told about it. Now there were simply small roads with square corners to them, roads that had been given names years before by someone in Pittsburgh. Most of the names were never used; some of them were never even known by the people in Rosemary. Many of those roads had turned back to dirt roads and then turned further back to grass paths that were used only occasionally by people walking, say, from a house in Rakestown or in Slabtown down to the river to fish, or by a child wandering or wanting to take a shortcut from where he was to somewhere else.

I enjoyed driving those roads, downhill toward the river bottom and the flat valley-land along which the railroad tracks ran. The carbide plant was built in this place so as to have access to railroad shipping, to use the river water to cool its furnaces, to use the river's electrical power from its dams upstream, to empty its sewage into the river. I had been driven back and forth to and from the carbide plant in cars with my parents, and sometimes my grandparents, for as long as I could remember. To be driving by myself, even if only the distance of a mile and a half between our house and the plant and even if in my father's car, I took as a sign that I was soon going to have my own life.

On the small road in to the carbide plant, speed limits were posted at fifteen miles per hour, another part of my father's safety campaign. I was careful to observe that restriction. I was always hungry to see everything around that place anyway. Driving slowly made it easier to look. Men I passed would raise a hand to me, or to my father's car. Their way of waving was different for me by myself than it would have been if my father had been riding with me. Either way, the gestures the men made were ones that I admired, a hand signaling an exact measure of respect and courtesy, of pride and humility. I was not able to duplicate their gestures or to make one of my own that would do. My waves seemed to me always a little too eager, too attentive. If I passed a group of men and waved to them, I imagined that my wave provoked them to talk about me when I had gone by. If I heard laughter from them, I became aware of my glasses; my neck and ears burned. I could make up the things they might say: "Not going to be the man his father is." "That's right. Little bookworm. Little horn-player." "His grandfather don't even know him, can't recognize him." They had their opinions of me, I knew they did, those men who worked for my father, with their rolling walks, their hats pushed forward on their foreheads, their sleeves rolled up over tattooed, veined, muscled arms.

I turned the car around beside the gatehouse, parked it with its nose pointing back toward home, turned off the engine but left the ignition key turned on. I had to hear one of my necessary radio programs, the request hour on the Madison station. Lots of kids who called in requests were my high school classmates, Madison kids mostly, but now and then somebody from Rosemary would get his name on the air. I was thinking about school, about how it would be to be able to drive a car there sometimes, because when the term started, I would be a sophomore. I kept the radio turned down to what my father would have called a reasonable level; he was very big on being reasonable and moderate, on exercising good judgment, in his discussions with me. I slumped down in the seat, looked out away from the plant and down into the field between the railroad tracks and the river. The water was running low and muddy, the way it always did during dog days. On the other side, the mountain rose almost straight out of the water, part of it upriver from the plant being sheer cliff-face of brown and gray rock. Out over the mountain the rolling column of carbide smoke rose, thick and solid-looking as spun glass, going out and up as far as I could see. I felt some-one touch my arm at the window and turned around to see Darcy standing there close enough to bite me if she'd been a snake.

"Reed?" she said. She wore a pleated white blouse and a skirt with small colored flowers on it. She had an earnest expression on her face. She didn't seem quite as poised as she had when she'd introduced herself to my mother that day. I nodded vigorously and reached to turn the radio off. I tried to think of something to say to her that she would like, something that would make her want to stay there. Because of her hair's being pulled back, I'd always thought of her eyes as small and slanted like an oriental woman's, but up close they were large and brown with flecks of green in them. "I don't know why I listen to that stuff," I said. I pushed my glasses up onto my nose and wished immediately that I hadn't done it, could see my toothy expression from her point of view.

"You're Reed, aren't you?"

"Yes, ma'am," I said. I didn't know why she was so concerned about what my name was. "The same name as my grandfather. It's his name, too. But nobody calls him that."

She smiled then, to herself, as if I'd said something that only she knew was funny. She crossed her arms in front of her, drew the white pleated blouse down tight over her chest, and asked, "How old are you, Reed?"

"Fifteen," I said. "I got my license last month."

"I'm nineteen," she said. "Just four years older."

"Huh," I said. I hadn't thought of her as being just nineteen. I'd thought of her as being a woman. It made me feel better to know she was just four years older, but I still couldn't think of anything to say that I thought would make her be interested in me.

"Your father's told me about you," she said, a tease coming into her voice.

"What did he say?" I asked. I really did wonder what my father told other people about me.

"Well, let me see," She put her finger on her chin. She was trying to act like she knew a lot, but I figured out then that my father hadn't really told her much about me, probably just my name.

"He said you played in the band." Darcy said that too eagerly, as if she were proud of herself for having remembered it.

"Yes, that's right," I said. "I play alto saxophone." Coming out of the gatehouse was my father. I couldn't help but let my eyes go past Darcy's shoulder to look at him, to see what he would think of her standing there talking with me. But he was listening to Mr. Atkins and Tommy Alley. I couldn't tell if he'd even noticed me. Darcy saw where I was looking, turned and looked too, then touched my elbow with her hand and said, "There's your father." When I caught her eye, we both realized what a dumb thing that was to say to me, and so we both laughed about it. "Time to go home," she said. "Goodbye, Reed." She pronounced my name very positively.

"See you, Darcy," I called out, as my father climbed into the car beside me. I wanted him at least to notice that I called his secretary by her first name.

"See you tomorrow, Mr. Bryant," Darcy called to my father, waving to him and walking ahead of us toward her own car. My father lifted a hand and gave her a smile, one that I knew he had to force himself to hang on his face, but as we pulled out it was easy to see he wasn't thinking much about Darcy.

"Have to change that," he said, looking at the new sign on the warehouse building we were driving past; it said THIS PLANT HAS GONE   DAYS WITHOUT AN ACCIDENT. In the blank space hung a metal plate with the number 109 on it.

"What?" I asked.

"Aw, Cecil Campbell," he said in a tone that if I hadn't known him all my life I would have thought meant anger of the deepest sort. "Got his fingers chopped off in the can shop this afternoon. These two." He lifted his own hand, with the middle and index fingers raised, to show me.

"God," I said. It was what we'd taken to saying at band practice when someone was out of tune or hitting a lot of wrong notes. My father gave me a look that registered for both of us how wrong it sounded in the car at that moment.

"The cutter in the can shop comes down every forty-five seconds to cut the tin. If your fingers are there, then it cuts them, too. Everybody who works there knows that."

"Nothing to be done for Mr. Campbell?" I asked. I swung the car into our driveway, another square corner.

"Nothing I know of," my father said, his voice tired. He settled back in the seat but didn't let his head rest the way he did sometimes. "Cecil Campbell was working in that can shop thirteen years when Tommy Alley's daddy lost his fingers in exactly the same way. You just can't get to daydreaming in the can shop. Cecil knew exactly what it meant when that cutter came down on his hand."

"Yes sir," I said.

"Fool," my father said.

"Sir?"

"They said he shut the machine off, scooped his fingers up with his good left hand, ran outside, and threw them across the railroad tracks there just outside the shop. They said he was cussing like a sailor."

"God," I said.

"But when I saw him in the first-aid room, he was as docile as a kitten. Kept saying, 'I'm sorry, Mr. Bryant, I'm sorry.' " My father put his head back then, took off his glasses, and put his hat down over his eyes, which didn't make sense since we were about to come around the last curve to our house. "I told him, 'Cecil,' I said, 'you don't have to be sorry to me.' "

At the end of August, just before school started, we traded cars. Mother said she was sure my father was doing it to cheer himself up. Two more accidents happened at the plant the week after Cecil Campbell lost his fingers, and union negotiations were coming up in October. Mother didn't object to the trade, though. It was a pleasure to see my father behind the wheel of his bright blue 1957 Dodge Coronet, with its streamlined fins going straight back from the rear window to the taillights, and with push-button drive. My father'd never had a car with any kind of automatic transmission, let alone push-button drive. He leaned back in the seat, straightened his arms at the wheel, and pushed the *D* button with exaggerated casualness.

The first time I drove it to the plant, Darcy came out of the gatehouse smiling like somebody was going to give that new car to her. She'd heard about it already, I could tell, but she asked me questions about it, talked with me enthusiastically. When my father came out, he did not go around to the passenger side as he usually did. He stepped right up beside Darcy and asked me to scoot over. When he got in behind the wheel, he stayed there talking to Darcy for a long while, leaning back in the seat with his arms straightened at the wheel. Darcy praised the car some more, then she bent down to speak to me across my father's arms. " 'Bye, Reed," she said. I found myself blushing with my father's eyes on me.

The first week of September I convinced my parents to let me take the car to Madison for a night meeting of the Beta Club. If it hadn't been an honor to be invited to join the Beta Club, I wouldn't have been allowed. In Madison the Rosemary kids had a reputation for being slow and stupid in school, but there were three of us from Rosemary whose averages had been good enough for Beta Club. Fat Bobby Sloan and Patch Whitacre, who had red hair and freckles and played trombone in the band, were going to ride over with me to the meeting. It was a Wednesday evening, just turning twilight as we cruised the highway, all three of us slicked up in our good clothes, ready to be honored for our intelligence.

The meeting, however, in the high-school cafeteria, was a disappointment. None of the Madison kids had dressed up, and Wayne Dillard, the president, called out, when we walked in early, "Hello, hicks." All three of us were used to being kidded about being from the sticks, being farmers, being hicks. But Wayne wouldn't have called out like that if Bobby Sloan hadn't been with us; Bobby really was kind of backwards in his manners. Because Patch and I were in the band, people sometimes even forgot that we lived in Rosemary. The Beta Club meeting lasted just long enough for them to call the roll and to swear in the new members. We were in a good mood from all the giggling and the horsing around and the yelling when the meeting was adjourned. When we walked out of the cafeteria, there was still an edge of red sunlight in the sky west of town. Bobby and Patch and I agreed it was a shame to go home that early, even if it was a school night.

Bobby asked us to take him down to the High Hat to get him something to eat. Patch and I laughed at him, told him he was fat, told him people in Madison would always think he was a hick if the first thing he did when he got to town was to go to the High Hat Drive-In and stuff his face with French fries. Bobby was embarrassed and said he hadn't had time to get any supper before he left home. Then Patch and I felt sorry that we'd said those things to him. We all went down to the High Hat and stuffed our faces. We stayed there for a while, kicking around the parking lot, talking to some people we knew, mostly older kids who came down there and hung around for a couple of hours almost every night. Bobby got tired of standing around other people's cars, and so he went to sit in our front seat to wait for Patch and me. Then we prowled around Madison for a while, driving past girls' houses and talking about them. Since Bobby didn't know where anybody lived, Patch and I gave him a town tour, so to speak. We hadn't been in any of those houses, the ones where the more famous of the junior and senior high school girls lived, but we'd had their houses pointed out to us by friends of ours in the band. I was careful on those streets because I'd heard that the Madison cops liked nothing better than catching somebody from Rosemary doing something wrong. When it was almost eleven, and most of the parking places on Main Street were empty, all three of us stopped talking. Bobby said, as if he'd been waiting a long time to bring it up, "Let's go home."

Out on the highway I tried to get back some of the excitement we'd had earlier in the evening. I ran the speed up on that Dodge just to show Patch and Bobby what it would do. Bobby stayed quiet, but Patch lit up a cigarette, switched on the radio, found the Wheeling station, and turned it up loud. Going that fast, it was too cold to keep the windows open, and so Patch and I cranked them closed. The highway was empty and straight out ahead of us. I didn't slow down again, just kept the speedometer on eighty and eighty-five, which was the speed where I could hold it steady. "Bobby, are you scared?" I asked him, and he said no, but I could tell that he was. The road was straight, and the new Dodge didn't show any sign of strain; it felt like it was riding about a foot higher off the ground than it usually did, like it was about to take off and rise up in the beams of light out ahead of us. Patch was saying how the speedometer was funny on those new Dodges anyway, the way there were little boxes that filled up with a bright red color, one box for every five miles of speed.

We came up over a hill. A car was pulling out down there, from a driveway, so slowly it seemed to be almost stopped halfway onto the highway. I could see the red lights, could tell they were barely moving, but it was a long way off. I touched the brake and felt the Dodge pull a little to one side. I put the brake pedal down and held it down, pressing harder and harder on it, seeing the red lights of the car down there get closer a lot faster than I'd thought they would. I felt the wheels go off in gravel, a heavy lurch sideways. Then the car was in a slow, gentle, merry-go-round spin, hitting into the ditch over on Patch's side, then just flopping right up onto its roof, so that all three of us were lying on the car ceiling, with the dash lights and the motor still on, the radio going, the headlights tunneling out at a crazy angle across a field. "Where's your cigarette, Patch?" I asked him. I turned off the radio and the ignition. The silence felt queer.

"I threw it out," he said, his voice calm, still perky, as if he were still having a fine time. Light from somewhere shone on his freckled face, making him look pale and spotted. Gradually I figured out how awkwardly our bodies lay on the car ceiling, how tangled we were with each other.

Then Bobby spoke up, his voice five notes higher than it should have been. "Are you all right? Are you all right?" he shrilled.

"I am," I said, but I didn't know for sure if I was. I couldn't find my glasses, but I hadn't noticed when they'd slipped off. Patch said, "I bumped my knee, but I think I'm O.K." Bobby rasped out loudly, "Thank you, God! Thank you, Jesus!" I tried to get my legs untangled from his. I remembered that Bobby Sloan sometimes went to the Pentecostal Holiness Church, and he was loathsome to me right at that moment.

"My door won't work," I said. Patch rolled his window down and started wriggling out of it. Bobby followed him and took a long time. I waited for him and hated his fatness until he was out of the car. When I got through the window, a man shone a flashlight on me, and another man was standing there watching me on my hands and knees. I still didn't have my glasses and couldn't see anyone clearly; they were shadows until light from the highway caught them. The one with the flashlight asked me if I was the driver. I told him that I was. He said, "Son, you're a damn fool. All three of you boys could have been killed." His voice had an edge of pleasure to it, as if he were saying something about a movie he'd seen and liked.

"Yes sir," I said. I couldn't see him well enough to know if he was the kind of a man I ought to be saying *sir* to or not. And it had not occurred to me until that moment that any of us were in danger. I started to tell the man that it wasn't as bad as he thought it was. But then there was a state policeman to talk to, a small man who came up beside me, spoke quietly, and didn't seem at all angry at me. He crawled into the car to shut off the lights and to be sure the ignition was off. When he started back out of the car, he held out my glasses from the window and called, "Whose are these?" I didn't say anything, just bent and took them from his hand. We all three went to sit in his car, me in front, Bobby and Patch in the back. He looked at each of us carefully, as if he were trying to make some judgment about what kind of boys we were. He asked me to tell him how the accident had happened. He'd parked so that his headlights shone through the dark over onto my father's upside-down car. While I was talking and while Bobby and Patch were talking to him, I had to sit there and look at the wheels and the underside of my father's new Dodge. By the time my father and Bobby's father got there, I had trouble making myself say any words at all. Bobby's father had had to pick up my father and drive him over to where we were. Mr. Sloan was sanctimonious and a leader in the union at the carbide plant. I couldn't look straight at my father.

We boys got out of the car. Bobby went over to talk with his father. Patch came over and stood beside me while my father climbed into the policeman's car to talk with him. Patch and I stood there and watched them through the back window, both of them nodding their heads, my father shaking his every now and then. When he got out, he kept his head turned toward the upside-down car instead of toward me. I decided he was waiting until we were alone. The wrecker came and pulled the car over onto its side and then right side up. The driver of the wrecker said that he was certain the car would be declared a total wreck. "Totaled that thing," Patch said quietly to me.

Bobby's father drove us all home, with only him and Bobby doing the talking, Bobby leaning up from the middle of the back seat to talk to his daddy, my father sitting silent on the passenger side in front. My father insisted that Mr. Sloan let us out at the bottom of our hill, down on the highway. The last thing Mr. Sloan said to us when we got out in the dark was, "We've got a lot to be grateful for tonight, Mr. Bryant."

"Yes, that's right," my father said. "We certainly do, Robert. I thank you for your help." When the car was gone, we stood for a while letting our eyes get used to the dark. We fumbled with the old gate down there, then decided to climb the thing. On the other side we had to stand still a minute to be able to make out the path up the hill to our house, and there my father touched my shoulder. He was awkward about it, and he didn't know what to say. He said, "Reed, Reed," as if he had something else to tell me, but once he'd said my name like that, in that tone of being sorry for both of us, there wasn't anything more for him to say. We went on up the hill in the dark. I told him I was sorry while I was walking behind him, and he said he knew I was, not to worry about it too much. He was out of breath and puffing by the time we reached the porch light my mother had turned on for us.

The judge suspended my driver's license for six months. He fined me fifteen dollars plus costs. He was a young man with short black hair going gray and a ruddy complexion. He said he would have fined me much more than that if I had been an adult, but he understood from talking with the investigating officer that my father would have to pay my fine for me. The judge said he didn't see any use in my father's having to pay a lot of money for my irresponsible behavior. He gave me a stern lecture, told me that the town of Rosemary didn't need any more drivers like me, that it had plenty of them already. He told me he hoped I had learned my lesson. I said I was certain I had. My parents tried to cheer me up, made jokes about how they hadn't liked that old blue car anyway. I told them solemnly that I never wanted to drive again. My mother said she understood how I felt. I doubted that she did, but I kept my mouth shut. We used my grandmother's old black '52 Chrysler for another week, until the new car that my father had ordered to replace the wrecked one came in. The new Dodge was green and white. My father didn't take as much pleasure in it as he had in the old one.

On the school bus, I became known as The Night Rider. The first several days after the wreck were especially humiliating. The bus drove right past my skid-marks on the highway and the wedged-up sod and dirt in the ditch where the car had landed. Rosemary high-school students had to catch one of the two buses that drove to Madison at seven or seven-thirty in the morning. Both buses looped out onto dirt roads to pick up county students from farms or back up in the hills. Kids from Rosemary and from our part of the county had a bad reputation in Madison: They didn't know how to act, didn't know how to dress, misbehaved in class, couldn't learn anything, never knew the answers, used crude language, fought, carried knives, weren't clean. Rosemary kids took a kind of pride in being the outlaws of the consolidated school, dressed like hoods or sluts, told stories about violent and reckless behavior. On my bus Janet Littrel and Judy Statler, who'd gone through grade school with me, clucked their tongues at me, rubbed pointed index fingers, and said, "Shame, shame on you, Reed Bryant." Herbert Blevins, who usually flipped my ears and dared me to do anything in retaliation, or who farted in his hand and then reached up from behind me to put the hand over my nose, asked me to tell him what had happened. I told Herbert that I didn't want to talk about it, but Patch, with whom I usually sat, gave him a full account. Herbert and George Oglesby and Botch Atkins all listened carefully and giggled and clapped me on the shoulder and called me The Night Rider. When Molly Whisnant got on the bus way out in Draper, she looked at me with a big smile on her face and said, "I heard about you, Reed Bryant." I kept my jacket collar turned up, looked out the window, wouldn't talk with anybody, just let Patch do my talking for me. But sitting there on that bus with those Rosemary kids talking about me, I began to feel good, began to feel like an outlaw. In the halls at school, rumors were that I had been traveling at well over a hundred miles an hour when the wreck happened, that I had been drunk, that what had really caused it was that I had been running from the cops.

Bobby Sloan stayed away from me after the wreck; he gave me to understand that he thought I was just fine but that his father had forbidden him to associate with me. But Patch and I became even closer friends. We were both in the band together, we both fancied ourselves pretty good musicians. Sometimes we sneaked out of Phys. Ed. to smoke a cigarette, or we smoked one before band practice or while we were waiting in the windy parking lot to practice the band's marching routines for the football games. Smoking cigarettes made me feel dizzy and powerful. I savored the looks of disapproval I received almost as much as the smoke itself. I imagined myself as having a casual deadliness of appearance with a cigarette in my mouth. I was somebody who'd totaled a car and lived to tell about it.

My mother caught me smoking out behind the garage one Saturday afternoon. She cried, said I was only fifteen, that if I wanted to smoke I had to wait until I was out of her house. I felt terrible. I promised her that I wouldn't smoke anymore. She and I hugged each other to seal the promise. Monday afternoon while Patch and I were waiting for the school bus, he offered me a cigarette, I took it, lit it, inhaled and exhaled, and was an outlaw again, with a smirk on my lips. On the bus, Patch and I went to the back to sit with Herbert Blevins and Botch Atkins, who carried a sharpened beer opener in his sock to defend himself against "Madison Twerps," as he called them.

I decided to switch saxophones. I put my father's smaller, shriller alto in its case, took it back over to the parlor in my grandparents' house, and stashed it behind the piano, where my father had kept it. Mr. Oliver let me use a horn that belonged to the school, an old tenor sax that was in bad shape but was larger, gutsier, jazzier than the high-pitched little alto. With Patch on his trombone, I began joining the older band members in their jam sessions before school, at lunchtime, and after school. The seniors laughed at us, they ad-libbed circles around us, but they didn't refuse our company. The band room was thick with cigarette smoke during those jam sessions, even though lots of times Mr. Oliver was sitting in his office right next door. Patch and I taught ourselves to play B-flat blues; we imitated the older kids. They were accustomed to giving each other solo breaks, to clapping, and to shouting encouraging or apprecia-tive remarks at the soloist, the way the members of Mr. Oliver's combo did, the way the professionals did. After Patch and I had been hanging around with them for several months, they started, for a joke more than anything else, to give us solo breaks. The first time it happened, Sult Watkins pulled his trumpet away from his mouth and shouted, "Reed, baby, Reed." I was startled and stopped playing, too, but Sult shouted at me, "You, man! Play!" I was scared. I merely squawked the major chord notes while Sult and Alan Hampton, the piano player, giggled to themselves and played along with the joke of my solo. Then Sult took his break, ripped up the band room with high notes and runs and professional-sounding licks, showing me how it was supposed to be done. But Patch and I caught on, getting off by ourselves and working at it. Then I found I could do it. I sailed for days, prancing through the halls at school knowing that was something I could do, improvise a jazz break, with people all around me, clapping their hands and listening to me and shouting at me, "Go, Reed, go," while I filled up the whole huge room with sounds from my horn. I had a fancy way of sticking my cigarette into the joint of my high F-key so that it wouldn't get in my way and so that smoke curled all around my face and head while I was taking my solo breaks. Sometimes, if the light was right, I could see my reflection in the windows of the band room, and I looked exactly the way I wanted to look.

Even though it was a lot of trouble, I hauled my saxophone case around with me almost everywhere I went. The case answered most people's questions about where I was going, what I was doing. All through that year of high school, I worked to make the sound of that tenor saxophone come out in patterns and shapes and tones that were just the way I wanted them to be. Even Mr. Oliver said I'd improved since the beginning of school. He began to select me to be in smaller groups of musicians, bands to do shows and special concerts, pep bands. I began to be able to feel the horn's sound when it started in the pit of my belly, came up through my throat and mouth and teeth, through the reed and mouthpiece, down through the body of the horn and out the bell; it was like knowing that I was strong, knowing that I could lift heavy weights.

At the end of April, I got my driver's license back in the mail from Richmond. Right away I started asking for the car. My mother reminded me that I'd said I wouldn't ever want to drive again. I told her it wasn't fair of her to bring that up. If I wasn't allowed to take the car to Madison, we had arguments at the dinner table. I'd found ways to get where I wanted to go when I hadn't had a license, had hitchhiked and bummed and begged friends to take me places. But now that I had the license, I was desperate to drive the car again. My father tried to stay out of the arguments I started, tried to let my mother make the decisions about what I could or couldn't do. But I found ways to turn everything toward him, to insist that he have the final word. He began dealing with me as if he had to be very careful not to lose his temper. He would say, "No, Reed," or "Yes, Reed," and I would know that he was thinking much more than just the small thing he was saying, would know that he was holding back.

In June, when school was out, I was restless. It was childish to be knocking on doors in Rosemary, asking ladies did they want their lawns mowed, did they want their flower beds weeded. But that was all there was to do. I stayed around the house a lot, practicing my horn (which wasn't the same all by myself) or reading, or sneaking cigarettes whenever I thought I could get away with it. Nothing was very satisfactory to me. I especially hated the nights when the whole family would watch TV, even my grandfather, who would walk over from his house in the dark to see Matt Dillon. I couldn't sit still then, would have to get up and pace into the kitchen or the study, fix something to eat, or else call Patch up to see what he was doing.

What I looked forward to was driving up to the carbide plant to pick up my father after work and seeing Darcy in her summer dresses. She came over to talk to me every day she saw me now, and I'd begun thinking a lot about her arms, which she usually crossed in front of her while she stood by the car window, and her calves and ankles, which I watched when she walked away from me. I liked to see her face, too, but I didn't think about it so much when I was away from her; her face seemed to me too cheerful and healthy to devote any time to daydreaming about. Those other parts of her body that I had seen appealed more to my outlaw self, my cigarette-smoking, jazz-playing self.

Now, when she came to the car to talk with me, Darcy would touch my elbow or catch my wrist or just put her cool hand on my arm and leave it there. Always her dresses were bright colors: yellow, blue, orange, pink, or once even white. Whenever I saw her, she was coming out of gray buildings onto a gray, dusty road. I noticed that even old sourpuss Mrs. Sharitz smiled at Darcy and waved good-bye to her at the end of the day. I could tease her a little bit, try to make her tell me who her boyfriend was, ask her when she was going out with me, things like that. Darcy claimed to be ready anytime I wanted to go out with her. I said I wanted to go out with her all the time. It was a joke, something to laugh about. I had matured enough so that I didn't mind the way the men looked at me in the car and her standing there talking to me when they walked by. One day I told Darcy they all looked the same to me, in their overalls and sweated-out shirts and carrying their dinner-buckets. I meant her to laugh about that, but she just asked me when band practice was starting up again.

On a rainy day late in June, two men from the plant, dumping a truckload of waste, were caught in a fire. There was a field some distance away where waste from the plant, mostly a gray, powdery dust, was dumped in piles. The field was locked up and marked with signs warning DANGER—KEEP OUT—NO TRESPASSING. Everybody in Rosemary knew that when carbide gets wet it generates acetylene gas, which is flammable. Boys I knew in grade school had told me that on a rainy day you could throw a rock into one of those piles where a truck had dumped the waste, and the thing would explode like in a war movie. On this day, the two men drove through the rain into the field, started to dump the load, and found themselves surrounded by fire. One man ran from the truck, through the fire, and got away with burns that would keep him in the hospital for a week or so. The other man had, in that instant of seeing the fire, decided to get under the truck to get away from it. The tires of the truck burned and went flat. The man was trapped under there until the rescue squad, the wrecking truck, a crew of men from the carbide plant, and my father could get him out. The man was conscious all that time, calling to the men who were working to get him out from under the truck.

When my father came home late in the evening, long after dark, I thought maybe he had somehow been injured himself. His color was pale gray. His skin glistened so that I could almost feel how clammy he felt. He shivered every so often. My mother fixed him a strong whiskey, and he drank that, asked for another one. She told him that she had kept supper for him. He told her he was sorry, he couldn't eat anything, he only wanted the whiskey. He wouldn't sit down. He just kept standing, shifting his weight, leaning against the mantel, so that we could see he barely had strength enough to keep on his feet. He told about it even though I was there and I knew my mother didn't want me to hear it. She didn't stop him, though. He said that the man had even been able to stand up and walk when they got him out from under the truck, but he'd been burned over most of his body. My father said that if it hadn't been for Darcy, he didn't know how any of them would have gotten through it. Darcy had made them coffee and brought it to them. Darcy had talked with them when it looked like they weren't going to be able to move the truck without killing the man underneath it. When the man's wife had come down there, Darcy had taken her away, out of the field, and quieted her, sat with her in the car. When it was all over, Darcy had driven the woman home and seen to it that she had somebody to stay with her. They didn't know if the man would live or not. They had taken him to the hospital. Finally my father went upstairs to bed. But all night long I'd wake up to hear him walking in the hallway, walking downstairs, opening and shutting doors. I'd see the hall light on and his shadow moving past my doorway.

For a long while after that accident I didn't like to see my father. His face was drawn. He looked at me with such a desperate expression that I thought he wanted something from me. I didn't know what it was. He lost his appetite, lost weight. Even while he sat at his desk in the study, with his back to me, I couldn't look at him without thinking of the fire in the field and the burned man. It changed how I thought about Darcy, too. I couldn't put together what my father had said about her with the vision I had of her, a pretty girl who liked to joke around with me about dating. For almost the whole month of July, I didn't go up to the carbide plant.

My birthday was not celebrated that year. Mother gave me a check my father had written out that morning before he went to work. The burned man had died during the night.

Patch had gotten some music from Mr. Oliver that we could work on, some duets for trombone and saxophone, and a couple of little dance-band arrangements. We started practicing over at his house. Usually his mother wasn't around. We smoked cigarettes right in his living room while we played. Patch offered me one of his father's beers from the refrigerator. I took it and drank it as if I were used to having a beer on a hot afternoon. Patch didn't make the offer but just that once; I think he might have had to account to his father for the missing beer. One afternoon when I was working under a hot August sun to weed Mrs. Peacock's pachysandra beds, Patch came running up there to tell me the news: Mr. Oliver had called him and told him that, starting that fall, he wanted both of us to be in his combo. We would have to start going to Madison right away to practice and learn the numbers. Patch and I yelled a lot and congratulated each other there in Mrs. Peacock's yard. I threw a dirt clod at him. Mrs. Peacock came out and said she thought I'd done enough for that day, how much did she owe me. I walked Patch home. Then he walked me home, both of us talking, neither one of us listening to the other one. We'd get paid for playing in that combo. We were going to be professionals.

Patch went with me in the car to the carbide plant. I surprised Mother by asking if I could go up there that afternoon. I thought taking Patch to see Darcy when she came out would be a fine way for us to celebrate. We were so jazzy. We sang be-bop riffs at each other in the car while I drove and while we sat waiting for the whistle to blow quitting time. I didn't tell Patch anything about Darcy. I wanted her coming over to the car to be a real surprise to him.

When Darcy came out of the gatehouse, she had on a bright blue dress, and her hair was down around her shoulders, but she kept her eyes on the ground, and she looked sad in a way that I'd never seen her look. I figured that walking that way she wouldn't even notice the car sitting there. So I called out to her, "Hey, Darcy," maybe a little too loud and casual. But she just lifted her head enough to glance at me and say "Hi." Didn't even say "Hi, Reed," didn't even use my name. And kept on walking. The last couple of steps to her car she ran, taking quick little steps in her high-heeled shoes. The whistle blew just about the time Patch asked me who she was. I said, "Oh, that's Darcy," like she wasn't anybody special to me.

My father came out but wouldn't take the passenger seat in front that Patch offered him, just sat in the back, studying his dinner-bucket, and wouldn't say much to either one of us. When I drove Patch to his house and let him out, my father still wouldn't come up to the front seat. I got after him to tell me what the matter was. I was still pestering him when we came into the kitchen, I don't know why. I was kidding with him, trying to cheer him up, but in another way I was trying to dig at him, get him mad. While he was washing his hands and trying to talk with my mother, I was still asking him questions. Then he lost his temper. He told me to get the hell away from him just for a few minutes. I went into the living room and listened to my mother ask him what was wrong while he was drying his hands. He let the silence stretch out for a while. I heard Mother go back to what she was doing at the stove; I guessed she'd decided she wasn't going to get an answer from him. Then he told her, "Bernard Oglesby and Mrs. Oglesby and Darcy."

My mother said, "What?"

He said, "Would you like to see the letter?"

Mother said that she would. I heard him digging in his pocket for it. Then he went into his study. I could hear both of them being quiet while she read the letter in the kitchen. She carried it into the study to give it back to him and said, "Oh."

I piped up from the living room, "I want to see it, too."

Mother said, "No."

My father said, "Yes, damn it, he wants to have his nose in my business. I want him to see it."

So I came in and picked the letter up off his desk and read it. It was written in sixth- or seventh-grade handwriting, on lined note-tablet paper. It was addressed to my father, Mr. Bryant. In it Mrs. Oglesby began by saying that Bernard had always spoken highly of my father. She said that Bernard thought my father was a fair man. She was just wondering if my father couldn't do something about the woman who had got Bernard so upset. Bernard was not able to pay attention to his family or do much of anything after work except go and buy Pabst Blue Ribbon Beer at Miss Tessie's filling station and take their family car and go ride around on the dirt roads of Mercy County. Mrs. Oglesby said that my father knew what woman she was talking about, she didn't have to call any names.

I whistled when I finished the letter. I set it back on my father's desk, right in front of him. But he swiveled his chair around to face me.

"Now," my father said, and gave me a look that was both angry and beseeching, "what would you do?"

"I don't know," I said.

"What did you do?" my mother called from the kitchen.

"I showed it to Darcy," he said. He was talking to Mother in the kitchen, but he was looking at me while he spoke. "She said that occasionally she speaks to Bernard Oglesby in the morning when she comes in to work, but she doesn't ever see him anytime except then. She said he stands by his car and tips his hat to her when she walks past him in the mornings."

"And then what did you do?" my mother asked, coming to the door of the study to be able to see him. We were both looking at him hard, feeling sorry for him but deadly curious at the same time.

"I showed the letter to Bernard Oglesby. Bernard said that he would take care of it this evening at home. I told him that if I heard of him lifting a hand against his wife, I would fire him. I told him that if I had any further reports of his drinking beer and driving around Mercy County in the vicinity of Preacher Webster's house, I would fire him. He said he didn't think that was fair. I told him I didn't give a damn about what he thought was fair, that was what I was going to do. Fire him. And he said all right."

"That's all?" my mother asked.

"That's all," he said.

When school started again that fall, Patch and I were members of the Mellowtones, a professional musical organization that played for dances in Virginia, West Virginia, Tennessee, and North Carolina. The other members of the band were Mr. Oliver on trumpet; Mr. Chambers, the band director from Oakley, on piano; Dr. Kahn, a dentist in Madison, on bass fiddle; and Mr. Webb, who ran a hardware store in Max Meadows, on drums. That quartet played all the numbers; Patch and I joined in, to add saxophone and trombone, on about half of them. He and I each had one solo number. Patch's was "Night and Day"; mine was "Love Letters in the Sand." We were paid half of what the other members of the band were paid. The Mellowtones worked a heavy schedule through the winter, Patch and I sometimes getting to bed only a couple of hours before sunrise during the Christmas and New Year's season. We did a lot of traveling with those men, always riding in Dr. Kahn's station wagon, Patch and I talking to him, keeping him awake while the others slept. The men assumed we both smoked, which we did. They told us dirty jokes, kidded us about girls. They looked the other way if Patch and I decided to accept a drink when we were offered one by somebody at a dance. We were surprised that it happened almost everywhere we played. But then we figured out that people who went to dances thought that people—even boys like us—who played in bands were immoral persons. Patch started wearing sunglasses so he would look less like a freckle-faced kid from Rosemary and more like a depraved jazzman.

Patch already had a notion of who was going to offer us a drink at the Soiree Club Annual Dance at the Madison Country Club. It was April again, we'd been several weeks without playing anywhere, and the members of the Soiree Club brought in with them through the doors gales of laughter, strong wafts of perfume and cologne, armloads of brown bags with bottles in them. Most of them were middle-aged people, doing the old-style dances, singing along with "Stardust" and "I'll Get By" and "Blue Skies," requesting "Sweet Georgia Brown" every set. They were folks who stood out on the dance floor in groups of six or eight, clasping each other, shouting and laughing between numbers. Sitting over in a corner, not dancing or talking with any of the others, was a couple who were friends of Patch's parents. Patch said they were real hell-raisers. They were giving him winks, lifting their glasses to him, clapping loudly after everything we played. Patch said they were getting loaded. Patch said at the end of the next break we'd go over to talk to them and see what happened.

Darcy came in. I half stood up to go meet her. I forgot for a moment that I had a horn strapped around my neck, that I wore the powder-blue-and-navy dinner jacket of a Mellowtone, that I was on the bandstand behind microphones, mutes, speakers, and lighted music stands. Darcy looked better than anyone there. She stood, unbuttoning her coat, smiling a little, and in the soft light of the room her skin was tanned, her hair a light shade of brown and shiny, held back behind her shoulders with a dangling yellow ribbon. A lull came in the noise. For a moment it looked like she had come to the dance by herself. But then a sandy-haired man in a dark suit stepped through the door behind her. When he closed the door and turned, he saw most of the people standing on the dance floor and sitting at the tables staring at the place where he and Darcy stood. The color of his face went darker.

We were about to start "How High the Moon," in which Patch and I had to play the opening eight bars. Mr. Oliver counted off by tapping his foot loudly, *one, two*. I held my horn ready and watched the man point Darcy over toward one of the side rooms. We startled the people out on the floor with the first notes of the number. Everyone began dancing, but I could still see the man helping Darcy off with her coat, see that her yellow dress came down in the back to below her shoulder blades. Mr. Oliver pointed his trumpet at me, blew "How High the Moon" right straight at me, and looked hard at me over the bell of his horn. Patch elbowed me and said, "He wants us to clap. He's been trying to get your attention."

I started to clap while Mr. Oliver stood up and ad-libbed his solo. Usually I enjoyed clapping while the rest of the combo played, but with Darcy there I felt stupid doing it. Even that was better than what we did on Latin American numbers. On cha-chas and rumbas, Patch beat on a cowbell with a drumstick, and I thwacked one ebony woodblock against another in a cadence that was sort of like *shave-and-a-haircut—two bits*. I always felt dumb doing that. I saw that Darcy was paying attention only to the sandy-haired man. He did everything he was supposed to do, checked their coats, found them a table, brought over a bottle of mixer, fixed their drinks, put the liquor bottle in its brown paper bag on the floor under their table, spoke to the people around them, shook hands, introduced Darcy. But he wasn't right for her. He had no grace or ease. You could see how much effort everything he did was costing him, as if having a good time were hard work.

Darcy, however, looked like she'd done nothing all her life but go to parties, enjoy herself, and make the people around her smile at her. Once I heard her laugh above all the other noise in the room; it made me smile while I was clapping. Then it was time for Patch and me to play the closing riffs. Riffs were fast little complicated variations on the melody, be-bop arrangements; we sounded like trumpet, sax, and trombone were improvising in perfect harmony. When we smacked those first, crisp notes, the sound picked up volume and energy. People turned their heads to watch us. I saw Darcy just then recognize me for the first time, saw her face brighten, knew she was glad to see me. Mr. Oliver took his trumpet away from his mouth just long enough to shout at me, "Settle down!" I calmed down then and played evenly. When we finished the number, Mr. Oliver grinned at me and said, "What's wrong with you, Reed?" He didn't want an answer.

We played "Stars Fell on Alabama," and almost everyone came out on the floor to dance, including Darcy and the sandy-haired man. They were exactly the same height when they danced, Darcy talking with him almost nose to nose. She gave me a big smile. I knew she was telling him about me. I saw him look at me a couple of times, saw him set his jaw and listen while she talked.

When we finished, Darcy led him over to the bandstand; she came directly to me and said, "Hello, Mr. Music Man." She introduced me to Phil. Then I tried to introduce Darcy and Phil to the others. It got awkward until they all just told each other their names. Phil shook hands with Mr. Oliver, but he only waved to the others, which was the right thing to do. We were still in the set, not taking a break. Darcy asked Mr. Oliver if he would let me off the bandstand long enough to dance with her. Mr. Oliver assured her that he would, next set or the one after that. When they walked back to their table, I saw Patch studying Darcy's back and shoulders the same as I was. He clapped me on the knee and said, "Hey, man." Then Mr. Oliver said we'd play "Night and Day," Patch's solo, for the last number of the set. Patch said, "Man, I'm going to blow them right out of their shoes." And he did. Standing up there, leaning back, with his eyes closed, he played the smoothest, gutsiest "Night and Day" any of us had ever heard out of him. I played the woodblocks, and Mr. Oliver shook the maracas. When it was over, all of us in the band applauded Patch, who was red-faced, sweating, and delighted with himself.

At the break I saw Darcy and Phil signaling me to come to their table. "See you later, 'Night and Day,'" I said to Patch. I was too aware of myself walking across the empty dance floor. Darcy was holding a chair for me, and I took it, beside her but across the table from Phil.

"Oh, Reed, I think you're really good." She beamed at me. I took off my glasses to clean them, hoping that would keep me from looking too smug. Phil chimed in with, "Pretty good sound there, boy." He was putting ice in a glass, fixing a drink. I asked Darcy how she liked my woodblock-playing. She didn't understand the sarcasm. I explained how I hated the woodblocks. She looked vague. "But they add to the music," she said. Phil handed me the drink. I took it, sipped it, tasted bourbon. I made an effort not to look surprised and said, "Thanks, Phil." I told them about the men in the band, who was who and what kind of work they did, but Darcy was the only one who listened. Phil kept looking around the room, even when Darcy tried to draw him into the conversation. She told me that Phil was just starting out with his own contracting business and that he went to dances all the time, in Roanoke and Bristol and all around. "You think Reed's band is as good as any you've heard, don't you, Phil?" she said.

"Sure do," Phil said, craning his neck to look around behind him.

Before I went back to the bandstand, I thanked Phil again for the drink. He told me that there were some people he had to talk to later on; he hoped I would be able to keep Darcy company while he did it. He gave me a grin and a wink. Darcy said, "Oh, poor Reed, he'll never be able to stand being with me by himself." It was our old joke, at the car window outside the gatehouse at the carbide plant. I laughed with her and mumbled that I thought I could handle it.

The next set was going to take us through midnight. Mr. Oliver explained to me that he'd let me have the last two numbers off to dance with Darcy. I asked him to make them slow numbers because I couldn't dance to anything fast. He laughed at me, said he'd thought I was a real be-bopper, he was disappointed in me. But he went ahead and put two slow ones at the end of the set. Patch smelled my breath and gave me the lifted eyebrows, which I thought was very juvenile of him. He whispered to me, "Nothing but ginger ale. I sat over there, listened to those two old birds the whole break. They gave me nothing but ginger ale." I told him that ginger ale was what a young fellow like him was supposed to drink. We played a good set: "Ain't Misbehaving," "Mood Indigo," "Tea for Two," "Cherokee," and "Woodchopper's Ball," in which I got a couple of solo breaks. I imagined that the bourbon had made me looser. I paid attention to how the whole band sounded, and I thought I played solidly. Mr. Oliver nodded at me, and then it was time for me to step off the bandstand while the others stayed up there. I could feel them watching me when I walked away from them.

"Here he is," Phil said when I came up to their table, and I thought he might have meant to be sarcastic, but I didn't pay any attention to him. I asked Darcy would she like to dance, and because it was something to do with my hands, I held her chair while she came out to the floor. Phil got up, too. "Have fun, kids," he said; he started making his way back through the tables toward the Players' Lounge where some of the older men had gathered to smoke cigars and talk. "Moonlight in Vermont," one of the numbers Mr. Oliver sang, was the first one Darcy and I danced to. I was nervous about touching her, about starting my feet moving, but it was easy after the first couple of steps. I decided everything was logical: music, dancing, having Darcy that close to me, having my arm around her waist, her arm around my shoulder. "You smell great," I said. Then I decided that was a crude thing to say. "I'm sorry," I said. Darcy gave me a light tap with her hand on my back and moved her forehead so that it touched the side of my chin. I felt my blood moving up through my body toward my head. "Tell me about your music," she said. "Not about those others." She motioned the hand I was holding over toward the band. "Just you."

"Like what?" I said. I matched my tone with hers, low and soft, as if we knew each other better than we actually did.

"Like how you got started," she said. "You know."

I stammered a little getting started, but then words started spilling out of my mouth. I told her about my father's old alto saxophone, stashed in behind the piano over at my grandparents' house, how he'd had it overhauled and put in perfect condition before he packed it away and started work at the carbide plant. Darcy was surprised that my father had played at all. I told her that he'd been very good, that he'd had his own orchestra in Rosemary back in the old days, had taught each person in it how to play his instrument. I told her about the picture in the study at home, of my father with his band, the two women in long, formal-looking dresses sitting at the piano, the solemn-faced men in dark jackets and white-duck pants sitting, holding their instruments in their laps, banjo, clarinet, trumpet, guitar, and my father standing up with his saxophone held in front of him.

"And he taught you, too?" she asked.

I told her that he had, that it had been hard for him because I was always getting ahead of him, learning things before I was supposed to but not practicing the things he wanted me to work on.

"Your father thinks you have a lot of ability," Darcy said. "Moonlight in Vermont" was coming to an end.

"You mean I make good grades in school?" I had to shout the question at her because everyone on the dance floor was applauding. "Thank you, thank you very much," Mr. Oliver said into the microphone. We wandered back toward Darcy's table, but Phil wasn't there, and so we didn't sit down. Darcy picked up her glass and sipped. "Want the rest?" she said. I took the glass and emptied it. She was frowning. "I think he meant more than just grades in school," she said.

The Mellowtones started playing "Laura," which Mr. Oliver knew was one of my favorite songs, one that he had asked me not to sing along with; he said that my voice had not matured enough for me to be much of a singer yet. Darcy and I went out among the other couples on the dance floor. We held each other and swayed to that slow ballad, our feet barely moving. She let her forehead rest against my shoulder. My vision closed down to just Darcy and me and the soft light around us. When it was over, Darcy said, "I could use some air." I said that I could, too, and I wasn't kidding; I felt like I'd been holding my breath for a long time. We strolled out onto the patio balcony. I felt the cool air sweep across the sweat on my forehead, and I was grateful for it. "What about Phil?" I asked her.

"He's a big boy," she said.

Other couples were there outside, some of them smoking. I took out the pack of Chesterfields I'd bought for Patch and me for the night. "I don't want one," she said, " and I don't want you to have one either." She took the cigarette out of my hand and dropped it over the railing. "Can we walk some here?" she asked. She put her arm lightly around my waist then, and I put mine around her bare shoulders. I was pretty impressed with myself for doing that. We headed for the steps that led off the balcony and down onto the golf course. It was too dark to see at first, but then we got used to being out of the light. The farther out into the dark field we walked, the more clearly we could see each other. Darcy's skin was gray, and her dress had become white, moon-colored. In her high-heeled shoes, it was difficult for her to walk. She leaned against me while we went slowly up a hill toward the dark shapes of trees. "You're lucky to have a father who has some respect for you," she said. "Mine doesn't think I have a brain in my head."

"I always imagined your father as a big man with heavy shoulders, thick, bushy eyebrows, and a loud bass voice," I told her. "Preacher Webster from Mercy County. I can almost see him on horseback, riding to turn sinners into Methodists." I said.

Darcy laughed. "No," she said. "My father's not as tall as I am, he's been bald ever since I can remember, and he has a soft voice. When I'm home, he follows me around from room to room, giving me advice, asking me what I'm going to do, offering to help me."

"So what do you do?" I asked her.

"Tell him that I'm a grown woman." I could feel her shivering, and because I'd seen Nelson Eddy do it for Jeannette MacDonald in the movies, I took off my jacket and put it over Darcy's shoulders. "Thank you." she said. She put her arm back around my waist while we walked. "I tell him that I appreciate his care for me but that I have my own life."

"What effect does that have on him?"

She laughed again. "None whatsoever. He says, 'Yes, Darcy, but,' and then keeps following me around advising and counseling."

"I don't think my father knows anything about my life," I said. I hadn't thought about it before, but it seemed true when I said it. We walked without saying anything for a while. Then Darcy spoke just as we reached the shadow of the trees.

"He'd surprise you with what he knows, Reed."

We both stopped walking and then stood like we were dancing in the shadow of the trees out there on the grass. We were both shivering. "You're wrong," I said.

"All right," she said. She headed us back toward the lighted windows of the country club. I was glad to be going back because I was cold.

"Will Phil be mad?" I asked her when we came to the steps.

"No," she said. "He's somebody I used to know a long time ago. He doesn't care what I do here."

I followed her up the steps. "You mean you don't know him anymore," I said. She stopped and turned around. I came up to face-level with her. She let me kiss her, but she didn't seem especially interested in it, just rested her hands on my shoulders.

"You know what I mean," she said. When we came up on the balcony, she handed me back my jacket. I put it on, and we went inside. I followed her to the table, helped her with her chair, sat down beside her. Phil wasn't anywhere to be seen.

"Do you want me to fix you a drink?" I asked.

"No," she said. She stared at the small candle-flame sputtering in its blue glass jar in the center of the table.

"Well," I said. But I couldn't think of anything else to say. I took off my glasses, cleaned them, put them back on, and watched the people in the room. Patch came up to tell me it was time to get back on the stand. I didn't want to leave Darcy there by herself, but she told me to go ahead, she'd find Phil. Up on the bandstand I got some fishy looks from Mr. Webb and Dr. Kahn. Mr. Oliver said, "O.K., young stud, let's see if you can get through 'Love Letters in the Sand.'" I thought I was playing my solo as well as Patch had played his. I didn't look out onto the dance floor, or anywhere except down at my music stand. I wanted to imagine how Darcy would look while she listened to me play. But when I opened my eyes at the end, I didn't see her anywhere. People out on the floor applauded, but the guys in the band didn't act like I had played it any better than I usually did. During the next number, I saw Phil with Darcy, getting their coats. I was playing then, going through some hard riffs in "Somewhere There's Music." At the door Darcy just lifted a hand to wave. She was wearing what I thought was a sad kind of smile when she went out with Phil.

It was the following Wednesday before I had a chance to drive the car up to the carbide plant. That afternoon, Darcy and my father came out of the gatehouse together, talking. They stood right beside me at the car window and discussed a report that my father kept insisting had to be gotten to New York right away. I watched him kick dust in the road while they stood there. Darcy didn't look once at me. Then, when she said goodbye to my father, she turned to me as if she were seeing me for the first time and gave me a wonderful smile. I said hello, and I was starting to ask her how she'd liked the party Saturday night, but she was saying goodbye, turning, and going toward her own car. On the way home I hoped my father would say something that would provoke me so that I could start an argument with him or say something hateful to him. But he sat quietly, looking out at the river, not much interested in talking with me.

One Saturday in mid-May, after a long marching-band practice, Patch and I pulled into the parking lot of the High Hat, and Darcy was there. First I noticed her car, and then I saw that she was in it, sitting behind the wheel, by herself. I asked Patch to back his father's car up beside hers so that I could talk with her out my window. The afternoon was bright, and I couldn't tell if Darcy was trying to smile at me or just squinting from the sun when she saw me. She said "Hi, Reed," and she asked me how I was doing. I got out of Patch's car and perched up on its front fender to make conversation with her. Something was wrong with her, something darkened about her face. She lit a cigarette. I told her I didn't know she smoked.

"Sometimes, when I'm in the mood, I do," she said. She offered me one, and I took it, clamped it between my teeth when I lit it. I asked her what she'd been doing. She shook her head like she didn't want to answer. Then she said, "Driving around, sitting out here, thinking."

"Problems?" I asked her.

"Nothing that won't go away of its own accord," she said.

I didn't like to think of her sitting there in her car by herself. I looked around the parking lot, which was empty except for two other cars. Even on a bright afternoon, this was an ugly place to be spending time. The High Hat Drive-In was a flat, squat building with Pepsi Cola signs and neon lights all over it. The place was right on the edge of Madison where the highway traffic was almost always heavy. "You want to go inside with Patch and me to get something to eat?" I asked her.

Darcy threw her cigarette out the window, shook her head, and ran her fingers through her hair. "Sure," she said, in a forced kind of way, as if she were determined to get herself in a better frame of mind.

Patch swung himself out of the car and hitched up his pants. "We're going inside and act like we're used to coming to the city," he said.

"You miserable hick," I said.

When Darcy got out of the car, I saw that she was wearing dungarees, loafers, and white socks. Her blouse wasn't even tucked in. She stuck her hands in her pockets, trying to give me a big smile, but it didn't work for her. Her face lapsed into an expression that was half getting ready to cry and half frowning. She watched the asphalt under her feet while we were walking to the door of the High Hat. I told her I'd never seen her in dungarees. I told her she looked good.

"Thanks, Reed," she said. She touched my arm and then let it go, which I took to mean that she appreciated my good intentions but she saw through my flattery. Patch bowed and opened the door for us. Inside was a line of booths on the highway side of the building, all of them empty, and on the other side a counter with a line of stools on one of which sat a waitress reading the paper and sipping coffee.

"Table for three, please," Patch said, coming up behind us. The waitress gave him a short look over the top of her glasses, jerked her head back toward the booths, and said, "Any one you want, Son."

Patch took one side of a booth; Darcy and I took the other. He was fidgety, took out his change and spread it on the table in front of him. After the waitress had taken our orders, Patch got up to play the jukebox. Both Darcy and I gave him money to put in for us. He stayed up there in front of the machine a long time, feeding quarters into it, punching buttons. I asked Darcy what was wrong. I told her I wasn't used to seeing her in a bad mood.

She shook her head again. "Take my mind off it, Reed. Talk to me. Tell me something."

I though hard. Everything I could think of to say was dull. "I haven't done anything fascinating recently," I said.

Patch came back and sat down, humming along with the Everly Brothers' "Bird Dog" from the jukebox. The silence hung over the table. Finally he said, "Something going on out there on that highway that I can't see?" He kept shifting his position in the booth, singing along with the songs on the jukebox, patting on the table with his hands. The waitress watched him grimly when she brought our chiliburgers and French fries and milkshakes and Darcy's coffee. Patch and I ate. After that it was easier to talk. Patch said something about how he wished the Mellowtones could play some newer music, and I agreed with him. It was an old subject for us, but we kept it going to try to perk up Darcy. Patch sang his rendition of "Peggy Sue" and got a smile from her. I was aware that I was trying to please her with my talk, describing things in funny ways, using special words. Patch gave me a couple of odd looks while I was speaking. After a while he stopped saying much. I kept trying to get him back in the conversation, but all he would say was "Yeah, that's right," or "O.K., man." Then we were all three quiet. "Saturday afternoon," Patch said and sighed and slapped the table. Darcy asked the waitress for another cup of coffee. After she'd gotten it and was sipping it, Patch said "Saturday afternoon" again. The jukebox ran out of songs. We sat there looking out the window at cars passing on the highway. Patch said he thought he ought to be going. I asked him what was his hurry. He said he wasn't in any real hurry. He'd been having a fantastic time all afternoon, he said, but he thought he could find a better way to spend his Saturday night than to sit over a table full of dirty dishes and watch the flies.

Darcy was smoking then. She was down to the bottom of her cup of coffee. She said, as much into her cup as to me, "Let him go ahead. I'll take you home." So I told Patch to go ahead, I'd see him Monday. He stood up and did a little dance to shake his pegged pants down his legs. He bowed to us. "I'll see you children later," he said. "Be careful in the big city." I felt strange sending him out like that, seeing him go off without me. After he'd driven out of the parking lot, Darcy and I talked about him. I told her Patch had been in the wreck with me. She said that my father hadn't said much about it to her or to anybody up at the carbide plant. So I told her about the wreck. I said a few things about Bobby Sloan that made Darcy laugh, about him saying "Thank you, Jesus," and being too fat to crawl out the car window. I went on talking about Bobby, told her how he represented everything bad that the Madison kids thought about people from Rosemary. "Except you said he was smart," Darcy said. She seemed more her old self.

"That's right," I said, "but he isn't really even that smart. He just studies all the time."

Darcy took up for Bobby Sloan, and I didn't mind. At least we had a conversation going. We watched it go gray outside and then deeper and deeper shades of blue. The waitress came to clear away our dishes, made us squeeze away from the table while she wiped with a gray cloth. People began coming in and talking loudly. "Want to go drive around some?" Darcy asked. "No law that says you have to stay in one place while you're waiting out your troubles." I was glad to be outside with her in the warm evening air. I stretched until my bones cracked. While we were walking toward her car, she handed me her keys.

"You trust me?" I asked her.

She just looked at me and went around to the passenger side of her car. It had been partially customized and was kind of a hot rod; she had told me before, in our carbide plant quitting-time conversations, that her brother worked on it for her. I had teased her about it then, told her I thought she was one of those Mercy County bootleggers, asked her did she know the words to "Thunder Road." When I started up that old Mercury, the exhaust noise was deafening until I let up on the accelerator. Darcy grinned and said she was sure I would get used to it.

We drove through town, up around the schoolhouse, then out to the Madison Country Club, which was locked up and dark except for a small light back in the kitchen. I pulled up in front of the front door and beeped the horn.

"Why'd you do that?" Darcy asked.

"Always beep your horn in front of a dark building," I said. I turned out the lights but kept the car idling. "I'm not so bad driving a straight shift, am I?"

Darcy said that I was terrible. We both fiddled with the radio to see if we could find music that suited us. When we were leaning forward together like that, her hair made a small tent for our faces. I told her that I liked her hair down like that. She switched the radio off.

"Come on, Reed. I don't need that kind of cheering up anymore," she said. "Let's get out of here before somebody thinks we're trying to break into this place."

"You don't want to take another walk on the golf course?" I asked her. She said she didn't.

We drove back to the schoolhouse. Every window in it was dark except for the exit signs at the doors. "The Old Schoolhouse," I said. I steered the car up over the curb and onto the sidewalk. I drove slowly all the way down the length of the building, past the band room, all the classrooms, the principal's office, the gymnasium, and the cafeteria. Then I drove back down over the curb into the teachers' parking lot. But Darcy was quiet the whole time, didn't even giggle. I didn't say anything about it either. At first I'd been proud of myself for thinking of such a droll thing, but then I decided it was childish and disgusting.

I headed us out the back way from town, as if I were going to Gantley the long way. When I saw Fish Hatchery Road, I turned off there and went along that dirt road slowly until we came to the fish hatchery. I turned in, stopped the car in the empty parking lot, turned out the lights, and turned the engine off. I did these things as they came to me to do; I did not plan them. The place was dark and full of frog noises. It smelled like water. Darcy opened the door like she'd been waiting for me to get her just exactly to that stopping place. I got out, too, and followed her.

It was warm out. There was no wind. In the dark I could make out Darcy, her hair hiding her face, just strolling across the parking lot toward the walkways and paths that led to the trout pools. Trees were all around us, mostly willows; they made it look like any direction we turned we would be heading into a wall of darkness. What light there was came down from the moon and stars; the trees scattered it like sunlight in patches on the ground. In the daytime, you could see trout in those pools, divided according to size, packed in so that the water was thick with them. In the daylight, you could see the markings on their sides, the light stripes of pink stippling on the rainbows, the red flecks on the brook trout. But now, in the dark, we could see only a yawning black rectangle that represented a pool, then white foam when the water was stirred up as we walked past each one. We could hear, even above the constant sound of fast-running water, the sound of water being thrashed and churned by fish.

Darcy and I passed along the tree-lined walkways, past half a dozen trout pools, until we came to the small park down at the very end, away from the main building and the parking lot. An area of smooth grass was surrounded by trees and benches. On one side was a small pool where only the largest trout were kept just for visitors to see and feed if they wanted to. Darcy stood over that pool, bending over and staring into the water. When she gestured toward it with her hand, the water made a sound like an engine picking up speed, and the surface of it became a white froth. "Those trout can take a finger off," I said to her. She looked at me over her shoulder, but she didn't say anything.

I sat down on a bench and waited to see what she would do. After a while she came slowly over and sat beside me. It was very dark. We sat close to each other, peering into each other's faces. I took off my glasses. "It doesn't make any difference," I said. "I can see you the same with them off or with them on." I spoke up loudly so that my voice would carry over the sound of rushing water. Darcy looked around us, at the dark trees, the patches of light on the ground. Over one of the pools, we could see mist rising in a shaft of soft blue light. "We could be under the sea, Reed. We could be at the very bottom of the ocean," she said. She stood up and took both my hands and raised me up with her. We went out onto the grass where there was an open spot of light coming down. We stood under the light and put our arms around each other, rocked and took slow steps, turning ourselves in a circle.

Darcy squeezed me hard, and I lifted her chin to kiss her. I was the one who kissed her, but she kissed back hard, opened her mouth to me, and pressed against me. We lay down on the grass together, pushing our mouths and teeth together, panting through our noses. Darcy pressed against me with her whole body and held me with more strength than I'd imagined she would have. We couldn't get close enough to each other, couldn't touch each other enough. I fumbled at the buttons of her blouse, she trying to help but getting in the way, finally both of us getting it open and the brassiere unclasped in the back. She pushed it up over her breasts and pulled me down. We were like two people fighting with each other, pulling at each other with our hands, breating so hard we were snorting. Then I undid the button and unzipped the zipper of Darcy's dungarees, and it all stopped. Darcy took her arms away from me and lay back on the grass, catching her breath. I scooted closer to her and put my hand on her belly. Darcy kept her arms still beside her. She looked past my shoulder at the sky.

I pushed closer to her, but she stayed quiet. She was breathing very calmly. "Will you do this with me?" I asked her.

"Yes," Darcy said after a long while. "Yes, if you want to."

"Don't you want to?" I said. I sat up and began to tug at her dungarees and her underpants, wanting to help her get them off. Darcy lifted her hips as I tugged, but she didn't move her hands to help me.

"No," she said.

I had her pants in a tangle at her thighs. In the light, her skin was the color of my grandmother's bone-china dinner plates, a length of smooth whiteness up to her unbuttoned blouse and loosened brassiere. I stopped pulling at her clothes.

"You don't want to," I said.

"Yes, that's right," she answered evenly.

"But you will anyway?" I asked.

"Yes," she said again, "if you want to," softly, neutrally.

I sat beside her there on the grass, in the pale light, looking at her for a long time. She lay still, watching me. The shape of her body, her breasts, the narrowing of her trunk from her hips to her waist, was the shape of a woman I thought I had dreamed. I put my hand on Darcy's ribs and then her belly again. Even then I wasn't certain either one of us was there with the other one. I stared at her so long that we both were floating, were being carried downstream in a heave of dark water. I shook my head. "All right," I said. I took my hand off her and put it on myself. I ached.

Darcy stood up then, used my shoulder to help balance herself. She slid the clump of pants, underpants, and socks down off her legs, took off the blouse and the brassiere, let them fall to the ground, and shook out her hair with her hands. Then she shook her arms and her legs like an animal shaking off rain. One piece at a time, she put her clothes back on, the underpants, the brassiere, the blouse, the dungarees, and finally her shoes. She picked up the socks and held them like she didn't know what to do with them. She muttered something about socks, I couldn't hear exactly what it was.

"What?" I said. I was unbuckling my pants, trying to get my underwear rearranged and my shirttail tucked in.

"Don't like them," she said, walking away from me, twirling the socks one in each hand. I walked over to the bench and recovered my glasses. When I looked back at Darcy, she was standing beside the pool, bending a little, dangling one of the socks up over the water. There was a whooshing burst up out of the water, a pipelike shape the size of the thick part of a man's arm. Darcy jumped back from the pool. The sock was gone from her hand. The water was churning as if someone had thrown a running outboard motor into it. Darcy hadn't made a sound, but when I came up beside her I could tell she'd been scared. The big trout continued to roil in the water, and though I couldn't see it, I imagined they had ripped that sock to shreds. "Those fools think it's food," I said.

"It's just my dumb sock," Darcy said. Then she saw she was holding the other one in her hand. She leaned forward and dropped that one in the pool, too. Again there came more splashing and thumping. "I bet they all get sick and die," she said. I hugged her shoulders, and she put her arms around my waist. We headed back to the parking lot, bumping our hips against each other as we went. When we came out of the little park, we saw the figure of a man standing stark still in the dark near one of the pools of smaller fish. "Damn!" Darcy said in a whisper. "Damn him!"

"Did you get an eyeful?" I called out at the shadow, but it made no sound. It gave no sign of life.

We were shivering when we got back to the car.

The next day was Sunday. I expected Darcy would be in church that morning, listening to her father preach. The thought of that made me smile to myself while I sat in our church with my father and mother. That afternoon I called Darcy. Her mother said that she was taking a nap, could I call back. When I called back, her father, in a thin, high-pitched voice, said that she and her mother had gone up to Gantley and wouldn't be back until late.

Monday I drove the car up to the plant. Darcy came out of the gatehouse and waved to me, gave me a smile, but she walked straight to her car. I started to call out to her, but I was too embarrassed to do it in front of the men who walked all around her heading toward their cars and trucks. I called her house that night. Her mother said she'd gone out with some young people from the church. She didn't know when Darcy would be back.

Tuesday in school, through civics, algebra, and study hall, I wrote

Darcy a letter. In the beginning of it my tone was angry; at the end of it I told her that I couldn't think about anything or anybody else except her. I said that I felt a great pressure of things I wanted to say to her, things I wanted to hear her say back to me. I apologized to her for my aggressive behavior. I said that I thought she could trust me from now on. I told her that if Bernard Oglesby was following her around, I was certain I could get my father to make him stop. I mailed the letter and didn't call her, didn't go up to the carbide plant all that week. I didn't get a letter back. I didn't hear anything from her.

I fell into a mood that surprised even me. In classes I found myself being noisy and as fresh with my teachers as any of the very worst of the boys from Rosemary ever were. Mrs. Yerkes, my algebra teacher, sent me to the principal's office two days in a row. Tall, pale Mrs. Lancaster, my English teacher, who sometimes had to leave the classroom because of migraine headaches and who praised my book reports, kept me after school to ask what had gotten into me. I didn't know, I told her, and that wasn't really a lie, because even though I knew that the way I felt had to do with Darcy, I didn't know exactly how it worked. Part of it was that since I couldn't see her or talk with her, I became less and less certain that it had happened, that we had gone with each other to that place. It was like a dream I'd had that was being taken away from me. Mrs. Lancaster gave me a long, kindly look and did not break the silence of the room for a while. I fiddled with my glasses and stared at the names scratched in the wooden desk where I sat: POTTSIE II, JANET, and GUTHRIE THE OGRE. Mrs. Lancaster said that she hoped my conduct would improve. She said that whether or not I liked it, I was an example to many of the other Rosemary students who attended Madison High School. She said there were only six of us from Rosemary who were in the College Preparatory Program. After each thing she told me, I said "Yes, ma'am." Finally she let me go out of the empty classroom.

But I didn't like being an example. I was at my worst on the school bus, with the others from Rosemary. I didn't like being thought of as different from them; I was one of them. I joined the school-bus fighting, which, as a good student, I'd always tried to stay out of. I'd had my ears gouged, my ribs thunked, my head slapped, and then turned around to see Herbert or George or Botch or Elmo Blair staring innocently out the window. Now I became a gouger, thunker, head-slapper. I joined the others in harassing the freshmen and eighth-graders and the older ones who held no rank on the Rosemary bus.

In that bus's history, there had been a running war between the boys and the girls, carried on in the past by older brothers and sisters, cousins and friends. After us, it would be fought by the younger ones who learned the rules of it from us. Sometimes a truce came about, especially if one of the boys started going with one of the girls and they sat together, holding hands or, if they were bold, kissing and petting. But mostly there was a constant effort among the hell-raising boys to make the girls lose their tempers. Seating had a lot to do with it; tougher girls, who enjoyed the battle, took the dangerous seats in back; more timid girls found safer seats toward the front. I began picking on those Rosemary girls; it was easy for me to get them upset. If one of them wore a new blouse or skirt or jacket, I would compliment her on it at length until everyone's attention fell on that girl. The same with a different lipstick or perfume. George Oglesby followed my example, and together with Herbert and Botch we succeeded in putting Janet Littrel in tears one afternoon. I also became a hair-puller, a bra-snapper, an ass-pincher, a trash-mouth. Those girls had known me all through grade school and the beginning of high school as a nice boy. They lectured me, told me to be ashamed of myself, asked me what my mother would think of the way I was misbehaving. I told them they were stupid. I called Molly Whisnant a bitch. George and Herbert and Botch were on my side, slapping my shoulder, speaking up for me. That afternoon, when the bus stopped at the bottom of our hill to let me out, Lenore Swenson and Harriet Weatherman held on to my belt and shirttail from behind when I started up the aisle. Judy Statler, who was almost as tall as I was and a good deal heavier, came back from the front toward me. She slapped my face a couple of times. When I had my arms up, clutching at my glasses, she punched me in the stomach. The others let go of me, Judy let me pass, and they pushed me up the aisle toward the door. I could hardly breathe when I stumbled off the bus. I could hear those girls jeering at me through the open windows when the bus was a long way up the road from where I stood.

A Saturday night toward the end of May, the Mellowtones played the Elks Club Spring Dance in Gantley. Patch and I got ourselves giggling-drunk on moonshine whiskey an Elks couple kept giving us, "to sample," they said. The woman, with her hair in an enormous beehive, kept asking us how we liked the stuff, we kept taking more, and her ruddy-faced husband watched us with his eyes dancing. Gantley was in Mercy County, near where Darcy lived; I hoped she would come into the dance and see me drunk and acting stupid with Patch on the bandstand.

Driving back to Madison in Dr. Kahn's station wagon, Mr. Oliver sat in the back seat with Patch and me and chewed us out. He said he was disappointed in both of us. He thought we'd violated the personal trust of the older members of the band as well as disregarded the standards of professional musicians. "You boys think anybody wants to hire a bunch of drunks to come in and play for them?" Patch and I said we did not. Mr. Oliver escorted us into the Madison Greyhound Bus Terminal and made us sit at a table and swill down coffee until he was certain I could drive home all right. As he left, he told us he would have a long talk with us soon to see if he thought we could be responsible enough to continue playing in the dance-band. He said he would have to discuss the matter with the other men first. On the road, all the way from Madison to Rosemary, Patch and I complained about how he had kept calling us kids and how they paid us only half of what they got even though we put in a full night's work, too. If they kept treating us as children, then how did they expect us to behave?

When I got the car into the garage and came in the house, I found my mother and father sitting up late. They weren't waiting for me, my mother said, they were just talking in the kitchen. It was three in the morning. Mother was in her bathrobe, but my father was still fully dressed. I told them I couldn't remember if I'd ever seen them awake at that time of the morning. They didn't say anything to that. They both looked serious, but they apparently didn't mean to carry on their conversation while I was there listening to them. I felt cranky anyway, from the moonshine and then the coffee and Mr. Oliver's lecture.

"What is the topic of our discussion?" I asked. I went to the stove and poured myself a cup of their coffee. Then I pulled out a chair for myself at the kitchen table and sat down with them. My mother sat looking at my father, and then she gave me a hard stare. "Reed!" she said.

"What?"

"You smell like a distillery, Son," she said.

My father didn't have anything to say to me. He looked at me over his glasses in such a way that it was clear he didn't have much use for how I was right then. He also looked like he didn't really want to have to address himself to the issue of my delinquency at that hour of the morning. I told them that Patch and I had accidentally got to drinking moonshine whiskey, that we didn't know what it was until we'd had right much of it. "You know it's clear as water," I said. My father and my grandfather like to tell Duncan and me about the old-timey moonshiners around Rosemary and Gantley, the ones who would throw horse turds in their mash to make it ferment faster. I knew I wasn't being overwhelmingly convincing, but they both looked so worn-out that I decided they were ready to buy just about anything I tried to sell them. I said that Patch and I had stopped at the bus terminal in Madison and drunk coffee until we were certain we were sober before we drove home. My mother didn't say anything when I finished that story, just turned her eyes toward my father.

"That doesn't sound so good, boy," my father said. He made me mad the way he said it. I looked him straight in the eye. He was really no bigger than I was, I thought. His skin was pale and mottled, he was losing his hair, his breathing had a rasp in it.

"Look," I said, "I'm tired of being a goddamn boy!" and I was shouting by the time I finished saying it. My mother lifted her eyebrows and looked first at me, then at my father. "You will have to excuse me," she said. "I think it's time for me to go to bed."

"I mean it," I said as she got up from the table.

"I know you do, Son. Goodnight." She reached across the table and patted my father's shoulder. "Goodnight," she said to him. She went out, leaving my father sitting there with me across the table, under the washed-out kitchen lights. We could hear her footsteps upstairs for a while, until she got in bed.

"Like for instance," I said, startling myself with the violation of silence my voice made, "before I came in here, you and Mother were talking about something important. And then you both got all hush-hush, like the child just can't handle the adult topics, you know. How do you think that makes me feel?" I took my glasses off and polished them with a napkin my mother had left at her place.

"Oh Lord, Son," my father said. I could tell he was tired. But I was making a point. I knew I had a momentum then that I wasn't likely to have again anytime soon. I didn't let up on him.

"Well?" I said. He looked at me over his hands, which he'd been using to rub his eyes. I kept staring at him, straight on.

"Darcy," my father said. "We were talking about Darcy. We were talking about whether or not I was going to have to fire Darcy." He said it like something he'd memorized, something he'd had to memorize that he didn't like. What he said surprised me. I kept quiet for a while. But he continued looking at me. I felt like he was giving me some kind of a test; if I handled myself all right through this conversation, then maybe he would start treating me with some respect. "What is your opinion?" he finally asked.

I let a few seconds go by before I answered him. "I don't know all the facts," I said.

"Mrs. Oglesby has complained again," he said, "that Bernard cannot concentrate on his family obligations without being distracted by Darcy Webster. Mrs. Agee and Mrs. Blevins have made telephone calls to me in the past week to make accusations against Darcy Webster. They say their husbands, who have both been excellent husbands in the past, have now gone to the dogs because of Darcy Webster." He waited for me to say something.

"Those are just accusations," I said. "What about you? Have you seen her do anything wrong?" I noticed that we were both speaking in formal tones, as if this were some kind of official proceeding.

"No," my father said. "I have seen Willie Agee hanging around Darcy's desk a good part of the day, and I have directed Willie Agee to keep his butt out of there since none of his duties require him to be in her office. I have seen Jake Blevins trying to engage Darcy in conversation, but it was clear to me that Darcy did not want to talk with Jake at that time and in that place, which was at lunchtime in the hallway just outside the women's bathroom. In my opinion, it's only Slick Mallory, whose wife has made no complaint, who might have some reason to devote any of his time to thinking about Darcy Webster. One afternoon I did see Darcy hand him an envelope as he walked by her desk. I do not know what was in the envelope."

"You've really been keeping an eye on her," I told him. I felt myself getting edgy. I couldn't help it. That vision of Darcy handing an envelope to Slick Mallory bothered me—even though I wasn't sure I even knew which one of the carbide men Slick Mallory was. I didn't like my father's telling me about it, either.

"Yes," he said. "I've had to watch her because people have been accusing her. I have thought that I might have to fire her. She has been a good worker. She was a great help to me and to several of the men that afternoon of the burning accident. From my experience with her, I find it hard to believe that she is not of excellent character. The envelope she handed Slick Mallory might have contined merely a letter he had asked her to type for him. If I am going to have to fire her, I want to be as fair about it as possible."

"You want to be in the right," I said. I could tell that got to him. I could tell I'd got him a good one with that. He'd been slumped in his chair while he talked before, but now he sat up straight.

"That's right," he said. "I want to be in the right." His glasses glittered at me, and his voice was tight, but he was holding his temper pretty well.

"I think she's kind of flirty," I said. I felt my stomach cramp. I barely had enough breath in my lungs to get out the last part of the sentence. I made my face hold still, made my eyes look directly at him.

"What?" my father said.

I shrugged. "On the bus," I said. "They talk about her. They say things."

"Who says things? What do they say?" My father's voice was up a half-tone from what it had been. I knew I had to be careful, had to hold steady.

"Just those guys," I said. "Herbert and Patch and George and T.W. They don't say much. Just they mention her name and then laugh. You know how they do it sometimes."

"No, I don't know," my father said. He was quiet for a while, and then he leaned back in his chair, folded his hands on the table in front of him. "Those are only accusations," he said. "Have you seen her do anything wrong?"

"Not really wrong," I said.

"Flirty, then," my father said. His tone was going back to normal. He was about to end the conversation, I thought.

"Yes," I said. "At a dance where I played. She came with one man, but she spent a lot of time with someone else."

"What dance was this?"

"The Soiree Club dance at the country club," I told him. "Last month."

"Who was the man she came with?"

"Phil somebody. I don't know his last name. That new contractor in Madison."

"And who was the man she spent a lot of time with?"

"I don't know him."

My father repeated it all to himself, as if it were a puzzle and if he went over it carefully, the answer would come to him. "She came with a man named Phil. She spent time with a man you don't know."

"Yes sir."

"You saw that with your own eyes," my father said.

"Yes sir."

"And you call that flirty?"

"I don't know what else you could call it," I said.

My father was quiet for a long while. Then he said very quietly, "She's not that kind of person. I don't believe you." He was speaking from way down inside himself, his eyelids half closed, as if he weren't even aware that I was sitting there across the table from him.

"Well, don't, then," I said. I got up from the table and went upstairs to my room. I hurried to undress, get in bed, turn the light out, but I was too slow. He was up there right away. I could hear his footsteps coming toward my door. He knocked, but he didn't wait for me to tell him to come in. He opened the door while I had my pants half off. I sat down on the bed and tried to glare at him.

"I want you to know I'm going to fire her," he said. "I just made up my mind."

"It's your decision," I said.

"I appreciate your helping me make it," he answered. And closed the door.

I stayed awake a long time that night thinking about him, how he wouldn't let go his hold on me. I imagined how he would have to speak to Darcy and tell her that she was fired. I knew she would cry: I could see her, in one of her bright dresses, standing in front of his desk, with her arms down, letting her tears come down her face. I knew she would ask him to explain to her why he was firing her. And I knew that would do some damage to him. Not enough, though. I expected he would tell me about the firing, make me listen to every detail. Finally I did hit upon something I could do that might shake him loose from me. If I embarrassed him in front of the men who worked for him, that would be a terrible thing for him, I decided.

We had a sullen Sunday breakfast. I ate methodically and tried to keep a pleasant expression on my face while I forked down my scrambled eggs. My mother asked my father if it was all right for her to have the car the next day, and he told her that it was. I asked, with elaborate politeness, if I might be allowed to be the one who drove to meet him there at the carbide plant that afternoon. My mother said, "Yes, if that's all right with your father." My father said nothing. I guessed he meant it was all right.

That Monday afternoon I drove slowly to the plant, enjoying the sunlight on the trees and fields and on the river where it turned the brown water into molten silver. I knew that when I saw my father I would call out something to him, loud enough for the men around him to hear it, about Darcy. I would shout at him and ask him if he had gotten rid of her, fired her, sacked her. I might even call her a name. I hadn't made up my mind exactly what I would say, but I knew generally what it was going to be. I would trust my tongue to improvise, to give the right words.

When I drove up past the warehouses and across the railroad tracks, I saw that Darcy's car was gone from its usual place and that her place was now empty. I knew for sure then that my father had fired her. Sometime around the middle of the morning she would have come out of the gatehouse, walked to her car, and driven home. I was sure my father had talked to her before lunchtime. He never delayed doing difficult things, liked to get them out of the way as soon as possible. I decided it would be a nice touch if I parked in Darcy's spot and waited for him there, with the car pointed toward the gatehouse where he would come out. I felt exhilarated while I tried to sit still there and wait for him. I knew something important was going to happen.

One or two men began to straggle out of the gatehouse, the way some of them did, knowing they wouldn't be reprimanded or docked any pay for leaving only a few minutes early. Then the whistle blew the official four-thirty quitting time, and the men began to stream out of the gatehouse. I watched them intently, noted their dark faces, their hats, the way their shoulders curled inward toward their chests, their sweat-marked gray and khaki and dark-blue clothes, the way they carried their dinner-buckets hooked down on the ends of their fingers as if they'd as soon drop them as carry them home. I made no attempt to greet those men, though I knew many of them. My window was open as they passed by me, but I did not speak to them. I noticed one or two men nod as they walked by me, but I did not think of nodding back or raising my hand. I concentrated on the men coming out of the door of the gatehouse where they appeared in thick packs of faces. I wanted to be certain I could see my father when he first appeared, to be certain I would correctly time whatever it was that I was going to shout out at him.

After a while I became aware of how tightly my hands were gripping the steering wheel and how they felt cramped and tired. I saw that the stream of men who got off work at four-thirty had passed. Only the late three or four were coming out of the gatehouse now. Most of the cars and pickup trucks were running and pulling out in the brief swarm of traffic and swirling dust that occurred every time the shifts changed. The lightness and excitement I'd felt a few minutes earlier turned into a gloomy anger. I felt as if I were holding a heavy object in the center of my stomach, just under my breastbone. No more men came out of the gatehouse. I made myself take my hands off the steering wheel, put them in my lap. I wondered if there'd been some mistake, if my father had called home to say he'd be staying late, or maybe had taken a trip to Madison or Gantley and had not gotten back yet.

Then I decided he was doing it to me on purpose, making me wait out there like that, as if my time had no value. He was keeping his hold on me. My neck and ears began burning while I sat there, and I decided I would leave him.

I started the car, but just then I saw him come out of the gatehouse, alone, his hat pushed back in that way he wore it when he was very tired, when he'd had the worst kind of a day. His clothes drooped on him. They were gray and his face was gray, carbide-coated. The car was running. I put it into drive and began coasting toward him. I saw him look at me across the hood of the car. I edged the steering wheel over toward him a little. I headed the car directly at him, pressing the accelerator just enough to pick up a mile or two of speed. It worked. He thought I was going to hit him, and he scuttled over toward the chain-link fence, took hold of it with his hand, and raised his foot. When I was almost on him, I flicked the steering wheel away, slammed on the brakes at exactly the right moment. The car slid to a stop with the door handle right at his hand. He leaned down to look in the window at me. I could see every line in his face, could hear him breathing hard.

"Joke," I said.

He kept staring at me, bending down to see in the window but not yet opening the door. His face was a way I'd never seen it before. It was a way I had known he was going to look at me, I had thought at one time, far out in the future.

"Joke," I said again, through my clenched teeth.

Only the Little Bone

T H I S   S U M M E R   our county has more cases of polio than any county in the nation. You catch polio from other people. Our parents decree that my brother and cousin and I must stay inside our yard. Until further notice we can't go out, and our friends can't come to see us.

Ours is an interesting yard, maybe an acre of mowed grass, an old tennis court gone to honeysuckle, and a bushy patch of woods far below the house that we call the jungle. If you had to spend a whole summer inside a yard, this one is better than most.

On the very day of the decree, we boys become bored and restless. Theoreticians of the small group advise that three is a lousy number, two against one the given dynamic. Duncan and I pick on Ralph, or Duncan and Ralph pick on me. Ralph is our cousin from Kingsport. Duncan doesn't get picked on, but he's the one who has to answer to our mother when she gets fed up with the whining.

Which is frequently. But since she interferes with our natural method of entertainment, she's the one we look to to provide us with peaceful activities. So she buys us comic books downtown, sometimes half a dozen a day. She hates it. She was raised to think of comic books as something that trashy people buy and read. I can't go with her to see her doing it, but I can imagine her standing down there at Mrs. Elkins's store in front of the comic-book rack trying to pick out ones we haven't read yet. She has to ask for the new Batman, the new Monty Hale. She's embarrassed and a little mad about it, but what can she do? She selects carefully, because if she brings us one we've already read, we howl and mope around the house for hours.

But she has to bake them before she gives them to us. The baking removes the germs. It also stiffens them, gives them an odd smell, makes them wear out quickly. Now she has acquired some skill at it, but she burned a few in the early weeks, charred a Sears & Roebuck catalogue pretty thoroughly by giving it extra minutes in the oven for its size. The baked comic books go along with the boiled water and the almost-boiled milk that tastes like liquid aluminum.

I commence a study of June bugs, those hefty green beetles. I tie threads around their legs and let them fly in circles around me. June bugs have shiny gold bellies and a sweet, oily smell. June bugs are uncommonly healthy, stupid, hard to kill, more or less blind, harmless. If you yank the thread too hard, though, you can jerk their legs off pretty easily.

This summer we are more than usually aware of our father's working too hard, always coming home tired. After supper maybe he'll toss the baseball with us or play a couple of games of croquet. But mostly what he wants to do is sit and rest. When he is home, though, we look to him to relieve us of our circumstance, all four of us hanging around him like hungry dogs. Our mother needs him to distract Duncan and Ralph and me, to give her a little rest, to let her go upstairs and take a nap. During certain late-afternoon and early-evening hours there is the radio, the Lone Ranger, Sky King, Jack Benny, Amos and Andy.

When we catch lightning bugs and when our parents aren't looking, we crush them and smear them on our hands, then make weird gestures at each other. More fun than lightning bugs is throwing brooms up in the air trying to hit bats. There are lots of bats swooping all around our yard of an evening, and Duncan claims to have hit one once with a broom. I doubt he did, but I have to admit it is deeply pleasurable to pitch brooms up into the air with the hope of knocking down a bat. Ah Lord, one can collapse with such laughing and fall down in the cool grass and gaze up at the first stars of the night sky.

Our mother is frazzled. Our grandmother comes to visit, to help. The situation is charged. Our grandmother is a small woman, mild-mannered for the most part, but a formidable Methodist. Our mother is also uncompromising in her Methodism. These two, mother and daughter, are temperamental and likely to fall out with each other. Anger and righteousness are directly linked in Methodist ladies of my mother's and grandmother's sort. If they become angry, it is because someone else has done wrong, and they relent only if the other admits the wrong and swears to change. On other occasions of my grandmother's visiting us, she and my mother have quarreled and taken to not speaking to each other. Nights, after we boys were supposed to be asleep, we have heard the two of them carrying on their argument by speaking through my father: "If she thinks she can come into my house and tell me . . . ," and "If she thinks that's the way a daughter can speak to her own . . ."

Our grandmother is good for canasta, the one card game, apparently, the god of Methodists must figure is O.K. Duncan and Ralph and I adore canasta, the huge hands, the double deck, the "melding" all over the table, the frequent occasions for clowning around, trying to get a laugh out of our stonefaced grandmother. Our grandmother is also good for Cokes. She drinks two a day, one at ten-thirty and another at a little after three in the afternoon. We boys usually don't get Cokes, but when our grandmother is there we get two a day. In the afternoon, we use our Cokes to make what in our family we call "foolishness," ice cream in a big glass with Coke poured over it.

But our grandmother is not accustomed to such intense exposure to my bother and cousin and me. On her other visits, our presence has been balanced by our absence: We go down thehill to Gilmer Hyatt's house to seine in the Rosemary branch for crawfish and minnows, or out to our grandfather's (our father's father's) farm to pester the men who work for him. This summer we are around her all the time, and our grandmother is more and more reluctant to accept our invitations to play canasta. She is more and more often in the guest room upstairs with the door closed.

Ralph and I sometimes sense Duncan sliding away from us. Sometimes he isn't laughing when we are. Sometimes we'll head outdoors, to the jungle, the trapeze, or somewhere, and Duncan won't be with us. He takes to spending time alone in his laboratory, the old back room upstairs where he put his chemistry set and a lot of junk that he said he didn't want Ralph and me getting into and ruining. Our mother tells Ralph and me that when Duncan is back there and doesn't want to be bothered, we are to leave him alone.

Ralph is homesick for Kingsport, but he can't go home because his mother is sick. He begins a series of temper tantrums, one a day, sometimes two. He blows himself up, gets red in the face, screams, breaks something that's handy if he's serious. I notice, though, that he chooses pretty carefully what he breaks.

I go into my pious phase. When Ralph does a tantrum, I counter with a lengthy speech about how they put people like him in reform schools and as soon as they get old enough they transfer them to prison. People who act like that. I tell him God's bad opinion of people who bust up their cousin's Army Command Post that he worked so hard to make out of glued-together used popsickle sticks from the trashcan at school. When grownups are around, I try to carry myself with dignity, to speak with unusual wisdom for somebody my age.

I have noticed qualities of my voice that are remarkably similar to certain qualities of the voice of Roy Rogers, namely a certain tenor, lyrical sweetness, and also the ring of rectitude. In seeing the films of Roy and in reading his comic books, I have sensed a special link between him and me. We share the same taste in holsters, saddles, hats, boots, and shirts. For Christmas I received an orange and white Roy Rogers neckerchief that I cherish as the outward and visible sign of my kinship with Roy. Wearing the scarf is what I do when I have other things on my mind, but my preferred use of it is to run with it in my hand, trailing it in the wind behind me. I wish only that I could see it better. When the wind catches that scarf, I know that I am in the presence of beauty.

In mid-August Mother hears that no new cases of polio have been reported for the month. She tells each one of us when we come downstairs for breakfast. She keeps explaining to us until we demonstrate to her that we are happy. Even our grandmother is cheerful. We decide to take a ride to Elmo's Creek to celebrate the end of the polio epidemic.

What should be very familiar landscape for my brother and cousin and me today is so new and vivid in the warm August sunlight that we are more or less quiet going out of our driveway and down the hill to the highway and then turning toward town. My mother drives slowly, chatting with my grandmother in the front seat. She asks my grandmother to keep an eye on Duncan and Ralph and me in the back seat because she can't really turn around, she has a crick in her neck. The slowness with which we travel on the highway out of town seems to me appropriate for the occasion, a decorous speed for three boys who haven't been out of their yard all summer and their mother and grandmother. Cars pass us honking their horns, but not one of us finds that trashy behavior worth remarking.

At the creek itself of course we boys must ask my mother if we can't go swimming. We whine just enough to let her know that we would in fact go into the water if she agreed to let us, but of course we all know she won't since we brought no bathing suits and since we all know how Elmo's Creek, with its bottom full of rusted beer cans, must be swarming with polio germs. Her denial is full of good cheer. We turn around and head back home.

Vanity is not the moving force behind all that follows. On the contrary, I am wholly without awareness of self, am without sorrow or desire, nostalgia or greed, am in that state of pure, thoughtless spirit that I later come to understand as aesthetic experience, as I hold my Roy Rogers neckerchief out the car window and watch it fly gorgeously in the wind. I have had to bargain with Ralph for the place beside the door, and I have had to exercise considerable discretion in sticking my hand and arm out the window. My mother's stiff neck prevents her from turning to see what I am doing, and I am sitting behind my grandmother, whose sense of well-being is directly proportional to the stillness of her grandsons. Even Duncan and Ralph, who are inclined to sabotage any pleasure I might be taking by myself, sit quietly regarding me and the neckerchief; I think of them, too, as being under the powerful influence of art.

Then the scarf slips loose from my fingers and flies back behind the car, curling in the wind, lightly coiling down to the gray asphalt. I am too stunned to speak, and anyway I have my whole head out the window now, looking back at what I have lost, but Duncan and Ralph speak up for me, cry out for my mother to stop the car, explaining to her what has happened. She does stop. She isn't able to turn completely around in the seat, but she sits and listens to my brother and my cousin and agrees that I can get out of the car to run back along the road and retrieve my neckerchief.

In the gravel and stubble I run along beside the highway, thinking that my neckerchief is much farther away than I would have imagined it and is strangely still there in the road after having been so lively when I held it in my hand. The day is hot and bright. The fields of Mr. John Watts's farm stretch out on both sides of the highway; even though Mr. Watts hung himself in his bedroom several years ago, the land is still farmed by his kinspeople. When I reach the scarf and hold it again in my hand, I am not comforted, as I had imagined I would be. I stand on a curving slope, a gentle slope but one that seems to be pulling me away back toward the creek, away from my parents' car that has begun slowly backing down the incline toward me but that seems such a distance from me that it will be long minutes before I can climb into the back seat with Duncan and Ralph and we can resume our stately homeward ride.

At the top of the hill another car appears, the sun flashing on its chrome grille and bumper. At a fair speed it heads down toward my family's car, which my mother has maneuvered into the middle of the highway in her effort to back up to me. I am concerned that there will be a collision, and I sense myself standing on the roadside, first on one foot and then the other. The strange car, a black sedan, doesn't slow down as it approaches our car. I can see the dilemma the driver faces, which way around my mother's middle-of-the-road-backing-up-vehicle he should take. He chooses the side that sends him directly toward me, not slowing and, once he has aimed himself toward me, not veering to left or right. Wanting to move but not being able to make my feet step in any direction, I stand on the side of the road, aware of raising my hands as if to ward off a pillow thrown by Duncan or Ralph. I catch a glimpse through the car's windshield of a Negro woman's face, looking directly at me, her mouth open and shouting something I can't hear. Then the car brushes me, I spin and fall and see the car sail over the fence into Mr. John Watts's alfalfa field.

I am surprised at what has transpired, intensely interested in the car in the field, all the doors of which are now opening, with Negro men and women climbing out and looking back at me on the roadside. Then my mother is there, so grimly calm that I barely recognize her. She wants to know if I am all right, and I tell her that I am. She tries to help me up, but I find that one of my legs won't hold me. It doesn't hurt—I tell her that, too—but I prefer sitting down in the road. She gathers me into her arms.

A Negro man with a kind face helps Mother carry me to the front seat of our car. He winces whenever he looks into my face, and so I tell him that I am all right, I just can't stand up. Someone brings me my neckerchief. My mother and the Negro man speak to each other with enormous civility. His name is Charlie Sales. He is from Slabtown. He will stay there with his car until the police come. My mother will take me to Dr. Pope's office back in town. The car door shuts. She holds me. People look in at us through the windows. My grandmother, in the driver's seat, says she can't drive our car, then puts it into low gear and drives it all the way to Dr. Pope's office.

The small bone of my left leg is cracked. At the Pulaski Hospital they pull a stretch-sock over my whole leg, then they wrap that with wet plaster-of-Paris bandages; the bandages are warm, and the hands wrapping them around my leg and smoothing out the plaster of Paris are comforting to me. My toes stick out, and a nurse holds them while the others work. I don't sleep well in the hospital that night, but my mother is there in the room with me to murmur to me in the dark, bring me water, put her cool hand on my forehead.

Charlie Sales had no brakes in that car. He feels terrible about what happened. My parents take no action against him; our families have known vaguely of each other for years. My mother takes her share of the blame for the accident because of her car being in the middle of the road because she was backing up but she had that crick in her neck so that she couldn't really see straight. When people ask her about the nigger that was driving the car that hit me, she says it wasn't Mr. Sales's fault. When they see my mother's attitude, they don't call Mr. Sales a nigger anymore. In the family, though, my mother wants it understood that it is her magnanimity that is saving Charlie Sales from being put in jail and losing every cent he has. Our family generally tries to do good in the world, but among ourselves we want credit for our excellence. Whenever anybody says that name, Charlie Sales, I see not him but that woman's face looking at me through the windshield, her mouth open, saying or shouting something I can't hear. Maybe she is Mrs. Sales. I don't know. When I imagine the accident again, it is graceful. The car brushes me, almost gently, and I spin a turn or a half a turn and fall. The car breaks the top strand of barbed wire on the fence when it sails into the field.

When I go home I have to stay in bed a week or two, and then I can ride in a wheelchair with a contraption that sticks out for me to rest my leg on. The cast is heavy for me, and someone must help me lift it when I move. The wheelchair is an old-fashioned wood-and-metal apparatus that is unwieldly in our house. I am always knocking into furniture or walls or something. I quickly learn that I won't be disciplined by my parents and that Duncan and Ralph are reluctant to do anything to me in my wounded state. I continue to think of myself as benign and heroical, in the mode of Roy Rogers during the few days he sometimes spends with his arm in a sling. But when

Duncan and Ralph are home I follow them in my wheelchair from one room to another, insisting that they play with me.

One day I throw my cap pistol at Duncan. I miss him, but our grandmother sees me do it. She wants me to be spanked. I can see her point, but I'm glad my mother won't do it and won't let her do it. The righteous anger of the Methodists sets in on both sides. They don't speak. The grandmother demands to be taken home. My father agrees to take her after the air show we've planned to attend in Pulaski on Saturday.

My mother and grandmother don't want us boys to know they are quarreling, and so they try to act as if the condition of their not speaking to each other and the grandmother's barely speaking to me while being warmly solicitous of Duncan and Ralph is the normal condition for us all to be in. We three boys pretend we know nothing, but we eavesdrop on all their conversations, which can take place only when my father is there. Our spirits can't help but be dampened in the presence of the adults, who sigh and gaze out the windows at mealtime. Ralph, trying to relieve the social anguish of one supper-time, slouches down in his chair to allow his mouth to come to plate level, and he scrapes the food in. Duncan and I find that pretty funny and register our amusement with sly grins. Our mother, however, sees the grins and sees the source of them, reaches over and whacks Ralph lightly on top of the head so that his face plops into his plate. Ralph looks up with bits of corn sticking to his face. All of us laugh, and for a moment the old family pleasure is there among us. Then our grandmother excuses herself but goes to sit only as far away as the living room. Solemnity comes quickly down again.

It rains at the air show. Many of the acts are canceled, others are invisible, though an announcer describes them to us through a static-crackling P.A. system. There is a parachutist who comes down close enough to our car to make us boys not want to leave the show. But mostly we sit in the car in a field full of other cars, and our grandmother and mother both cry, sitting beside each other in the front seat while my father tries to make himself invisible with his hat down over his eyes. We boys whine to get out of the car into the rain and whine for refreshments and whack and pinch each other, writhing in our state of misery and hilarity. Duncan and Ralph must be wary of my leg in the cast. I have the advantage over them.

You'd think things would improve immediately with the grandmother gone, but they don't. For one thing, Duncan has taken to exercising what he sees as his "adult privileges." Eating breakfast one morning, he calls our mother by her first name, and she throws the empty dish-drainer at him. For another thing, I become so impossible in my behavior and demands that it does become necessary for my mother to spank me. This is very hard on her. And finally, I become much more mobile. My cast has gradually lightened its pull on my leg. Sitting on my butt, I can scoot up and down the steps without assistance. And my grandfather has made crutches for me. These are sturdy crutches, just the right size, probably made with the help of three or four of his men. I am delighted with them and launch myself around the house on them.

And take a fall immediately. And continue falling several times a day, great splatting, knocking-into-furniture-and-breaking-things falls that cause everyone in the family to come running to me, my mother frequently in tears. My grandfather has forgotten to put rubber tips on the ends of my crutches. When we figure this out and buy the rubber tips and put them on the crutches, I stop falling. But by then the bone-set that was coming along nicely has slipped, and the doctor has ordered me back to the wheelchair for another several weeks, has ordered the cast kept on for an additional month or five weeks.

The missing crutch-tips are the first clue I have to this peculiar family trait, one that for lack of any better term I must call "flawed competence." We Bryants are a family of able and clever people, industrious, intelligent, determined, and of good will. We are careful in our work. Remember, my grandfather measured me on two occasions before he made the crutches. But we usually do something wrong.

Four years later I become increasingly aware of "flawed competence" when I develop a plan for converting our old grown-over tennis court into a basketball court. My grandfather is always interested in plans, and in this planning session, we decide that he will make the hoops, and he will help me make the backboards. Clearing the ground and smoothing the surface will be my tasks. So I rip out honeysuckle and hatchet down a few little scrub cedars, working a couple of hours a day after school for a week. It becomes clear to me that there is at least ten times more work to be done here than I had in mind originally, but I hold fast to my plan and continue the work. We Bryants are known for setting our minds to things.

Then my grandfather delivers the hoops. They are beautifully designed and constructed, metalwork of a high order for such amateurs as my grandfather and his men, who are mostly talkers, cursers, storytellers, spitters, and braggers. But the hoops are twice as big around as ordinary basketball hoops.

I say, simply, that they are too big. I am not ungrateful, not trying to be hateful, not in my opinion being overly fastidious. I am simply describing a characteristic of the hoops. But my grandfather's feelings are damaged. No, they can't be made smaller, and no, he's not interested in helping me with the backboards now or with any other part of my plan. He's sorry he got involved in the first place. This, too, is a corollary of "flawed competence." We are sensitive, especially about our work, especially about the flawed part of our work.

At the place where I work twenty-eight years after the basketball hoops, I am given a new office, a corner one with two large windows and a view of the lake. There's a string attached, though, and that is that I have to build my own bookcases. I commence planning with enthusiasm. That's another, less harmful family trait, that attraction to making plans. I measure, I look at other people's shelves, I get a guy to help me attach brackets to my office walls.

It is while I am cutting a notch in one of the uprights to allow access to the light-switch by the door that I suddenly think of my grandfather and those basketball hoops. I feel a light sweat break out on my forehead. A pattern of genetic fate reveals itself to me: I'm going to gum up these bookshelves just as my grandfather before me would have gummed them up. This very idea I'm working on, the notch in the upright for the light-switch, is a Granddaddy Bryant kind of idea. No doubt I'm sawing the notch in the wrong place. This epiphany comes to me at night in my new office with a fluorescent ceiling light shining down on me and my reflections from both windows mocking me full-length while I stand there with the saw in my hand.

The whole time I work I wait to see where the screw-up is going to come. I imagine what my colleagues will be saying about me in the hallways. Did you know that Bryant built his shelves so they tilt? Did you know that Bryant's books rejected the color he painted his shelves? But the screw-up doesn't appear. I paint the shelves red, and they look O.K. (Grandaddy Bryant once painted yellow a whole row of company houses he built.) I paint a rocking chair blue and red, and it's a little silly-looking, but it picks up the blue of the carpet and the red of the shelves. The vision isn't nearly as impressive as I thought it would be, but then what vision ever is? We plan-makers are accustomed to things turning out not-quite-as-good-as-what-we-had-in-mind. Our *Weltanschauung* includes the "diminished excellence" component. Diminished excellence is a condition of the world and therefore never an occasion for sorrow, whereas flawed competence comes out of character and therefore is frequently the reason for the bowed head, the furrowed brow. Three months later, when I try to turn the heat off in my office, I discover that I have placed one of the shelf uprights too close to the radiator to be able to work the valve. The screw-up was there all along, but in this case I am relieved to find it. I am my grandfather's grandson after all.

In the spring, on a visit to my parents' home, I am out in the toolshop behind the garage. Up in the rafters I find those old basketball hoops. Since I have so recently thought about them, I take them down and stand for a moment weighing them, one in each hand. My grandfather has been dead for twelve years now, and I have this moment of perfect empathy with the old man: the thing he worked on so as to be part of my life was no good; when I told him, "They're too big," I pushed him that much further away from me and that much closer to his own death. Those old hoops are monuments to something. They're indestructible, and perfectly useless. God knows what some archeologists of the future will make of them when they dig them up out of the rubble.

Stashing the hoops back up in the rafters, I find this other thing, too, the cast from my broken leg. When the doctor sawed it off, somebody taped together the two parts and gave the thing to us to take home. It is a child's leg, slightly bent at the knee, grayish-white, not much larger than my arm. It is at one and the same time utterly strange and utterly familiar. The little bone of my leg was broken one day because I'd dropped my Roy Rogers scarf out the car window when we were taking a ride to Elmo's Creek to celebrate the end of the polio epidemic the summer we had to stay inside the yard and my mother couldn't back up straight because she had a crick in her neck, and so Charlie Sales, whose car had no brakes, had to swerve and miss her and therefore hit me. Holding that cast in my hands, I can almost understand the wacky logic of that accident.

That light, hollow little leg that is somehow my own calls up layer after layer of memory in me. Both my mother and my grandmother have softened their tempers, have taken on that Methodist sweetness that you feel in hymns like "Bringing in the Sheaves" and "A Walk in the Garden." Whatever wrongs that grandmother might have committed, she has been harshly dealt with, first with glaucoma and then with a skin cancer that works on her slowly. I doubt she even remembers the day of the rained-out air show when she and my mother wept in the front seat while my father pulled his hat down over his eyes and Duncan and Ralph and I writhed in the back seat.

My mother still remembers when Charlie Sales hit me, still holds herself responsible, still takes on a sober expression and a sad voice when she speaks of that day. And once at a party in New York, I met a black woman who spoke to me of people she was related to, Saleses from Madison County, Virginia. That seemed so significant to me. I told her the story about Charlie Sales hitting me with his car and breaking my leg. I told the story in such a way as to make it seem all my fault and my mother's, Charlie having to choose which one of us to hit. I thought the story would make an incredible impression on this dignified black woman. I thought she would acknowledge our deep and lasting kinship. I still remember her face—serene, interested, kind, polite. Yes, she said, it was probably her kin-people who came piling out of that car, she said, she didn't know for sure, she hadn't been back there since she was a child. And she turned away from me to talk with someone else. But, in my memory, her face became the face of the woman I saw in the front seat of Charlie Sales's car, just before it touched the little bone in my leg. Memory and fact are old cousins yammering away about whether or not there even was a strand of barbed wire on that fence for the car to snap when it flew into the field and how could I have seen it anyway, having just been knocked and spun around by the car.

I stand there holding that cast in my hands, reading something somebody in my third-grade class wrote on the side of the knee, and I know that everything that happens is connected to everything else and nothing that happens is without consequence. I am washed by one memory after another like ripples moving backwards to their source. All of a sudden I am no one. Or I am this stranger standing in an old toolshop with memory trying in its quirky way to instruct him. A man came home to visit his parents, a man who got an office and built bookshelves, a man whose grandfather died and who was a soldier for a little while, a boy whose leg was broken by a car and who did not become a basketball or a football player, a boy who stayed a summer with his brother and his cousin inside his family's yard. The moment of my disappearance passes, and I come back to myself. Now, holding this cast in my hand, standing just in this one place, I feel like I could remember all of human history. If I put my mind to it.

From *The High Spirits* (1989)

Playing

B I L L Y   H Y A T T is a prodigy of the alto saxophone. The summer between eighth grade in Rosemary, and ninth grade in Madison, Billy's mother drives him to Madison High School so that he can practice with the band. Before practice and after practice, and during practice if it's possible, Billy talks to girls, plays games with girls, chases girls across the fields of mown grass that surround the brick school building. One day just after the morning marching session, Billy finds himself shoved up against the rough wall outside the band-room door, Bob Kerns holding him there with one hand against Billy's chest and the other held back like he means to make a fist and maybe decorate the bricks with Billy's brains.

"Frieda Goforth is my girl," Bob Kerns instructs him. "You need to know that."

Billy nods. It wouldn't be something he'd argue even if Bob Kerns didn't seem ready to snuff out the bright flame of his candle. But he understands Bob Kerns's reasons. Billy, after all, has noted the billowing curls of Frieda's reddish-brown hair and her skin which is the color of a just-peeled apple. Billy has had the nerve, once when he peeped down the collar of her blouse, to imagine the whole shape of one of Frieda's breasts, though in this moment of confronting Bob Kerns and Bob's anger, he reminds himself that he did not imagine them both, only the one most apparent to him in the instant of her bending over to pick up a dropped piece of sheet music.

Bob drops both his held-back hand and the one pushing Billy's chest. Billy guesses he's looked so afraid that Bob is ashamed of himself. He should be. Bob Kerns is a junior, a big boy who plays a sousaphone. He hasn't so much as spoken to Billy before this, and now with deep contempt he's saying, "You really like the girls, don't you, Hyatt?" Bob shakes his head and walks away before Billy has a chance to answer him.

But he wouldn't have answered anyway. What Bob Kerns says to him falls on him like prophecy. In the core of his fourteen-year-old brain he knows it's true, he's a fool for girls. This is the moment he realizes that it's O.K. to like them, but not to like them as much as he does.

God knows why any girls are interested in gangly, pimply-faced Billy anyway, though they are. Every day at these band practices they call out his name when his mother lets him out of the car. When the whole band loads up on buses and goes to band camp for ten days, Bob Kerns's sad mockery still rings in Billy's ears every time he catches himself trying to look up the skirt of one of the flute players or that sleepy-eyed eighth-grade girl in the clarinet section.

"The saxophone is the sexiest instrument," Valerie Williams tells him one day during a break, squinting her eyes against the sun to be able to look up at him, a light sweat broken out across her freckly forehead.

If somebody like Valerie Williams says something like that it must be true. She's thirteen, the new majorette. She's short, with straight black hair that's shiny as a crow's wing, and a shape like those cartoon girls he studies in his grandfather's *Esquire* magazines. She's Larry O'Dell's girlfriend, but she's been recently discussed intently by every boy Billy knows—by now he's fifteen and already the first chair tenor saxophone—with the consensus of opinion being that Valerie Williams is something else.

Something else, something else, his mind chants for him all the rest of that afternoon. It's August. They're practicing their marching routines in a dry, stubbled field. Out in front of the band the majorettes prance, twirl their batons, pitch them up at the cloudless sky, fail to catch them, grimace and say shit not quite loud enough to have Mr. Banks yell at them. They get tired. Only Valerie Williams lifts her knees almost to her chin every time they go through the show. By four-thirty the others are walking through it, Valerie is still lifting those knees, and Billy, back in the fourth rank, is still listening to his old brain chant for him, something else, something else.

Nighttime at band camp is hot, and the air smells like the sassafras leaves are cooking in the dark. "What do you think?" Valerie whispers to Billy. He's got a hand up underneath her blouse, her breast in its bra cup in his palm. Billy's in a state. If he speaks or moves, he's going to shoot off a load in his pants. They're sitting out on the steps at the back of the main building, where they can hear the music from the scratchy forty-fives somebody's playing so that kids can dance in the little social area around front. "One early morning . . . ha-ooo . . . I met a woman . . . ha-ooo . . . we started talking . . ."

"Cigarette?" Billy asks Valerie. He calmly removes his hand from her blouse at the same time he discharges enough sperm into his jockey shorts to impregnate every mildly fertile female within a radius of thirty miles. He lets his face show nothing but wonders if she'll be able to smell it. Leaning forward, unintentionally over his crotch, she's tucking her blouse back in her shorts. "Yeah, sure," she says.

He drops several smokes, shaking them up then out of the pack, but it's dark, and probably she can't see anyway, and so he lets them lie there. Hospitably he extends the pack toward her, and she takes one. He has a lighter. His hand shakes. She coughs. He cautions her against inhaling if she hasn't done it much before.

"Valerie Williams! William Hyatt!" Like a figure from the Old Testament, Mr. Banks bursts upon them. He confiscates Billy's pack of Chesterfields. He extracts a vow from Valerie that she will never, ever smoke again. He dispatches them around the building into the lighted area where Billy can't stay because he has to go change his pants.

But they are impelled toward each other. When the band comes back to town, school starts, and Billy starts riding the bus twenty miles there and twenty miles back every day. Most of the hours of the day he's got a hard-on and Valerie floating through his frontal lobe.

Valerie lives in Madison. Her mother won't let her wear shorts downtown. After school Billy finds excuses to stay in town so that he can walk home with her, drink milk and eat cookies with her in the kitchen, then go downstairs with her to play Whistle-Stop in the basement. That girl can't whistle worth a damn. Billy's fingers make it all the way up under the hem of her shorts before she so much as raises one faint note. Billy's hand goes behind her back untucking her blouse, and she gets a pensive look on her face like she's thinking about something else.

Valerie's little sisters sneak around and spy on them through the windows. Valerie plays "Peggy-Sue" on the record player again and again, Billy trying to sing along, never getting it right. In shorts Valerie walks him downtown where he catches his ride home with Walter Sawyers whom he must pay a quarter for each trip. Billy rides with his books in his lap, figuring out how to explain to his parents why he stayed in town this afternoon. Valerie's mom raises a holy ruckus when she hears Valerie was downtown in her shorts again. Valerie's dad, the manager of Piggly-Wiggly, gives Billy that look every time he sees him; they both know what the look means, but they make their manners just the same.

Billy gets into a dance band. These guys his brother knows at the radio station need a sax man. Billy can play a couple of jazzy tunes, but he hasn't tried it much. They say they'll teach him. They buy him sheet music they can't read but he can. What they can do is fake it behind him. They practice and work up a program, make a date to put it on the air on Saturday at four o'clock.

Billy tries to tell Valerie who they are. Al Kravic, the newsman, claims he's learning how to play this expensive set of drums he bought in Abingdon. Johnny Wilson, the station engineer, plays steel guitar, leans heavily toward hillbilly stuff and those Hawaiian numbers that make Billy want to puke every time he hears them; but Johnny's a virtuoso of his own kind, even Billy can discern that. And Birdy Z. Pendergast, the station's morning man: Billy can't make him clear to Valerie at all, a little rat-faced man you just know was a sissy all the time he was growing up—a moody, fastidious, mildly effeminate, high-pocketed, pot-bellied genius of the cheap piano not tuned for years.

"I'm serious," Billy tells her, liking the way she's laughing at him, "if it was a new Steinway somebody had just tuned, Birdy Z. would sound like the clunker he really is." It's Saturday afternoon and they're buying popcorn and Pepsis to take into the two o'clock movie at the Millwald Theater. It's September but hot as July. Valerie talked her mother into letting her wear Bermuda shorts to the movie. Billy'd rather she wore a skirt, but he keeps his druthers to himself.

"Birdy Z., Birdy Z.," she says and laughs loud enough to make people turn around and look at her. Valerie wants the rest of his popcorn. She's got an appetite. When the movie starts—it's a western—they slump down in their seats and hold hands and lightly rub the goosey insides of their arms together.

It's five minutes until four when they walk into the radio station together, rubbing sweaty palm to sweaty palm, Billy's ears ringing and Valerie's face crimson. Up in the studio Al Kravic and Johnny Wilson take one look at the kids and commence grinning at each other, but Birdy Z. is in a fury. When they go on the air, Billy's sticking the neck into his sax and going to have to try to get it tuned while they're playing the first number.

When they switch off the studio mike to run a couple of commercials, Birdy Z. bursts out, "God almighty, that sounded like a piece of warmed over rat shit!" He's looking straight at Billy. Billy knows Valerie is watching them all through the studio window. He blows a cute little riff she can't hear, looks up at the acoustic tiles of the ceiling, tries to act like nothing's wrong. "Don't know as I would dignify it to that extent," murmurs Johnny, giving Billy a wink and echoing Billy's riff on the steel guitar, using it as a segue into one of his Hawaiian numbers.

Billy notices the faces of his old mom and dad bob up beside Valerie's in the studio window. Thank God they'll introduce themselves. Billy's relieved he doesn't have to perform his manners for his mother. He wails out two choruses of "O when the saints," Johnny takes his two—making it sound like something you ought to strum along to with a ukulele, Birdy harangues the studio with about thirty-thousand piano notes, and they yield to Kravic's pitiful version of a drum solo. When the program's over, Billy hauls his sax case out into the waiting room and finds Valerie and his mom, their legs crossed and leaning forward toward each other, sitting on vinyl seats by a plastic fern in the corner.

Birdy Z. comes out, all sociable and Mr. Public Personality, and makes a joke out of it, but he damn sure lets Billy's old man know Billy was late getting there for the program. Taller than Birdy by an inch or two, Billy hates him standing here in his rat-man glasses.

Billy's old man doesn't say anything to him when they're giving Valerie a ride home—country folk in town, driving slow as farmers in a field, Billy leaning forward in the back seat doing all he can to give the car foward momentum, Valerie and his mom carrying on their chatting like a little song they both make up as they go along. It's all deeply, deeply embarrassing. Billy walks her to the door but they don't touch so much as an arm hair when they say good-bye with his parents watching them from the car.

Coda for the day is the lecture Billy's old man has for him on the slow, slow drive back out into the county to their house: Billy's heritage of six known-generations of responsible and decent men on both sides of his family is what he'd better be carrying on his shoulders for the foreseeable and so on. Billy bites the inside of his jaw to keep himself from offering any smart mouth.

"So he told, did he?" she says. "The damned old queer." Valerie says she never cared for Birdy Z., even when all she knew about him was his voice on her mom's radio in the kitchen. "You can just hear it in somebody's voice, somebody like that. A thirty-five-year-old tattletale. What're you doing, Billy? Listen, let's turn him on now and spit on the radio," she says, but it's not Birdy on the air, it's Kravic stumbling through the news like it was written in a foreign language. And what Billy's doing is backing Valerie up against her mom's refrigerator. They don't know what it is about that refrigerator, but they like it against her butt bracing them pelvis to pelvis. "Let's go downstairs," Billy whispers. "What do you guess is down there?" she asks him and pulls his mouth toward hers again so that he can't answer.

Her little sisters' names are Connie and Florence, Coco and Flossie. They are eight and ten and geniuses of hiding places with an angle of vision on Billy and Valerie. They could be down there doing their homework all afternoon and never hear a peep from the siblings, but let Billy get a hand up under Valerie's sweater or let them lie down on the sofa and from somewhere there'll come a twitter. Or else one bright little girl's blue eye looking straight down on them when Billy chances a glance toward the door or the window. "What would we do without them?" Billy says, standing up trying to rearrange his pants to get some comfort.

Valerie opines she has to go outside and practice her baton routine anyway. She goes up to her room, puts on shorts and a spiffy little white T-shirt. From the porch Billy watches, torn between admiration for her physical skill and resentment of the energy she devotes to keeping that two-foot rubber-tipped aluminum rod spiking through the air.

"I gotta go," he says, finally. Valerie's out of breath anyway, talks him into staying and having some lemonade with her on the porch. She's worked up a light sweat. He marvels at the fragrance of her. They talk about how much they hate the Z. "Let's go turn him on," she says, and they go into the kitchen and snap the switch on. He isn't. "Shit," Valerie says, lacking authority in her swearing, because she's just turned fourteen. Billy likes it anyway, gets a thrill from her trash mouth. "What're you doing, Billy?" she asks, but he knows she knows what he's doing. Behind her, the refrigerator makes its barely discernable humming. "Mom's gonna come in here any minute," she whispers. "That's cool," he says.

Billy turns sixteen and gets his driver's license the very next day. The band gets a job playing for the Moose in Hillsville. "God, I didn't even know they had the Moose in Hillsville," says Birdy Z., chortling, "but the man calls me up and offers us a hundred and fifty dollars. He heard us on the air."

"I'm surprised he didn't send us a bill for a hundred and fifty dollars, if he heard us on the air Saturday," Johnny says, diddling that little chrome bar up and down the strings.

"We're getting better all the time," pipes up Kravic, but he's not. The man has reached a permanent plateau at the zero-beginner's level.

Birdy Z. and the D-Jays is the name Birdy gives them. Kravic can't argue because he has no status, Johnny doesn't argue because he doesn't give a fat rat's ass, and Billy makes a face at the name because secretly he wanted it to be Billy Hyatt and the High Notes.

Besides, Birdy is the one doing the driving. "Can you believe a Studebaker?" Billy asks Valerie. She says she wouldn't have believed anything else. It's October. She has on a sky-blue sweater that spot-welds her torso into the base of Billy's brain. Mythic, downright mythic: if he could have her both naked and in that sky-blue sweater at the same time, that's what he'd choose for his deathbed vision, for the last image his eyeballs would ever shoot to his brain.

In the Studebaker, the four D-Jays drive to Hillsville, Galax, Max Meadows, Rural Retreat, all around the county. They get a reputation, not for being good, but for being cheap and for taking short breaks. All these dances are the same, boozy old guys and dames with bottles in brown bags they set on the floor under the tables, stepping through dances that went out before Billy was born. "Trying to drink themselves back to your age," Birdy Z. tells Billy. Nowadays Billy doesn't hold back his smart mouth. "How do you know, Bird? You don't drink."

"Reason I don't is that I do," Birdy Z. tells him. "Or I did." Then he tells Billy all about it.

Through a snowstorm, Birdy Z. crawled from the street where

somebody dumped him on the sidewalk around back of his house and up onto the porch where he slept, got frostbite, almost lost a couple of fingers. He takes a hand off the steering wheel now and wiggles its fingers for Billy. Lost a job somewhere, got a job somewhere else, showed up drunk, lost that one, too, and no money to get home with. His wife wouldn't let him back in the house when he did get there.

It's a long drive through those mountains from Galax to Madison. Johnny and Kravic sleep in the back with Kravic's tom-tom on the seat between them. Birdy Z. tells Billy places in the house a drunk will hide his bottles. Highway's empty; nobody's out that time of night. Talk in the front seat of a car takes on intimacy. How can you hate a man who explicates for you the three dozen ways he has been humiliated?

But Billy can't explain it to Valerie. There's something about the man she can't stand; she takes him as her personal enemy. Another night he's meeting her late, after the D-Jays get back to Madison and let him out at the bus station where he's parked his dad's car. Instead of heading straight home—it's after two now—he drives up near her house, douses the lights, parks, sneaks into her backyard, taps on her window. Her face appears, her lips move, she's gone again. In three minutes she's slipping out the screen door of the back porch. He can't hold enough of her to keep her warm. She's in shorty pajamas, without even slippers on her feet. Can't stay, can't stay, crazy whispering out by the swing set in the backyard.

He's never encountered her without her bra on, now he doesn't want to stop touching her breasts under the thin material of that pajama top ("They're free," he says, "they're so free!"); but if he lets her go to do that she gets cold immediately, the pale, almost full moon over them both the ice and fire of the moment. He holds her, wraps the sides of his dumb band-jacket around her, tells her about Birdy Z. crawling through the snowstorm to his back porch, but Valerie's feet and legs are so cold she's about to cry. The story and how cold she is, how mean it is that she has to go in, make her hate Birdy Z. even more.

Monday morning, standing by her locker at school, Billy tells her, "Valerie, he doesn't care what we do"; but she's sure he does, sure he's the one who called and told her mom she was with him downtown in her shorts that day. "He's a queer, Billy, don't you know that?" she tells him. And Billy says no, he's not, suspects immediately that maybe Birdy is; but then a queer is somebody despicable, and now that Billy carries with him these stories Birdy has told him, he holds responsibility for the man, feels he must defend him, says again no, he's not. When Valerie tells him everybody in town has known that about Birdy Z. for years, it's only because Billy's from Rosemary that he doesn't know that, Billy argues that maybe Birdy used to be queer when he was a drunk but he isn't now, he's certain of it. He isn't at all.

Birdy Z. and the D-Jays need somebody else, another horn player or something. Elliott Pugh, this big-lipped kid in Billy's classes at school, is a clarinet player the band director is trying to switch to alto sax. Birdy Z. knows the kid, lives near him, asks Billy about him. Billy says the kid knows no music but classical, which he knows is an exaggeration, but he doesn't care. He reminds Bird that Elliott has taken piano lessons since he was old enough to sit up by himself. "Beethoven is the kid's personal hero, if you can feature it," Billy says. Birdy shrugs, says all they need is somebody who can play the harmony part, a second sax. "Might be just the man for us," Birdy says, "talk to him, see what he says, see what you think." Billy's the one who makes the contact. Billy's the one who actually hires Elliott Pugh to play sax and clarinet with them.

Valerie can't believe it. "Elliott Pugh?" she says. She took ballroom dancing with Elliott from old Mrs. Tyson when she was eight and he was ten. "No one I ever met had less rhythm," she tells Billy, tossing the baton twenty yards straight over her head and catching it already spinning in her hands. Billy lugs her books, the price he pays for the milk and cookies he's got coming to him. The baton twirls in the air around Valerie, going hand to hand to hand, cutting swathes of air around her, buzz-saw, propellor, finger-bruiser if you so much as reach to touch her. Valerie doesn't like Birdy Z. Billy doesn't like the baton. Elliott Pugh they figure doesn't matter to anybody.

Elliott himself couldn't be happier. He's humbled by the invitation and gives Billy more big-lipped grins than Billy has seen on his face in a year's worth of knowing him. Elliott Pugh is the only kid in the whole school who wears unpegged—pleated, for God's sake!—pants, belt buckle riding about navel high.

"They're both high-pockets," Valerie tells Billy. "Probably queering each other every chance they get." She and Billy are riding the second of two band buses back from the Martinsville football game. Good bus to ride, Susan Sweeney and Annabell Sparks up front picking out the songs and getting them going, telling who to sing what part: "Blue Moon," "Tell Me Why," "Down By the Riverside," "Try to Remember." Sweet voices come out of even the toughest kids, Maynard Johnson and Delano Phillipi doing the doom-da-da-dooms of "Blue Moon" pretty as can be. Best bus to ride, no doubt about it. The couples kiss for long miles of highway, boys in the darkest seats getting as much bare titty as the girls will allow. Billy doesn't want to talk about Elliott Pugh and Birdy Z. Pendergast, wants instead to be carrying out an inventory of the goosebumps on the inside of Valerie's thigh.

"What do queers do, Billy?" Valerie seems struck suddenly by the intellectual aspect of the whole thing. Billy's got vague ideas, but he guesses he doesn't know. "Play Whistle-Stop?" he suggests, puts a hand on her knee. She whistles three notes, loud and clear. "I mean really," she says.

"They're not queers," Billy whispers into the curly hairs around her ear. "They're just . . ." But he doesn't know what they are.

Elliott and Bird do have this understanding. Rarely do they have to talk. But two more disparate musicians couldn't exist. Elliott so stiff, precise, not an ounce of fudge, fake, or syncopate in his bones; and Birdy Z. who never in his life read a note and/or hit the right note on the right beat on pure intuition could fake a Mahler symphony. Rehearsing "Woodchopper's Ball," Billy witnesses at one and the same time Elliott tapping a big foot like a metronome, Birdy Z. diddling both heels and slapping randomly at the pedals with his toes.

"Stars Fell On Alabama," "Blue Hawaii," "Little Brown Jug," "Rock Around the Clock," "Your Cheating Heart," "Night and Day," "Cherry Pink and Apple Blossom White," "Stardust," "Laura," "Blue Monday": Birdy Z. and the D-Jays have no shame about what they'll play, and no matter what the tune, there's one of them in the band who can sabotage it. At the kind of dances they play, nobody cares; you could take a dishpan and a hammer in those places and somebody'd pay you to knock one against the other so they could get out there and step around the floor with their arms around somebody.

They fire Kravic and get Cecil Taylor—a kid who looks like he was put together with drinking straws—to become the rhythm section. A certain ruthlessness sets in as a result of how they improve themselves. Billy and Elliott, tenor and alto, loose and stiff, reckless and cautious; not such a bad pair on two or three numbers, but Elliott can't ad-lib, no matter what they tell him to try to help, just can't do it, would rather sit, red-faced, with the sax in his lap and study his charts than to stand up and try to make up some ditty as it goes along. Something about that failure pisses Billy off way down deep. He commences a sabotage on Elliott, making him look bad, making him sound bad, mocking him, overtly condescending. "Stand up and blow that thing, sucker!" he'll shout when he knows Elliott's going to sit there, big-lipped, hair combed like an old-timey photograph, eyes cast down like a shy girl's.

"Don't pick on him," Birdy Z. tells Billy.

"You're the one they made hire him, why don't you fire him?" Valerie asks him at lunchtime, out in Billy's dad's car, the two of them out there fooling around, sneaking cigarettes. Would be a hell of a thing, damn right it would, Billy allows, chortling to himself, slumped down in the driver's seat. "You're fired, Elliott Pugh, your ass is gone!"

"You're fired, Elliott Pugh, your ass is gone!" Billy says Wednesday afternoon in the studio where they're rehearsing. Elliott's just said he's not going to play harmony or anything else on "Burn That Candle," he's sorry. To air the words, Billy has said he's fired. Elliott blinks at him. Nobody else says a word. Johnny slides the chrome on his strings, evokes the swaying hips of Hawaiian girls in grass skirts, pays no attention to anybody. Cecil's new, keeps his mouth shut, looks into the other studio where the evening man is holding forth at the board. Birdy watches, watches, a look on his face like he's ready to start slavering at the mouth and taking bites out of somebody's arm or leg. Elliott looks around at them. Nobody's got anything to say. "Haul your ass on home, Elliott," Billy tells him and knows now he's got the power to do it, knows he is in fact doing it and getting away with it.

Elliott starts blubbering while he packs up the alto. If Billy had a gun he doesn't know whether he'd aim it at Elliott or himself, but wishes he had the choice.

Small town dances are on Billy's mind. How the women put their arms up around a man's neck and let their breasts lift up against his chest is the gesture Billy begins to dream about, again and again, fat women, thin women, all of them reaching upward in that heartbreaking willingness to give themselves over to some man and politely dance with him.

Teenage master of sneaking-around foreplay, Billy's destiny is blue-balls, sperm-spotted underwear, stained crotches of his khaki pants, wet dreams, the rightful heritage of any high-school boy. He's sixteen, Valerie's fourteen, they're so clearly too young for it that even they, had they been asked to speak responsibly, would have said of course they shouldn't do it.

They do it. On a rainy night in the spring in the front seat of Billy's dad's Dodge, they park out behind the Madison country club, so close to the clubhouse door that from its window the light from the Coke machine shines on them. It's after a concert for which Valerie has ushered. She has on crinolines, stockings, a garter belt. Billy has on a suit that six months ago fit him pretty well. They stretch across that seat, managing legs and clothes and body parts as best they can, and somehow manage a penetration. To neither one of them does it feel even as good as a dry-lipped kiss on the cheek. They talk a little and lie sweetly to each other and disguise their diappointment. The rubber he probably didn't even need Billy throws out the window for the club pro to find in the morning when he opens up the shop.

Nothing changes. Billy drives home and next morning wakes up with a hard-on and smelling lilacs from the front yard. At school, standing at her locker, talking with Annie B. Loomis, Valerie gives him a grin that tightens the muscles in Billy's thighs. He has English first period and tries to change his seat so he won't have to sit beside Elliott Pugh. It's been three days since Billy fired him, but Elliott's face, like some weepy girl's, still looks tear-stained, bruised. Miss Lancaster won't let him change. Elliott hands him an envelope with Billy's name typed on the front. He doesn't open it until lunchtime, in the car by himself now, Valerie not able to sneak past Mr. Banks who from the band room doorway keeps an eye on the parking lot. Dragging hard on his Marlboro—Billy's brand now—he makes himself read a sentence or two—*want to know what right you have . . . think you are such a . . . let me tell you what a real musician would . . . will never know*—of Elliott's typed letter to him; but he can't go on with it or he'll be crying out there himself. He'll go in and find Elliott before Algebra and apologize and hire him back—if they gave him the power to hire and fire Elliott, then he knows he has the power to rehire him. But when he sees the god damned high-pocketed, big-lipped queer-ball standing and scowling just outside the door to Miss Damron's room, just waiting for Billy to say one word to him, Billy stares him down, walks right past him without speaking, and takes his seat.

Billy's cool; he's got his collar turned up, his tightest pegged pants on slung low down on his hips, he smells like cigarette butts, and he's got money in his pockets from last week's gig, money coming to him this Friday and Saturday night from gigs in Abingdon and Fries. But what cool he's got he needs—and maybe a little more besides—when he has to face Birdy at rehearsal that night. The man has a way of beaming his eyeballs through those thick-lensed glasses of his like he means to blowtorch straight through Billy's zit-pocked forehead. "I thought Elliott might come tonight," he finally says quietly.

"You want him to come," Billy says, putting a cigarette in the corner of his mouth and pretending he's got on sunglasses, "call him up."

The Bird says nothing, nor does he move toward the door to go call Elliott. Mechanically they work through the rehearsal, hardly a sociable word among the four of them. Once running through "Till There Was You," Billy hears Elliott's harmony and for a moment thinks he's hallucinating it until he sees Johnny is playing it exactly with Elliott's play-it-by-the-numbers phrasing, grinning as he runs the chrome bar over the strings. It's tasteless of Johnny to make a joke like that, Billy feels, but he says nothing when at the end of the thing, Johnny winks at him. "Billy, you want to stay a minute?" the Bird asks him when they're packing up, and Billy dreads it.

In the studio alone with Birdy now, Billy is aware of how the place cuts off every sound from outside, and he's jumpy, trying to face down the Bird, who's just looking at him in that purse-mouthed way. "I think we need somebody else, Billy," Birdy finally says. "The sound's too thin. Don't you think so?"

In about three seconds flat, Billy has to reevaluate everything he thinks about Birdy and himself and his place in the band and the world. That Birdy would consult him, would actually talk with him as if his, Billy's, opinion were the one that determined how things would go is simply outside the territory of Billy's imaginings. He's thought they were letting him hire and fire Elliott as a joke, because he's the kid of the group and because they didn't want to take responsibility for dealing with another kid besides himself.

"What do you think of Jack Lamereaux?" Birdy asks him.

Billy thinks Jack Lamereaux probably wouldn't want the D-Jays even to play for his old cat. But what he says aloud is that he'd be surprised if Jack would be interested in becoming a D-Jay. Birdy nods slowly, holds onto his rat-man philosopher face, and assures Billy that Jack would like the chance to play with them.

Before Billy makes it out the studio door, Birdy turns half around on the piano bench, with his right hand plinks out a tacky little riff, sighs, and says he wishes he was a drinking man again, he's got a hankering for a cold one. Billy wants to get out of there and so doesn't even pause. "Yeah, well, good night, Bird," he says, already clearing his mind for the project of meeting Valerie at the Shaefers' apartment where she's baby-sitting.

"These guys think I'm better than I am," is how he explains it to Valerie. Still it doesn't add up for him. "It's true, I read music, and they can't. And it's true I'm the coolest one ever to grace the corridors of that sorry radio station," he tells her, walking toward her in mock pursuit while she backs away in mock retreat all around the kitchen.

"Oh yeah?" She parks herself against the Shaefers' refrigerator lifting her eyebrows and giving him to understand she's waiting for him there, but when he lunges toward her, quick as a single-wing tailback she's gone. Billy acts like all he meant to do was take a peek inside the fridge. He pulls out a can of Miller High Life, closes the door, rummages in a couple of drawers until he finds an opener; though he's never done it before, he punches holes in the thing, turns it up and takes a big swig.

"See?" he says, but then the foam backs up in his throat.

"Yeah, I see." Valerie points a finger at him. "The coolest one ever to grace the corridors of Anna Shaefer's kitchen can't handle a little sip of beer. Give me that," she tells him. When he hands it over, she takes two reasonable sips. "That's how you do it, young fella." She sets the can on the counter in front of him. "Want me to get you a bowl of Cheerios?" she asks. When he comes toward her again, she's out the door and down the corridor, telling him no, leave her alone, she didn't mean it. Then they're rassling around on the Shaefers' big bed, trying to stifle their giggles so as not to awaken and traumatize the sweet-dreaming little infant in the next room. With Valerie flat on the bed, Billy half on the floor and half on top of her with his head pillowed on her beskirted, beslipped, and bepantied pubic bone, he says, "Hey, Val, you think this is what queers do to each other?" He kisses her skirt right there and feels her relax, her whole body go loose.

"Don't do that," softly, dreamily, she tells the ceiling above her. "Don't you even think about doing that."

So he doesn't.

Jack Lamereaux knows a lot of good jokes to tell in the car on the way home from dance jobs. The one of Jack's that Billy likes best is about the tall, dark stranger; it takes miles and miles of highway to tell it, and the punchline is "You better cut that shit out." Johnny Wilson knows a lot of jokes, too, and with his intellect aroused by the jokes Jack tells, Johnny takes to matching Jack joke for joke. He makes it even tougher on himself by sticking only to farmer's-daughter jokes. Billy's never heard men do this before, but he recognizes that he is being included in some significant way. Birdy's jokes, mostly puns, seem to him insipid, but he snickers politely along with the others.

So Billy tells the one joke he knows himself, about this retarded guy trying to seduce an extremely seducible girl, the punchline being the retarded guy's repeating after the girl, "lower, lower," in a bass voice. If Billy begins telling his joke in the spirit of manly fellowship, as he tells it, he feels himself drifting out into intense isolation and ends it feeling deeply humiliated. He tells the joke badly, his voice won't go down to anything approaching a bass register, and he's a sixteen-year-old boy performing for grown men. They don't laugh, not even politely. Billy has the middle seat in the back, between Jack Lamereaux and Cecil Taylor. His neck and ears burn. He'd like to die. Short of that, he'd like to machine gun Birdy Z. and the other three D-Jays. They ride for a long time without saying anything. Then Jack Lamereaux tells a joke about queers, lisping and making an effeminate gesture with his hand. Billy makes a point of not laughing at that one, not saying a word to any of them all the rest of the way back to Madison.

Parked with her down by Brice Memorial Middle School he explains to Valerie his relief at having the decision-making responsibility pass on to Jack Lamereaux. Jack really does know the music, really does know what kinds of arrangements they can play, how to set up the numbers in a set, even how to use Johnny's steel guitar to the band's advantage. Billy is happy to be just one among them again, but he wonders about it a lot. "It was like for a little while I was the boss of these grown men; I didn't want to be, and they didn't want me to be, but it just came about. I don't know why."

"You're the coolest one," Valerie tells him, with an edge to her voice that Billy knows is not generous. She is smoking a Marlboro now, one of her own, and they're working on a six-pack of Schlitz that earlier tonight Birdy bought for Billy at Billy's request. Valerie and Billy have had sex again a couple of times. Tonight they could have it if they wanted to, and they're choosing not to, because it's like an appliance they've bought that just doesn't work. They've taken to just sitting in the car and talking, smoking cigarettes and drinking beer if Billy has been able to get it.

He knows something that he's not supposed to know officially, though they both know that he knows: Valerie has been out several times with Pete Ratcliffe. It stands to reason because lots of times when there are parties and dances at their school, Billy is out with Birdy Z. and the D-Jays in some godawful Odd Fellows Hall playing from nine until one and even later if the old dames and geezers can come up with the cash to keep the D-Jays going. Pete's a nice enough guy, and Billy figures Valerie's entitled to a decent time. He has no doubt that Valerie only likes Pete, while she loves him.

Later, he explains all this about Valerie to Birdy Z. while the two of them sit in Billy's dad's car after a Friday night dance job. Birdy has surprised him by joining him for a beer before Billy drives home. Billy was just joking when he invited the Bird, and he thought the Bird's saying all right, he would do that, was also just playing around. But now Billy works the church key on the little can of Country Club and hands it over. Birdy holds it, grins at it, shakes his head, and then turns the can up for a hell of a big swig. He belches, and tells Billy he ought not to be sure of anything with any woman, he's here to tell him that. Billy watches Birdy grin at the beer can again and wonders if now that he's drinking with him Birdy Z. is getting ready to propose queering him. On the contrary, Birdy tells Billy he's going to have to come home with him some night soon and meet his wife. If he's going to be having a beer every now and then with Billy, he's going to have to tell his old lady; it'll be easier if Billy is there with him.

So after the gig on Saturday night they go up to Birdy's house and Billy meets Lannie. She's a big, loose-jointed woman, taller than the Bird by a good three or four inches, with blonde hair going dark at the roots, buck teeth, and blue plastic-rimmed glasses. Billy likes her a lot in her faded blue pajamas and maroon bathrobe. Lannie looked really worried when the Bird brought in this bottle and set it on the counter and asked her if she'd like to join him and Billy in a little nightcap. But then she sighed and said, "Oh God, Birdy, if you just knew how tired I was getting of drinking that Sanka with you at this time of night anyway. I guess I'll have one with you." So now they're standing in her kitchen at two-thirty on a Sunday morning, the three of them finishing off a fifth of Smirnoff's vodka, mixing it with the breakfast-juice from the refrigerator.

The house is a mess, as far as Billy can tell, at least the downstairs is, evidence of kids messing into everything, scattering toys everywhere, even into real stuff like the Pendergasts' magazines, the jars under the kitchen counter, the books, and ashtrays. Billy wonders why Lannie didn't clean some of the mess up while she was waiting to have Sanka with Birdy Z. She fires a lot of questions at him, about where they play and how the people act and dance. While he's telling her, she gets this dreamy look on her face and sighs and says she wishes she could get out and go to these things with Birdy Z. Before they had kids, she used to go with him and have a great time. She gives Billy this big horsey grin and winks at him. He can just imagine Lannie out there on the floor, dancing to a fast one, letting it all out, flinging those long arms and legs of hers every which way.

"I guess that's the last of this," Birdy says, pulling the bottle down from his mouth. Billy watches Lannie's face change when she sees what the Bird has done. It does occur to him that the bottle was at least half full when they brought it in, and he and Lannie have had just one drink apiece.

"How do you feel, Bird?" Billy asks him, swirling what's left of his ice in the Bugs Bunny glass Lannie gave him.

Birdy Z. grins at them both. "I feel fine, kids, I feel god damn terrific."

Over the next several months Billy sees a good deal of Birdy and Lannie. It's a little deal they've struck—Billy wanting to be careful not to let his parents find out he's drinking, Birdy and Lannie not wanting anybody to know they've gone back to drinking—and so they drink with each other after rehearsals, after gigs, once or twice just when Billy comes up and has supper with them and the kids. They're full of good cheer, as if they've come into money or found a secret pleasure. One night Billy takes Valerie over there, but she doesn't have a good time and doesn't change her mind about the Bird one bit. "So what if he's got kids and that goony-goony wife? So what if he's nice to you? I don't have to like him, do I?"

Well, she doesn't. And the truth is, Billy has begun to wonder if she even likes him. Nowadays, without milk and cookies, they go straight down to her basement. When he untucks her blouse and reaches a hand back there to unhook her bra, she sighs, sits up straight, and says, "Here, let me do that, for goodness sakes." Then she sits back looks at the ceiling while Billy puts his hands on her. Billy still likes her breasts, but he can feel little messages being passed from every cell of her skin to the palms of his hands, "Get away from me, get away."

"Val, have I done something to you to make you mad?" He takes back his hands to his own self.

"No, but I'll tell you what." She starts crying like she just realized she was in pain.

He's ready for her to tell him something he won't like, such as she's sick and tired of him and she's decided to accept Pete Ratcliffe's invitation to go steady. What in fact she does tell him is that she's pregnant. He feels like she's taken a sledge-hammer to his forehead.

"And I'll tell you what else," she says, too, from this posture she has taken of leaning forward with her face in her hands. Billy can't imagine what else there could be after what she's just said.

"It could be your baby or Pete's, I don't know which." Until this moment, Billy has never imagined sex between Valerie and Pete; now the image of them doing it in a car seat stuns him into a long silence during which he merely gapes at Valerie. She won't look back at him.

Billy goes through the motions of asking her questions—yes, she's seen a doctor; yes, her mother knows; no, her father doesn't know yet; no, she hasn't told Pete yet, but she's going to tonight—but all his mind will do for him is chant *you're not even seventeen yet, she won't be fifteen until March, you're not even . . .*

Billy slides through a couple of days like a brain-damaged kid. In

230

the hallways at school, his pals are constantly putting their hands on him and pushing him this way, directing him that way. His teachers are bemused. "Go sit down back there, Billy," Mrs. Lancaster, his English teacher tells him, and he does. But the next thing he knows is he's in Pete Ratcliffe's dad's car with Pete driving and Valerie sitting between them, and they're heading out to the Pendleton stone quarry after school to figure out what's to be done, all three of them smoking Valerie's cigarettes and shaking so bad it doesn't even occur to them to get nasty with each other.

Billy hears himself yelping, "A god damn coin-flip? I cannot god damn believe this!"

Valerie cries at some length while sitting between the two boys. Pete finally blurts, "If you know a better way to . . ."

He and Pete get out of the car. It's a Ford, a new one, pretty, with the sun glazing its waxed hood, shining on the chrome bumper up there where he and Pete stand to do the flip. It's Pete's quarter. They agree that Pete gets to flip it, Billy gets to call it while it's in the air; they'll let it fall in the grass beside the road. One throw will decide the whole thing. One throw, one toss, what the hell—Billy feels like he's about to float out into space. Just before Pete flips that thing up in the air, he looks Billy in the eye and asks, "Did you use rubbers?"

Billy nods, then asks, "Did you?"

"Damn straight I did!" Pete spits to the side. They shake their heads at each other and press their lips together hard. Pete tosses the quarter, Billy calls tails just before it hits, then they're both leaning down to look at it, a little metal disk in the scrubby grass. It's tails. When they get back in the car Pete is the one who has to tell Valerie that he is the one.

On the way back into town not one of the three of them has a word to say. Billy has scooted over as close to the door as he can, and Valerie has scooted over beside Pete as far as she can. Billy asks Pete to take him to Birdy Z.'s place. When he steps out and says, "See ya," it's as if he's a hitchhiker they're just dropping off. Walking up Birdy's sidewalk with his hands jammed down in his pockets, Billy's whispering, "That didn't hurt. That didn't . . ."

Inside the Pendergasts' house, Lannie sits him down at the kitchen table and tells him she should have known it, she's a fool, she's got to get the Bird on the wagon again or he's going to lose his job at the station. They smelled it on him the other morning, and they warned him. The Bird is out for a walk, mulling it over. Billy and Lannie sit there and smoke. Billy wants to tell her what he's just gone through but knows better than to put that on her shoulders. He knows she wouldn't like what he really feels about the whole thing, as if he's been accused of some crime but found innocent in court. And while he sits there with her, he knows Lannie knows the Bird would have never started drinking again if Billy hadn't gotten him going. He tries to think back over that night when he joked and asked the Bird to have a beer with him and the Bird joked and said, well all right.

When Birdy Z. comes in from his walk, he's chewing gum and smells like Juicy Fruit. Billy and Lannie know he's loaded. While he goes to wash up, sitting there at the table like parents of a wayward kid, Billy and Lannie give each other a long look. "Stashed a bottle in the garage, I expect," Lannie murmurs.

"Do you want me to go look?" Billy offers.

Lannie tells him he won't know where to look, and Billy tells her a long time ago Birdy told him all about stashing bottles. She tells him to go find it then and pour it out and come on back in for supper. Out there, behind a can of charcoal lighter fluid, Billy finds a half-full pint of Old Mr. Boston gin. He takes a big slug of the stuff, grimaces, decides what the hell, he wasn't hungry anyway. He finishes it in three more swigs, and starts walking out to the edge of town where he can hitchhike home.

The next day Pete and Valerie are absent from school, and the day after that it's all over school about them running off to Sparta, North Carolina, to get married. Kids look at Billy funny in the hallway. He feels resentful and smug at the same time. Next week they're back. Billy and Pete manage to nod grimly at each other when their paths cross; but he goes out of his way not to see Valerie, and he expects she's doing her best, too, to keep from seeing him.

Billy feels like he's chasing his life. Jack Lamereaux raises the fee the D-Jays charge for playing a dance, and they get more jobs. He raises it again, and they get still more jobs, at higher-class places. "We are god damn much in demand," Birdy Z. says in the car on the night of the day he has received final notice from the radio station. "I can make a living on my music."

"You can't do any such god damn thing," Johnny Wilson leans forward from the back seat to tell him. They are headed to the Hotel Roanoke where they will make a hundred dollars apiece for their night's work, a little dance for the Southwest Virginia Hollins Alumni. Jack Lamereaux is the one who drives them to the jobs now, though because they all still defer to him, the Bird always rides shotgun.

The Bird turns up his bottle for a quick swig and chortles and says, "Johnny, you old fart, you just lack the guts to set yourself free."

Johnny sits back. He's not saying anything, but he's grinning at Billy and Cecil Taylor on either side of him.

By eleven-thirty, Birdy Z. can't sit up straight at the piano bench. They have been hired to play until one. Two numbers too soon Jack declares the band to be on a break and helps Billy escort the Bird outside where they walk him around in the parking lot. "Can't fire me, you fuckers," Birdy tells them, giggling, his arms pulling heavily on their shoulders. "Band's named after me."

"Yeah, Bird, yeah," Jack Lamereaux tells him. Jack's pretty disgusted. "Can you handle him, Billy?" Jack needs to go back in and stall for time before they start the next set. Billy keeps walking the Bird up and down the aisles of cars under the streetlights that make everything look bluish gray, especially the skin of Birdy's face and hands.

"Billy?" the Bird says, hauling his arm away from across Billy's shoulder.

Billy's happy to see him getting hold of himself this much. "Yeah, Bird?"

"You love me, Billy?" Bird stops suddenly and stands there in the parking lot with his eyes locked on Billy. His shirt's untucked; his tie's loose and skewed around under his collar.

"Let's keep walking, Bird." Billy reaches for him to turn him back in the right direction.

Birdy brushes his hand away. "I asked you a question, Billy." He's even put a little parental authority into his voice, so that Billy has to shake himself to get a hold of exactly what the situation is.

Billy studies the Bird and knows he's not going to get off easy here. Now is the time that Birdy Z. is going to try to queer him. He isn't afraid of it anymore. He sighs and says, "You're my pal, Bird."

"God damn it, Billy."

"Lannie loves you, Bird."

"You like Lannie, Billy?" Birdy's voice takes on a smooth, interested quality that sends shivers up Billy's back.

"Hey, Bird," Billy tells him, no-nonsense now, "Time to go back in and play the last set, man."

The Bird stands there and stares at him. Finally he does say, "You're not my pal, Billy. I don't want anything to do with you. I don't want to see you around my house any more. You understand?"

Billy's relieved. He figures it's just drunken palaver, just what came into the Bird's brain at the moment. And if it isn't that, then what the hell, he can do without the whole mess of Birdy Z. and his drinking. "You ready to go back in and play the last set, Bird?" Billy asks him.

"You're god damn right I am," Bird says and takes a step. Billy reaches toward him to steady him. "Keep your god damn hands off me, O.K.?" Birdy says and walks into the back of an Oldsmobile, falls forward onto its trunk, then slides backward onto the asphalt. Billy can't get him up and so trots back into the hotel to get help. All the D-Jays come out and have a look at Birdy Z. laid out like a dead man in the parking lot.

"You free now, Bird?" Johnny murmurs while they are lifting him into Jack's car, but of course the Bird can't respond.

They try playing out the job without a piano player, but nobody argues with Johnny Wilson when he starts packing up and says that even by his standards they sound embarrassing. Jack accepts half the fee they agreed to originally, and the D-Jays head home early. By the time they pull up in front of his house, Bird has awakened and sobered somewhat, but he has nothing to say until he's out and standing on the sidewalk, glaring down at the car full of them. "You fuckers are fired!" he shouts at them. Jack pulls away, but they can hear the Bird shouting after them, "And I don't want you using my name anymore! You understand that?"

"Set us free, too," Johnny Wilson murmurs, looking back at him, as they all are, even Jack Lamereaux, using the rearview mirror. Billy is the only one of them who giggles, but he thinks it may be because he feels almost crazy.

Jack stops beside Billy's dad's car, parked in front of the bus terminal. The four of them sit there talking for a little while, finally agreeing that it's not worth it to try to keep the D-Jays going. "We're disbanded, man," Johnny says, laughing. Jack says, "Yeah, man, that's exactly what we are, disbanded as hell."

Before he gets on the road, Billy walks into the bus terminal to take a leak. While he's in the men's room facing the urinal, he hears a stall door slowly creak open behind him. He turns to see a man's face slowly extend toward him from one of the stalls. It is an unremarkable male face, not one Billy has ever seen before, but the sight of it scares him. He hears himself saying in a voice he hardly knows to be his own, "You son of a bitch, you fuck around with me, I'll fucking kill you!" The face recedes into the stall, the stall door creaks closed, Billy rushes his urination and leaves without washing his hands.

Driving home at three in the morning, he's wide awake now, shivering and wondering about the voice that came out of his own chest and throat in the bus terminal. When he said what he said, he knows he felt a power in his arms, hands, and fingers; whether or not he actually had it in him to kill the man who peered at him, he knows he spoke out of animal certainty that he could do it. "Would do it," he whispers to the green light of the dashboard, "would do it." He wonders what Birdy Z. would have done if Billy had spoken to him that way. Then he feels a gush of affection for the Bird, imagines himself back in the parking lot, admitting to the Bird that he did indeed love him, walking toward him and embracing him. It wouldn't have had to be queer, he thinks. He entertains the idea that if he had done that, they could have gone back in and finished the gig and ridden home telling each other jokes.

At school Valerie is absent for an entire week; Pete is out of school, too, one day, back another, then absent another. Billy's friends and acquaintances talk about Valerie and Pete so much that the hallways ring with their names, every laugh sounding to Billy as if it must be on Pete's and Valerie's account. But he himself is not included in their conversations, hears no information, asks no one about them. He's almost seventeen. His days now seem full of the grim injustice of his having been cut off from everyone.

On the day she comes back to school, before homeroom, Valerie walks straight up to Billy at his locker and hands him a note that instructs him to meet her outside the band room at lunchtime. She's so quick and definite about it that what she's done goes almost unremarked by anybody but Billy himself. She's pale and puffy-faced, doing what she can to smile and speak to kids who come up and ask her how she's doing. She looks back over her shoulder at him when he's had a chance to read the note. He nods at her.

He knows the place she means, out by a side door where few

people rarely pass by, even at lunchtime. She's waiting for him when he walks back there, but she's got no smile for him, not even a hello. It's late April, a damp day. Underneath her band jacket she's got on a new white sweater that sets off her dark hair and that he likes, but the way she's standing there she looks like a tough girl. She drags hard on her cigarette, then starts speaking to him in what he figures is a speech she's worked on for a while. "The doctor was wrong," she says. "That bastard. Sunday afternoon I started hemorrhaging. What I have—what I had—was a cyst! Can you believe that?"

Her eyes drill Billy as if she's holding him responsible for what's happened to her, but he knows it's just because she's willing herself not to cry. Or maybe she does think it's his fault. Maybe it is. He can't say anything, and so he reaches toward her to pat her shoulder or something, but she backs away from him and keeps looking at him. He can't say anything for more than a minute; then he gets some words up out of his throat: "Are you and Pete going to stay . . . ?"

"Yeah, we are," she says vehemently. "My parents don't want me to, but Pete thinks we've made fools enough of ourselves now, and he doesn't want a divorce. What he thinks is what I go by since he was the one who was man enough to—"

"Valerie, it was a coin flip!"

"Yeah, tell me about it," she says and keeps her eyes on him, waiting. Billy feels the weight of enormous injustice coming down on him, but he knows better than to complain about it to her. He tries to hold her eyes, looks away, tries again.

"I just wanted you to know," she says finally.

"Yeah," Billy says.

"Can you keep it to yourself?" she asks him, and he nods. She reaches toward him—for a second he thinks she means to punch him in the ribs—clasps his hand and squeezes it. "Take care," she says, then walks away from him fast, stretching her navy-blue skirt with every stride.

Just before marching band practice that afternoon, Elliott Pugh, like a soldier reporting for duty, walks over and stands in front of Billy. "I'm playing with Mr. Pendergast now," he says.

Billy drags on his cigarette and looks at Elliott but doesn't make an effort to meet his eyes. In the last couple of days he's had about all the hostile eye contact he can stand. Still, he can't help witnessing Elliott's presence here in front of him. Billy would still like to take back his betrayal of Elliott those months ago. He figures he has some options: One, he can warn Elliott of Birdy's drinking and tarnish the prize Elliott thinks he's won; or two, he can politely wish Elliott luck. He chooses number three and tells Elliott to go fuck himself. When he sees Elliott grin maliciously at him, he knows that number three was the best for both of them.

Billy puts his cigarette in the corner of his mouth and keeps standing off more or less by himself, comfortable with the horn at his waist hooked to his neck strap like a little attached shelf for him to rest his arms on. Elliott's down at the other end of the ranks with the clarinet section, all of them toodling like free-lance musical idiots. If for no other reason than that the big queer is a clarinet player, Billy knows he was right in what he told Elliott. He snorts to himself, drops his cigarette, and stomps it. Up front chatting with the other majorettes, Valerie has changed into shorts but she's still got on her band jacket, and Billy imagines she's feeling the wind on her legs. "Val, Val," Billy hums to himself and shakes his head and smiles.

More than a hundred kids are in this marching band with Billy. He is one among them. He thinks of Birdy, home at this moment, probably sleeping off one binge, getting ready for another, and Lannie, probably sitting at her kitchen table, smoking a cigarette and trying to figure out what she's going to do about the Bird and the kids and her life—their lives. That's the thought that comes to him just about the time Mr. Banks hollers at them that break is over, put out the cigarettes, dress right dress! Billy takes his place in ranks, still thinking about how Lannie really does have to look after her kids, how she probably figures she has to do what she can for the Bird. Elliott has just hitched himself to the Bird's fate for at least a little while. Valerie is up there in front, a married woman but bouncing her baton on her toe now like a kid.

Mr. Banks pokes the whistle into his mouth, lifts his arms and gives them a shrill blast. Billy puts his teeth to the mouthpiece of the saxophone, ready to play. He's in the center of a rank, kids in front of him, behind him, and to either side of him. Mr. Banks blasts the whistle again, plunging his arms downward, and in unison with them all Billy steps forward, releasing a huge exhalation into the horn. The sound that comes forth is an enormous, rich billowing of vibration that swells up out of the moving formation of more than a hundred musicians. He keeps perfectly square in his rank and in his file. Stepping out crisply to John Phillip Sousa's "King Cotton," Billy's exhilarated. He feels so free he can hardly stand it.

The Beautiful Gestures

AN INVITATION has come to me to speak at Portland State University. While there I will see one of the first good students I taught here in Vermont. Susan Larrick has become a teacher, and my suspicion is that she's a considerably improved version of the teacher I was sixteen years ago. I'm forty-six now, and through all this time I have carried in my mind a sort of paraphrased version of the poem she wrote for my class that convinced me she had talent: It was called "Tight End," and it documented a college girl's drunken behavior on a football weekend. I loved the title's pun, and I was thrilled by the nerve of this girl who wasn't afraid of presenting to her classmates a somewhat slatternly self for the sake of a poem. When I mentioned "Tight End" on the phone to Susan last week, she said that she had long ago disowned the thing and destroyed all her copies of it.

When I was twenty-nine, I weighed 175, had gaunt cheeks, and imagined that I would write novels that would rival *The Sound and the Fury* and *The Sun Also Rises*. I might have been a dashing figure in the eyes of a literary-minded sophomore with a lousy social life. Susan was always struggling with her weight. She had a tendency to grin in most circumstances, and toward hooting laughter—though her mirth was often on the edge of weeping. As the fall 1971 semester went on, and I came to know her, I began to understand that Susan was frighteningly well-suited to be my student. She was amused, moved, or disgusted by what amused, moved, or disgusted me.

"That's because she has a crush on you," my wife said while the two of us were eating supper and I was singing Susan Larrick's praises. I couldn't deny that, but it seemed to me that at least some of Susan's ability to apprehend what I had to teach came from natural inclination and ability. I hadn't put into Susan the gift that enabled her to write a terrific villanelle. But it was true that Susan's laughter

238

at my little classroom jokes was loud and long. True, too, was that the grin she gave me each morning when I walked into my classroom usually got me off to a terrific start.

Intimacy is a necessary condition between teachers and students of any art. If a student is good and a teacher wishes to serve that student well, then the teacher must be prepared to be intimately connected with the student. Nineteen seventy-one was the fourth year of Marie's and my marriage. As to kids, push was coming to shove: Marie thought she wanted them, and I thought I didn't. If you're moderately constant and sociable, you can get through five years of marriage without children; ten years is another question, and it was one Marie and I were just beginning to address. Everything was relevant to it. My accord with Susan Larrick was especially relevant, though Marie and I acknowledged this only in subterranean levels of our separate and maritally bound consciousnesses. When just two of you eat dinner together night after night, your unborn children sit there at the table with you, and so does your terrifically talented student who has a crush on you.

Susan had a couple of pals who would come with her to visit me during office hours. I liked the pals, but in my office those girls made me nervous. Bea Thackston was tall, buck-toothed, and gawky-limbed, the kind of girl you think of as a genuine *gal*, and she had a laugh that echoed up and down the English department hallway. Candace Winters was lithe and silky-haired; only partially aware of it herself, I think, she generated the purest sexual energy that has ever fueled my imagination. Susan was usually in the company of only one of her pals at a time. But when I remember those fall afternoons of 1971, I place the four of us there in my mop-closet of an office—Candace's skirt riding up her thighs, Bea spouting riffs of laughter, Susan grinning at me and making nervous wisecracks while she poked around the stuff on my desk. All the while I was sweating it out, trying to act cool but hoping to hell they'd make an exit before someone walked down the hall to complain to my chairman.

Toward the end of that semester she handed in a poem that troubled me; about her father, it included a couple of lines describing his inclination to touch people and how, when he had had his evening cocktails, he was inclined to touch Susan in ways that she found offensive. She did not ask me to consider the poem privately; in fact she presented the poem routinely for discussion by the class. Students in undergraduate writing workshops are completely unpredictable: they'll devote hours of class time to arguing about capitalizing each line's first letter, but in the case of Susan's poem, not one sensitive soul brought up what it had to say about incest or child abuse. Throughout the discussion Susan squirmed in her seat, red-faced, and with sweat broken out on her forehead and upper lip, but that was how she'd appeared in discussions of all her previous work.

I knew Susan was much taken with the work of Sylvia Plath and that she had the kind of fondness for Plath's "Daddy" that her peers would have had for a Neil Young or a Van Morrison song. In my office after class, without the company of Bea or Candace, after we'd sat a moment or two without talking, I said something like, "That's pretty serious stuff you're writing about in that poem"; and she replied with something like, "Yeah, I know." I didn't know how to direct the conversation to any further illumination, and I wasn't sure I wanted to know anything more. Plath's poem is a mean-spirited fiction, and Susan's might well have been an imitation of something I had directed her toward admiring.

Among the ways in which I am responsible for Susan is my having infected her with my taste (in those days) for a certain trembly lipped strain of literary document, Plath's poetry being high on the list of work I admired and read aloud to my classes. Faulkner's Nobel Prize Acceptance Speech, Tillie Olsen's "I Stand Here Ironing," Theodore Roethke's "Elegy for Jane," and W. C. Williams's "Dedication for a Plot of Ground" were other favorites of mine from that early period of my teaching. Nowadays I'm partial to more densely constructed and restrained work. I have come to love design at least as much as conviction. Robert Hayden's "Those Winter Sundays" is what I wish I'd directed Susan toward appreciating rather than Plath's adolescently exhibitionistic "Daddy."

There were boys she hung around with—there were a couple of bearded, raggedy-dressing literary boys who even gave her some halfhearted romantic pursuit, but throughout her four years at this university Susan's social life was generally pretty sad. She kept me informed on this subject as if I were somehow responsible for what a lousy time she was having. She didn't help matters with her inflated standards of male acceptability; a girl so basically human in her appearance couldn't afford to be as choosy as she was. Bea Thackston had a deadly handsome pre-med boyfriend with whom, according to remarks she and Susan let drop, she enjoyed such a vigorous sex-life that both their dormitory roommates had requested reassignments. And in the area of romantic success, Candace Winters had begun surprising us all.

Candace had been one of the first people I met on the first day I walked into the department office. She was the niece of our secretary, Mrs. Hansen, as well as being an English major, and so she felt at ease around that office. "Have you met Professor Puckett yet?" she asked me when I told her who I was. At the moment, she was sitting up on the belly-high counter surrounding the secretaries' desks; she was wearing a miniskirt, and I was using all my willpower to direct my eyes no lower than her chin. "Professor Puckett," she explained happily, "is the other creative writing teacher here," as if with that piece of information I had the key to a successful career. When she turned to Mrs. Hansen for confirmation of Puckett's significance, I snuck a look up her skirt and thus have never forgotten that first encounter with her.

One reason Candace didn't try to hide her adoration of Scott Puckett was that she knew it was absurd for her to hope that he would be interested in her. Everyone would have agreed with her. Puckett was just not a romantic figure. Short and muscular, a fireplug of a man, he spent every free moment in the gym playing squash and lifting weights. He was reticent around everyone and almost catatonic around women, so much so that I wondered how he ever managed to meet Sally, his wife, who was a very personable young woman. Puckett attended her as knights of the fifteenth century attended their ladies.

From the beginning, because he and I were "creative" types, we had things to talk about, business to transact. Among the department's thirty-some literature Ph.D.'s, he and I with our writing M.F.A.'s were foreigners of the same nationality. And maybe because we were both tacitly aware that our colleagues would have been delighted if we had become enemies, he and I became friends in spite of Puckett's difficulty with intimacy. He even tolerated my wretched squash-playing for so many hours that I became a decent opponent for him. After our matches and after our showers, we had many a good talk, sitting under that huge maple tree at the corner of the gym. When you've cooled off, but you're still too tired to want to do anything, you can sometimes get right to what you really want to talk about.

With Puckett and me in those days, our topic of choice sometimes was Ms. Larrick and Ms. Winters. He began it by speaking well of their writing. I'd shared Susan's poems with him, and Candace had shown me a couple of her stories from her classes with Puckett. My perception of their talents was that Susan was the real thing, but that Candace was your basic above-average undergraduate proser. When Puckett praised the two of them equally, I was surprised and a little irked. I took his high opinion of the two of them in fact to be a diminishment of Susan's value. Couldn't he see what a remarkably mature poem "Tight End" was for a college sophomore? But the subject was touchy, and I had the accidental good sense merely to question him further.

"She's made me step back and think," was his remark that signaled to me that the man was experiencing marital slippage. Which in itself was only mildly shocking. What struck me was that he was taking Candace Winters's attention seriously—that he was elevating a child to the status of a woman. Well, she wasn't a child. I have to confess that I'd carried on a flirtation with her since I'd met her that day in the office; and though her interest in me was purely casual, I had thought I understood her pretty well. I had thought she was going to pine impossibly after Puckett, all the while polishing up the nugget of her sexuality—polishing it up until around graduation when she'd haul off and marry some up-and-coming young Republican and for the rest of her life she'd hold onto this romantic past history of the silent man who had remained out of her reach.

I had it all wrong, unless Puckett anchored himself back into his marriage. He and Sally had no kids. Sally Puckett hated all forms of athletics, she loved fine clothes and restaurants, and she gave one to understand that she loved dancing, though Scott was a nondancer. Sally was from Texas, and she also gave one to understand that she'd had some high old times before she met Scott and "came north." She had a way of saying the word "north" that I thought charming. I liked her. Marie and I sometimes called them and had them over for a few drinks late in the evening. Scott would be yawning and wanting to go home, but Sally was a terrific midnight boozer. She was funny, reckless, and full of peculiar opinions in that southern way of colorful talkers. She knew I liked Faulkner, and she liked to rag me about him; she spoke about Faulkner as if he were her reprobate uncle. She knew his work almost as well as I did, though she certainly thought less well of it.

Neither Candace nor Susan had been around for the summer. When they returned to school in September, both of them seemed to have gained strength. They no longer needed each other's support to come to our offices. Walking past Puckett's office, I'd see Ms. Winters in there holding the man's total attention, even though he might have a couple of students slouched in the hallway outside his door, hoping for a chance to see him. I'd think, those students know what's going on in there, why doesn't Puckett wake up? But then when Ms. Larrick was in my office talking about a book of poetry she'd borrowed from my shelf, I'd glance up and see Puckett walking past my door, giving me a little grin or a wave, and sweat would break out across my forehead. What did students waiting outside my office door think? And there was one significant difference between us: He had tenure, and I didn't.

Bea Thackston had come back to school, too, but she didn't find her way to my office. According to Susan's hints, what kept her away was what Bea and her med-student fiancé did with every minute of their free time, in his room with a chair propped under the doorknob. I don't know if what she suggested was true. Those were peculiar times. The sexual freedom of the sixties was being joylessly translated into seventies pragmatism. Middle-class kids screwed to improve their social skills. Or if they weren't as comfortable with sex as fashion instructed them they should be, then they told their friends they were screwing a lot. I liked it when Susan, grinning and checking her watch, suggested that Bea and Kelly, right at that very moment, had sent his roommate to the library so that they could get it on during the free half hour they had between her major's seminar and his Organic lab.

But God knows what was actually true and what wasn't. The culture sent messages to all of us about what we were supposed to be doing. A female colleague in the department made overtures to Marie and me that we took to mean that she and her husband wanted to do a little spouse-swapping. At a lawn party we'd attended that summer, another colleague—a male and a rather large one at that—a specialist in the nineteenth-century American novel, had worn bright red lipstick. Except for that detail his behavior was normal and his appearance exemplary—he'd worn a blue seersucker suit, a tie, and nicely polished cordovan shoes. No one said anything to the man about his lipstick; it was almost as if it had been drawn on his mouth by someone else as a joke.

Those were the days of streaking. Naked young men or women would suddenly dash through crowds of people. Streakers usually performed alone or in pairs; men streaked with other men, women with other women. I never heard of an incident of cogender streaking, though it always seemed to me something that couples might want to do together.

The point of all this is that people did shocking things in those days, or said they did, though I have a great deal of doubt about whether such acts were really what we wanted. It was an odd time in the nation. We were pulling our troops out of Vietnam, but Nixon had mined Haiphong Harbor and stepped up the bombing of the North, and even though we were still meddling around with it, we'd begun shrugging off responsibility for that war. In the sixties there was conviction. In the early seventies there was phenomenon, but it did not necessarily reflect the truth of anyone's thoughts or feelings.

Of course, every age tests a person's sense of identity. One day when she was bemoaning Bea's efforts to fix her up with one of Kelly's pals, I remember telling Ms. Larrick, "You have to figure out who you are and proceed. If you let your pals tell you who are, you've got some sleepless dark nights to pass through." I advised Ms. Larrick that if you write, you've got something to brace you up against the outside world. I'm afraid I let her know just how talented I thought she was, which wasn't good for keeping her humble or for keeping her out of my office. One day when I told Susan that another student was waiting in the hall for an appointment with me, she said, "He can wait until I finish telling you this." She wasn't kidding, though it was to her credit that at that moment she had been telling me something she'd figured out about a Theodore Roethke poem. But right then I began worrying about how insufferable Susan would become if I kept on trying to nourish her poetic talent.

Though Ms. Larrick and Ms. Winters carried out separate visitations on our hallway, apparently they talked with each other a good deal when they were away from the English Department. They cooked up a plan for having a Halloween party—a four-person party to be held Halloween afternoon in Ms. Larrick's dormitory room. When I recall those times, I wonder just what Puckett and I were doing to let ourselves be talked into a scheme like that. I want to think that both of us acted freely and courageously, but I have my doubts. I remember that a day or two after I got the hand-drawn and lettered invitation ("to a 'spirited' party"), I stopped by Puckett's office to ask him if he was going. He shook his head, a much-used Puckett mode of communication, but then he said he wasn't sure, was I going? Without saying so, we both knew that if one or the other of us refused the invitation, there'd be no party, or worse, one of us would be going by himself to a dorm room to socialize with a female student. It would be a good deal less shocking if there were two of us. At the end of the week, when he stopped by my office to check with me, I told him I thought I was probably going; and he shook his head again but then said, yeah, he thought he probably was, too. In that very moment we must have been daring ourselves to do something improper.

Kissinger was trying to negotiate peace. Puckett and I were going to take an afternoon stroll over to the dormitory they called the Shoebox. Ms. Larrick and Ms. Winters were going to throw a little wine-and-cheese party. The nation's fate was not in our hands.

It was a day full of weather. Wind sailed battalions of clouds overhead from horizon to horizon. First the sky darkened, then a patch of light opened out over the lake and came sweeping over the city and up the hill toward the university. When the sun was out it was hot. When it clouded over, the day was brisk and chilly. Wind was the one constant. I remember that wind as one that, if it were with you, pushed you, almost pummeling at your back.

Walking with Puckett across campus that afternoon, I joked about our teacher-costumes. We both had on jackets and ties—ties the wind snarled around our necks and flapped over our shoulders as we walked, heads down, hands in our pockets, toward the Shoebox. I was wondering if I'd be feeling so foolish if I'd been by myself, and I thought he was probably wondering the same thing, though he said little. The nearer the dormitory we got, the more aware we were of students casting their eyes on us.

Entering the Shoebox and climbing its stairwell, Puckett and I were solemn as pallbearers until we'd located Ms. Larrick's room, number 307 according to our invitations. Then we exchanged grins, realizing that like responsible adults we'd both brought the cards with us, folded up in our inside jacket pockets. In unison we lifted our hands to the door; I grinned and dropped my hand while he rapped crisply three times. Instantly the door swung open. We faced two goblins in full regalia.

Susan and Candace had bought devil costumes (red face-masks and red paper-cloth capes) for Puckett and me, which of course we refused to put on. There were crackers, cheeses, and an ice chest containing beer and bottles of Chablis and Chardonnay. The beer was the one Puckett liked, the wines were ones I thought acceptable. There was a stereo, and there were records that demonstrated that Ms. Larrick and Ms. Winters had studied Puckett and me carefully enough to know our tastes in music.

Through our first hour of awkwardness, the young ladies teased us and giggled. Puckett and I slugged down beverages. It wasn't long before we were enjoying ourselves. Around three o'clock, I struggled up from the floor where I'd been sitting being entertained by Susan's tossing grapes toward my mouth. "I'm gonna try on my silly-assed costume," I announced. Puckett stood up beside me—Candace had been rubbing his shoulders—and said he was going to try his on, too. So for the rest of the afternoon we were two devils and two goblins. Though we did nothing really wrong, we nevertheless had a very comical and affectionate time of it until around four-thirty, when Puckett and I knew we had to start heading back to our houses and our wives.

Getting out of the costumes took a bit of time, as did calming ourselves down enough for us to believe we were leaving the room with some decorum. I remember that I accused Puckett of being a rowdy man and that he loudly denied it. Ms. Winters and Ms. Larrick wouldn't hear of Puckett and me going back to the English Department by ourselves, and so, stifling giggles like a pack of high-school sophomores, the four of us clattered down the staircase of the Shoebox.

The outdoors was sobering. The wind had picked up a bit, and though the huge cloud banks had broken up, small clouds still sent shadows skittering across the landscape like fast-moving ghosts. And the yellow light of that afternoon was so intense it was almost palpable. "It's like Sauterne," I told Puckett while we stood there outside the dormitory, blinking. Before us was a small quadrangle of grass, criss-crossed by sidewalks and recently planted with pear and crabapple trees, wind-whipped as in a Van Gogh painting.

"Race you!" Susan said to me. She'd been jittery ever since we'd decided to end the party. Her eyes were wide, and her grin was a grimace. I took off running the instant she did. The spectacle I was making of myself did occur to me, an English professor sprinting across campus with the wind almost ripping his jacket and tie off his body; but the running was ecstasy. The first twenty yards or so I outdistanced Susan. Then my legs felt odd, as if they were suddenly aging. She caught up with me, so that only by exerting myself far beyond what I knew was good for me did I manage to touch the door of the English Department building before she did.

Gasping for breath, grinning at each other but unable to talk, Susan and I leaned against the brick walls and waited for Ms. Winters and Professor Puckett. When they walked up to us, they were shaking their heads in disapproval that was not entirely joking. Then discretion and common sense seemed to occur to all four of us, and we said quiet thanks and restrained good-byes before the young ladies turned back toward the Shoebox and Puckett and I headed upstairs to our offices. He and I could hardly face each other. When we'd retrieved our briefcases and topcoats and come back downstairs, I knew he was just as relieved as I was to be alone for the walk home.

My dread of facing Marie was wasted energy. She'd left me a note asking me to get supper started and reminding me of a neighborhood pre-trick-or-treat meeting she had agreed to attend. I was dicing carrots and humming along with the radio when she came in, full of news about who had said what at the meeting. All evening, taking my turn to hand out expensive little candy bars to trick-or-treaters, I felt as smug as a man who's found money in the street. What remained in my mind for many days afterward was not anything that happened in the Shoebox room (which almost anyone else would have construed to be the "good stuff") but running shoulder to shoulder with Susan through the yellow light of that windy afternoon.

Puckett and I never talked about Ms. Winters and Ms. Larrick's Halloween party, but around each other I think we were both embarrassed by the memory of it. And we were both aware of having stepped back from the afternoon's intimacy among the four of us. Cold weather set in earlier than usual that year. Nixon's landslide re-election had provoked a "winter of the consciousness" in the university community. When Susan came into my office one afternoon to tell me her father had announced his plan to divorce her mother, it seemed to me news in the spirit of national events. Kissinger seemed on the verge of negotiating a peace at the same time that we were heavily bombing the North Vietnamese. The troops were coming home, but the Watergate scandal was breaking open like rotten timbers in an old house. Susan's dad had taken up residence with his receptionist; Susan's fifteen-year-old sister, whom she claimed to be "the only decent one in the whole god damn family," was expelled from school for being drunk in homeroom. On April Fools' Day, the last American prisoners of war were released in Hanoi, and Susan brought me in a letter from her mother asking her to withdraw from the university and come home "to help out."

Although Marie and I were carrying on the most quotidian lives in our little two-bedroom apartment, the world beyond our front door battered us in ways we weren't aware of; we suffered a kind of invisible damage. Like most educated men and women, we needed to make sense of our lives, needed to understand our tiny places in the larger scheme of history. Thirty hours a week Marie did social work in a nursing home, helping old people as best she could, and I taught poetry-writing to twenty-year-olds. What did our petty little jobs mean in connection with the resignation, at the end of April, of four members of the staff of the president of the United States?

Marie is a tall woman with crow black hair and such a presence that people often rudely stare at her, but back then I found myself looking straight through her, talking with her and immediately forgetting what we'd said. I had lost track of myself, too. Almost nothing I said or did interested me. I had stopped showing Marie the little bit of poetry I was writing. We were this standard American couple grabbing toast and coffee in our apartment before we went to work. If one or the other of us happened to glance at a newspaper headline, it might stall us out for ten minutes at a time, not so much reading the story in detail as trying to figure out what planet we were standing on.

Susan Larrick asked me to write her mom a note saying she should at least finish out the semester at the university. I did that, but as I composed my little argument, I kept wondering if one thing might not be as good as another—Susan going home to hand her mom

Kleenexes or staying at the university to read Ezra Pound, what difference did it make?

The springtime that came to us that year was unmerciful. Here in the upper regions of the northeast, spring is usually a weatherman's notion of black humor. "Mud Season" is the polite name for three relentless months of slush, chilly rain, constant mist, and soggy gray-green ground. Not so in 1973. We might have believed we were on the coast of South Carolina, the way the balmy breezes caressed our faces when we went outside, and the tulips, daffodils, hyacinths, and lilacs turned promiscuous that summer. A university campus in that kind of weather goes "a little sweetly crazy," as I phrased it to Puckett. (I'd been composing in my mind as I walked up to the office that morning.) Puckett and I had just scurried into the building, having witnessed more than we could stand of America's upper-middle-class youth cavorting outdoors in shorts and T-shirts. "Speaking of springtime images, did you see Nixon's face on the front of your newspaper this morning?" I asked him as we walked up the steps, and he laughed much louder than the remark warranted. When we reached Puckett's office, Candace Winters, in a white sundress, was waiting for him.

The change in weather brought a hard season to Marie and me. That spring she knew she wanted to start having children—right away—and I was more certain than ever that I wasn't ready to be a parent. In fact I was wondering how much longer I was going to be able to stand being married. I wasn't romantically inclined toward anybody else, and I supposed that if I had to be married, Marie was a better wife for me than anyone else I knew. But something was driving me crazy about that apartment when I'd walk home through those gorgeous afternoons. Marie wouldn't even be there when I'd come indoors to our composed living room, our coffee table with the day's newspaper and two stacks of magazines, our wedding-gift lamps, pictures of our parents, and our combined collections of records. Something in me wanted to start pitching things through the windows.

One particularly luxurious early evening, Marie came back from a downtown shopping expedition looking as stricken as I'd ever seen her. She didn't even return my "hello, darling,' or come to the kitchen counter where I was working. She stood in the kitchen doorway and studied me from that distance. "I saw Scott and some student," she told me as if accusing me of betrayal. "Yes?" I said, perfectly casually, but I knew what she'd seen and knew how it had affected her. "Something's going on," she said. When I met her eyes, she knew that I knew what she was talking about. "Tell me about it," she said.

I told her the truth, that I hadn't wanted to suspect anything but that in spite of myself I did. It was odd discussing the Pucketts and Ms. Winters with Marie, because as I realized then, I'd wanted to have her opinion all along. The talk was charged. It was my night to cook, and I didn't get dinner on the table until almost nine o'clock. By then it was dark outside. Marie lit candles, I suggested opening a bottle of Beaujolais I'd been saving, and so we picked up the flatware I'd put out and reset the table with our wedding silver. It was one of the most tender evenings we'd shared in a long while; but when I handed her her brandy, Marie shivered and said, "Frank, do you think we're celebrating the end of the Pucketts' marriage?"

"Of course we're not doing that," I told her, but I couldn't think of what else to say to reassure her.

There was a phase in which Candace and Scott were seen frequently together in public. In the English Department hallways my colleagues and I talked ravenously about them. People assume scandalous things go on all the time in English departments, but for years, apparently, ours hadn't had so much as a stolen kiss. Now there was an associate professor holding hands at a poetry reading with a voluptuous student. That spring, Ms. Winters had become round and rosy, so sultry in her movements that I knew I wasn't the only one who'd considered running a hand down her back just the way you'd stroke a longhaired cat. As if to show the entire university they weren't hiding any longer, Professor Puckett and Ms. Winters started taking bag lunches out to the quadrangle in the noon hour. When we looked out our office windows and saw the two of them together out there, we understood the power of biology or of romance, depending on how we thought about such things.

The way Marie thought about them was with increasing anger. She visibly seethed the afternoon of the English majors' party, to which all the faculty spouses were invited and most attended. Sally Puckett's absence was conspicuous; Sally had always had a pretty good time in previous years of this party, and I know I wasn't the only one who missed the sound of that Texas accent loudly riding over the other voices in the room. You could almost tell that Scott Puckett and Candace Winters had taken vows to stay away from each other during this party but that they were finding it difficult. They stood by the hors d'oeuvres table, a yard apart, but watching each other eat little blocks of cheese. "I'll swear to God!" Marie snorted under her breath at me and strode away from me.

As Ms. Winters blossomed that spring, Ms. Larrick seemed to undergo a shriveling of the spirit. She was able to persuade her mother to let her finish the semester at the university, but she was no longer able to joke about it. She remained on speaking terms with Candace, but her own parents' divorce made her unable to take any joy in Candace's having snared the affections of Professor Puckett. Susan gained weight and took on a bad color. I didn't see her much; though a couple of times, when I went out into the hallway, I found her wandering around out there with her jacket collar turned up as if to hide her face. The second time, I made her come into my office and sit down. She requested a Kleenex and blew her nose forcefully. Then, as if she were bored and impatient, she said, "Whaddaya want?" I just looked at her; as I did so, her eyes welled up and tears began splattering her jacket front. I tried getting her to talk, but she would only stare at her lap and shake her head. I called the university counseling service, set up an appointment for her, and walked her over there.

And as Professor Puckett and Ms. Winters drew the forces of that outrageous springtime into their lives, Marie and I felt a gradual diminishing of the pleasure we took in each other's company. Our dinners were filled with uneasy silences. Marie spent many hours with Sally Puckett, and although at first she had shared her impressions of "how Sally was taking it" with me, she came to say less and less about what she and Sally had done or said. Agnew was much in the news those days; his jowly face seemed a cruel joke visited upon us in our time of personal difficulty.

Susan Larrick's therapist advised her to continue talking with me. We were both relieved that now when she came to my office, we were carrying out an officially approved task. Susan's mood was darker than I'd imagined. She gave me to understand that she had been suicidally inclined enough to persuade the university's counseling service to pass her along to a private therapist. This therapist was encouraging Susan not to sever the ties she'd established with her university friends, but Susan still wasn't able to bear the company of Candace Winters.

The last week of school Susan and I met each day for at least an hour. I felt privileged to be allowed access to so much of Susan's inner life, and in thinking that these talks were helping her, I felt the smug pleasure of a do-gooder. But a bond was being forged between us that made me somewhat uneasy. Susan and I had begun to understand each other and to communicate at a very subtle level. That intimacy made my life with Marie even more painfully absurd in those days of our barely being able to smile when we said good-bye to each other before we went to work.

I still think of that spring as having been hexed. In mid-May Susan told me that Bea Thackston had asked her to stay a couple of weeks to tend the plants in the apartment she and Kelly were renting. Though I was aware of Susan's mother's desperately wanting her to come home, I didn't question that arrangement. I knew Bea and Kelly were getting married that summer; I knew they planned to move things from both their dormitory rooms into the apartment. Then Marie informed me that the following weekend she intended to fly down to Boston with Sally Puckett. Though she told me very little about what she and Sally planned to do in Boston, I didn't question Marie because obviously, if I chose to resist the idea, she stood ready to argue with me. As I remember it, my thinking then was that Marie had taken on a kind of generalized husband-anger— I remember thinking up a German word for it, *Übermanngeraucht*, or something like that. I knew that it behooved me not to give her any cause for moving from the general sentiment to a specific fury toward me.

Marie allowed me to take her to the airport, but I gummed up the occasion of our good-bye hug by saying, "Maybe things will be better for us when you get back." Marie pushed away from me, gave me a look, and opened her mouth to speak. Though the words never came forth, I heard them anyway: "Don't count on it." Well, at least I still understood her well enough to know her unspoken sentences.

In the airport parking lot I felt like a neutralized man. Airports conspire to genericize human experience anyway; and in this case I was an exemplary victim, your basic citizen climbing into his basic car having put his basic wife on the plane to Boston with her basic friend. I felt empty of emotion or personality or consequential thought.

With Marie in the apartment, I enjoyed solitude, the kind available to me in my study with her in the living room listening to public radio or working the crossword puzzle from the *Times* Sunday magazine. With Marie out of the apartment, I felt a lonesomeness like the constant high whine of a violin note. I tried reading, listening to records and then the radio, tried every channel on the TV several times, opened a bottle of good burgundy and finally had a couple of brandies. I never was able to settle down and relax. All through the early morning hours, I kept waking, aware of Marie's absence in the bed. Late Saturday morning, when I finally did haul myself out of the sack, I felt exhausted and headachy. Then, opening the drapes, I faced one of those mean windy rains slashing at the trees and shrubs.

It takes superior inner resources to get through a rainy Saturday in a four-room apartment by yourself. The baseball games on TV were all rained out; you'd have thought rain was battering the entire United States of America. The public TV station was doing a Nixon story, showing photos of his boyhood and college years, playing the old speeches, and so on. I sat there and gawked at the image of Nixon lifting his hand to be sworn into office as Eisenhower's vice-president. I felt utterly absorbed by what I was seeing; as my personality diminished, Nixon's seemed to be swelling before my eyes.

All through the day I hung around the apartment, hoping Marie would call. By six I knew she and Sally would be heading out to eat in one of the Boston restaurants. I envisioned the two of them, dressed up and enjoying the looks they'd be getting from city men. I put on my slicker and went downtown, took a sandwich at a bar, had a glass of the house wine at one place and then another. Whenever my eyes met someone else's, the other person looked away quickly. I knew despair must have been on my face. All the more troubling was what a cheap brand of despair it was: I was no returned Vietnam vet, burdened by all the buddies he'd lost in battle and the Asians whose ears he'd cut off; I was just a husband who couldn't get through a day or two without his wife. At ten o'clock, I lost conviction and went home.

From the foyer I heard our phone ringing. I rushed unlocking the door and ran to answer it, certain that Marie was calling from a pay phone in some theater lobby. It was Susan, calling from her borrowed apartment. "I'm scared, Frank," she said. "I've been trying to get you for hours. I'm really scared. There's this noise."

I wish I could say I was disappointed that it wasn't Marie calling. The fact is I was probably happier that it was Susan—Susan calling me by my first name, she needed me and wanted my company in an hour in which circumstances had forced me into such a devaluation of myself that I felt almost invisible. I didn't quiz Susan. I told her I'd be there in a minute or two. I hung up, turned the light out by the phone, walked back out of the apartment, and locked the door.

Though Bea and Kelly's apartment was only five blocks up the hill, I drove the car there; and though it didn't seem unusual at the time, it does seem so now as I think back over that rainy night. As clearly as if it had been a film, a vision came to me of Scott Puckett entering an apartment where Candace Winters was living. So far as I knew, at the end of the semester Candace had gone home to her parents' house in Montgomery Center, and so this fantasy of mine was all the more untoward: Candace was in Puckett's arms before he'd even gotten the door shut behind him. He was slipping the nightgown off her pale shoulders, following it with his mouth down her chest. That was the kind of thing I was witnessing mentally— while the windshield wipers slapped the rain this way and that—and I strained to see the entrance to the parking lot behind the apartment building. I remember chiding myself to "stop it" and forcing myself out of the car and into the heavy rain so as not to sit there and carry on my lewd imaginings.

In an old bathrobe pulled tightly around her waist, Susan met me at the door and backed quickly into the shadow of the little foyer when I stepped into the apartment. She led the way to the living room where a single lamp burned on a low table. "I feel silly now that you're here," she said. The calmness of her voice made me immediately understand that on the phone she'd been exaggerating about how scared she was. I didn't mind. I smiled at her.

"Listen," she said, cocking her head. I was relieved that she wasn't lying about there being a noise. But it wasn't hard to locate the source of it—a tree branch brushing against the window of the small bedroom in which Bea and Kelly had stored boxes of their things. (Or perhaps Susan had pushed all their boxes in there to clear the other room for her living quarters.) I called Susan to come in there and look out the window. When I pointed to the waving branch, she said, "Oh yeah!" in such a forced way that I knew it wasn't a revelation to her.

"I *was* scared," she murmured.

"I believe you," I said. I did my best to make up a kind of generalized fear Susan might have experienced that she couldn't have described for me in any literal way.

I was following Susan's broad back into the living room when she turned and made a gesture with one hand that I remember with extraordinary vividness through all these years. It was a curving, ripple-fingered rise and fall of her hand that conveyed a history of her many hours spent arranging everything in the room so that I would see it in just that certain way.

A packing crate was her bedside table. She had purchased bookends that were miniatures of the "Thinker" bookends I used for special books on my desk at school. Copies I had absentmindedly given her of the little journals that had printed poems of mine were aligned with books I had recommended to her—the Williams *Selected Poems*, the Roethke *Words for the Wind*, a couple of thin volumes of Sylvia Plath's poems, and Baker's biography of Hemingway. Blotner's two-volume biography of Faulkner was on the floor as a kind of step up to the table. I knew enough of Susan's financial circumstance to know that buying such books had been no casual matter for her. The picture taped on the wall at the other side of the bed was of Marianne Moore and Muhammed Ali sitting at a restaurant table; where she'd gotten that photograph I couldn't imagine, but I clearly remembered telling her the anecdote that I'd read about somewhere, of Ali's insisting that he and Miss Moore work on a poem together when they met at Toots Shor's.

I know that I stood there with Susan for quite a while, letting my feelings evolve as they would. In a way it was devastating to be made to see what an overwhelming effect I'd had on Susan, and though it played on my vanity considerably, her arrangement of these effects also demonstrated the paltriness of my offerings to her. What she must have thought to be a grand education I now saw to be a small portion of what she'd need to get her through the years that were coming to her. What in God's name did I think Williams and Plath and Roethke and Hemingway and Faulkner had to say that would be of use to Susan? Especially in the light of that little table lamp on the crate by Susan's books, I saw what a wretched life I had made for Marie and me—how I had failed to make any happiness for us in our marriage and had instead taken us both to a point of mere sullenness with each other. What had the books that I claimed to love done for me, and what right did I have to teach anyone anything?

It seemed to me that the only thing to do was to leave Susan's apartment, go walk in the rain all night, and in the morning type up my resignation from my teaching position at the university. It came to me that what a man like myself should be doing for a vocation was deliver the mail. I needed to be functional but not to be in any position to have an influence on people. When I turned toward the dark foyer and the door, I felt Susan's hand touch my forearm. "Don't go yet," she said in a voice that in my coldest moment I wouldn't have been able to refuse.

She walked heavily into the kitchen and in a moment came back with two opened bottles of beer. She handed me one of them, went to her bed, sat down, and directed me to the one chair in the room, by the desk in the opposite corner. In silence, we both drank for a while. It amused me somewhat to observe how our postures suggested a couple of workers taking a break on a construction site. Then she put her bottle down, crossed her arms in front of her, looked at me and said, "I want you to stay here with me tonight." It was not a romantic request, she clearly conveyed that. There was in her voice something so straightforward that she might have been asking to borrow a sum of money.

"I can't" were the first words that occurred to me because they would have been appropriate on almost every previous night of my acquaintance with Susan. I sat there not saying those words, knowing that if I did say them, Susan was ready to ask me why not. In one corner of my brain I was trying to figure out how Susan knew that Marie was out of town. The only answer I could come up with was that the information had come to her by way of Candace whom Scott would have told because Sally and Marie were traveling together; that made me wonder if in fact Candace was in town somewhere and if she and Scott were carrying out carnal adventures in somebody else's apartment at that very moment. I felt a chill. I was about to stand up and say something like "I'm sorry, Susan, it's just impossible" when Susan lifted her hand and opened her palm to me. She held it like that only for an instant, but the effect on me was dizzying, as if she had lifted a shroud in my brain: I knew that I could stay with her and that there would be nothing carnal about it. "All

256

right," I started to say. Then I understood that I didn't even have to say that. She was grinning ever so slightly, in that way of hers, and so I grinned back.

Susan left her bathrobe on, and I kept my pants and T-shirt on. It wasn't an easy night's sleep, though we curled around each other in ways that were comforting. Still, we weren't used to each other that way. I kept waking, and whenever I did, I saw that she was awake, too. But we made it all the way through until daylight, and when we climbed stiffly out of that little bed, it was as if we'd taken a long bus ride to somewhere we both wanted to go and now we had gotten there.

Susan fixed us coffee and juice. (I said I didn't want pancakes or toast.) We chatted at the kitchen table for a while, and then I said I'd better go home. At the door we kissed awkwardly as if years ago we had been lovers.

That Sunday afternoon when Marie came home (Sally having given her a ride from the airport), I heard her steps in the foyer and met her at the door. I meant only to help her with her luggage, but when I saw her face, I knew immediately that something had changed; where before she left I'd seen simmering rage, now I saw longing and regret. I still don't know if the change was in her facial expression or in my perception of it. And whatever else the results of my night with Susan meant, it seemed to have eliminated my ability to mask my feelings in the presence of Marie. We could hardly get ourselves inside the door fast enough. Even now, fifteen years distant from that afternoon, I still remember exactly how we moved from the overheated foyer into the cool shadows of our apartment, how I carried Marie's suitcase with one hand and with the other pulled her by both her hands, laughing, behind me into the bedroom.

That summer of 1973, Scott Puckett had me help him move his belongings out of his house; Sally wasn't there, and I didn't know if it was something they'd agreed on or if Scott meant to be sneaking his stuff out in her absence. At any rate he moved into an apartment on the other side of town; before he and I had got everything un-loaded from the rental truck and moved indoors, Candace Winters was there with a bag of groceries, offering us cold beer from a six-pack. I think Scott was a little embarrassed at how familiar she was with him and me and the new apartment. As usual, though, he had little to say. Candace was chipper, I'll say that much, as well she should have been, knowing the future as she did: she and Scott have a real pistol of a daughter, almost ten years old now.

Scott Puckett is still my good friend, but here in our middle age, we've both given up squash; so even if we wanted to, there's little occasion for us to talk. That old history that gave us what lives we have now is this undiscussed subject between us; it is what holds Puckett and me close at the same time it keeps the distance between us.

If Scott or Candace were telling this story, they'd probably be saying what a pistol of a son Marie and I have. They'd mean the fourteen year old, Steve, who in my opinion is more of punji pit than a pistol: With him it's not a shoot-out in the street, it's guerrilla warfare. Of all the difficult human beings I've known in my forty-five years, Steve is the most difficult by a factor of three or four. He's smart enough, though, that when I'm ready to kill him, he's gotten Marie on his side enough to defend him, and when she's ready to kill him, he's gotten my sympathy. If the kid ever gums up his timing and gets both of us mad at him at the same time, he'd better barricade himself in that wasteland of a room of his. Our other boy, Charles, is eight, and his main project is making his older brother look bad; thus Charles maintains a pretty clean image around here, but it's clear he's taking instruction from Steve as to what he can expect to get away with as an adolescent.

I keep on receiving instruction about how kids anchor us into our lives. Just the other day, Marie got a letter from Sally Puckett, now Sally Dalton, remarried and living in Austin, Texas. She wrote to Marie that she's finally been able to forgive Scott, because even though he didn't mean to, he let her go home. She enclosed school pictures of a kindergartner and a second-grader. "And to think," she wrote, "I used to be so certain I didn't want kids! Tell Frank I feel like I've finally been granted tenure or something."

Susan Larrick Parisi has begun learning all this, having just become the mother of a hefty little boy, one Michael Joseph Parisi. In her letter to me giving me the news, she says, "We would have named him Frank, after you, except that I never got used to calling you by your first name anyway, and I could hardly name him Professor Berry, now could I?" Susan met Paul Parisi when she moved out west, and they lived together for years, finally getting married a year or two after Susan's father died. Paul is now in his second year of coaching the football team and teaching phys. ed. at Columbia High School. Susan herself is taking a leave of absence from her job—teaching four sections of freshman English a semester at Portland State, where, as I say, I've been invited to speak.

This little topic I've worked up, "The Place of Creative Writing in the Study of Literature," turns out to be attractive to college and university English departments that like the idea of literature still being the most important item they have to offer. In it I talk at some length about how differently students come to understand what is commonly called "symbolism" once they try to engineer some symbolism of their own in their stories and poems.

The example I use is the hypothetical one of a student who would write a poem about the Vietnam War: With only a crude understanding of literature and symbolism, the student might very well use a rose, an eagle, or a sledgehammer as his or her imagery. And what a good creative writing class might teach this student would be how to look into the subject matter itself for a more natural kind of symbolism; thus, a helicopter, say a UH-1, might become an image suggesting both assault and flight. I will call to my audience's mind the last American helicopter's departure from the embassy rooftop in Saigon, will lift my hand upward in the gesture of the abandoned ones who failed to scramble aboard. If I find that audience out west especially responsive—and I hope Susan will have found a babysitter so that she can attend my little talk—I may go on to mention the helicopter that whisked Nixon away from Washington after his resignation in August of 1974. If I am feeling especially loquacious, I will speak of Nixon's retreat to his California mansion, Ford's pardoning him for all federal crimes that he "committed or may have committed." I will demonstrate how the helicopter might be used as a symbol for the flight from responsibility for one's actions. "What do you suppose," I will ask my audience, "the American people made of the sight of their highest elected official—the father of the nation, so to speak—boarding that aircraft?" (Actually, now that I am entertaining this scenario, I think I prefer for Susan to bring the infant Michael with her to my presentation.) "Do you remember, before he flew away, how Nixon turned and smiled and waved, as if he'd just done something marvelous for us?" I will ask, and of course I will lift my hand and wave.

From *Intimates* (1992)

Little Sawtooth

M Y   L I V I N G   R O O M is twelve feet wide and twenty-five feet long; it feels both large and cozy. I work there in the hours just before and after dawn, the hours when my wife and daughters sleep most deeply in the bedrooms upstairs. Since my laptop computer screen is lighted, I don't have to turn on any lamps. I write while sitting on the sofa with the fireplace opposite me and the empty wing chairs facing me as if they held ghosts whose duty is to watch me struggle with my early morning compositions.

More and more, my writing has caused me to examine my past— or maybe more accurately, my past has begun to examine *me*. Surprising things have come back to me for no discernible reason.

Someone I knew at the University of Idaho twenty-two years ago has been paying me some memory calls this past month. She's a woman I knew from what was a particularly harsh period for me, the beginning of my separation from my first wife. I was finding living alone almost unbearable, but I was afflicted with Recent Divorcee's Syndrome, the symptoms of which are simultaneous desire and hostility. It's a good thing I'd enrolled in graduate school, because anything more structured than that would have had me committing crimes of violence.

Michelle Gonyaw was the young woman with whom I fell into acquaintanceship. She, too—though it took me a while to see it— was a case-study in pain that year. I of course thought I was the only human being on the planet who'd ever been so severely singed by love. After our Whitman-and-Crane seminar was over each Tuesday and Thursday afternoon, I'd catch up with Michelle and chat with her while we walked toward town. Actually I was doing most of the talking and most of it about myself, but of course that's not what I thought I was doing. And she wasn't friendly either, which is probably why I persisted.

A few years younger than I was, Michelle dressed in the plainest, darkest, loosest clothes she could find and kept her black hair cut short. She tried to make herself invisible, but people noticed her any-way—I did at the very first meeting of our seminar. She couldn't hide her big violet eyes and her skin that was the lightest I've ever seen on a healthy person. At the time I took pride in not being sexually attracted to her—I just thought she was odd and probably an out-cast like me—but my guess now is that her way of presenting herself allowed me to be sexually attracted to her without my realizing it.

"You know you dress like a god damn nun," I told her one after-noon, walking toward town. That was the tone I used with her most of the time.

She snorted, the first time she'd shown any sign of being amused by me. "Yes," she said. "That's exactly what I am, a god damn—a god *damned* nun."

I looked at her while we walked, but she didn't say anything else. After a while I said, "That's a mystifying thing to say."

She shrugged, which marked the end of our conversation for that afternoon.

But I persisted, and though she remained detached in her attitude toward me, Michelle did begin to let me accompany her inside her apartment. I had to ask her if I could come in; after she stopped saying no to that, then I had to ask her if I could have a cup of tea. Later on I even got to where I'd ask her if maybe she had a sandwich or something to eat. But the point is that she obliged me—usually with a shrug, as if she didn't care whether or not I came in with her, or whether or not she had to put the water on to boil or to make a sandwich.

Our acquaintanceship proceeded just this way for months. I did all the talking and most of the tea-drinking and sandwich-eating, while Michelle sat at her kitchen table and stared out the window. I got used to seeing how the fall light—and then the winter light—shone over her hacked-off black hair and her pale face on which there was never a trace of makeup.

One Thursday afternoon in Michelle's apartment kitchen, while she was staring out her window, I asked her if I could borrow a stamp. Not even glancing at me, she told me to go into her living room where I'd find one in her top desk drawer. I took that as a sign of her getting used to me, letting me rummage in her stuff like that, and I'll confess I was more than a little curious about what she'd have in her desk. A minute later she walked into the room where I was absentmindedly holding this pair of glasses in my hands and looking at them.

When I glanced up at her, I couldn't imagine what was wrong. She stood sort of tilted forward with her mouth gaped. Still, it might not have come to anything except that I noticed what her eyes were focussed on. "Michelle, whose glasses are these?" I asked her.

She spun back toward the kitchen door, but she didn't walk out of the room. Instead, she put her face in her hands. I set the glasses down on her desk, walked over to her, and almost put my hand on her shoulder. I didn't of course, but I was surprised that she even continued to stand that near me because nothing I'd seen in her up to that point had indicated that she had it in her to cry like that or to let anyone give her comfort.

"What's the deal here, Michelle?" I asked her. She shook her head. But then she said, "Yes, I'll tell you. But not right now. Please." In another moment, she moved away from me—not rudely but just in a this-has-gone-on-long-enough kind of way. She walked over to her desk, picked up the glasses, returned them to the drawer, and turned back to me, by which I understood her to mean that she wanted me to leave her alone.

"So I'll come by for you tonight," I said on my way out. She didn't say anything. "We'll go get a drink," I said with the door open. She didn't say anything. "Around ten," I said from the hallway. She shrugged. I took that to mean that she'd go with me, and I shut the door behind me.

That was the beginning of phase two of our acquaintanceship. We started walking down to the Moscow Hotel for drinks around ten or eleven almost every night. And Michelle started telling me about the glasses. Again, I had to be the one who made it happen. I'd show up at her door and knock—but then it wouldn't take her long to get ready to go. At the hotel bar, when we had our table in the corner and our drinks in front of us, I'd ask her a question, and she'd start talking. If she stopped, I'd ask her another question. Sometimes I wanted her to go on, and sometimes it was fine with me for her to stop and let me think about what she'd told me. It took quite a few nights to get the whole story out of her.

From Spirit Lake, north of Coeur d'Alene, where she'd grown up, Michelle had gone to college down in Boise. She wanted to be a teacher. She had what she thought of as a standard liberal arts education until her senior year when she signed up to take English History from a new instructor, just out of graduate school at the University of North Carolina. He had all these fancy fellowships—and had even studied at Cambridge University in England—but Professor Hammett Wilson had never taught any classes before he showed up for his first one at Boise State.

He spoke about English history the way revivalist preachers talk about Jesus, except that instead of repeating everything three or four times and shouting and carrying on, Hammett Wilson was brilliantly articulate. Michelle said he'd be broken out in a sweat, pacing the floor and gesturing, but he'd be speaking with this incredible lucidity and precision.

According to Michelle, he wasn't anything special to look at, a man of medium height and build, average taste in clothes, brown eyes, brown hair that fell over his forehead, and glasses, which he wore all the time, except when he lectured. Michelle said you could almost hear the whole class exhaling when Hammett Wilson set all his books and notes down on the desk, stood up straight, smiled at them, and took off his glasses.

What happened between Hammett Wilson and Michelle Gonyaw was that one morning when he took his glasses off to begin lecturing, he was looking straight into Michelle's eyes. He seemed to want to look away but to be unable to manage it for a long moment. For the rest of the class Michelle felt paralyzed. Hammett took up the lecture in his normal manner, except that again and again his eyes came back to Michelle's. At the end of class, he walked over to her desk to ask her to stop by his office that afternoon. He hadn't even learned her name, so that he had to ask her that—"Sometime after two o'clock, Miss—?"

Michelle said she knew she shouldn't have gone, but she had no more choice about it than she did about taking her next breath. She knew Hammett was married. He was the kind of man who, even though he'd been in town only a couple of months, had taken his wife and two young boys with him to everything on campus that might be of interest to a new teacher. Michelle had been raised a Catholic. She said that in the student union snack bar she sat alone like a hypnotized person until two o'clock. When she stood up to walk over to Hammett's office, she knew her old life was over.

His door was open, but she knocked anyway, standing just inside the threshold. He'd been looking out the window with his back to the door. When she heard her, he stood up and turned. They stayed like that a moment or two, until he finally stepped around behind her to close the door. Michelle wouldn't spell it out for me, but I gather that he let his hand brush across her shoulders when he turned back from the closed door.

"What he mostly did was whisper—because the walls of his office were so thin," she said. "But it was very intense whispering. He liked to have long talks like that, the two of us standing there holding each other, whispering with our mouths almost touching each other's ears." Michelle said she thought it was strange, but she didn't mind it.

She also said, "I was the one of us who was more physically aggressive," meaning me to understand, I think, that she wasn't some innocent country girl who had let herself be seduced.

But I think nothing much more than whispering, kissing and maybe a little touching happened in that office. How many times she visited him there is not clear to me, but I doubt if it was very many. No one suspected them of anything. It was still early enough in the fall for them to think about taking a drive out Sunset Peak Road toward the National Forest.

Having been a member of the Outing Club since her freshman year, Michelle had come to know that mountainous countryside between Boise and Sun Valley. About fifty miles out of Boise, there was a place called Little Sawtooth Falls that she wanted Hammett to see. Michelle considered it her own private park. She had the idea they could talk there in their normal voices.

That second week of October Hammett's wife had taken their two boys to visit her sister in Portland. When Hammett told Michelle that his family was leaving him at home for a couple of days, both of them were quick to say that it wouldn't do for Michelle to visit his house.

The arrangement they worked out was that after his Thursday afternoon class, Hammett would walk from his office a few blocks over to a shopping center parking lot where Michelle would wait for him. Her aunt and uncle had just given her a second-hand car for her birthday because they'd promised her one if she wouldn't smoke or drink until she was twenty-one.

I was amazed that anybody could get to be twenty-one without smoking or drinking, but Michelle just shook her head at me and muttered, "I never thought about it. It wasn't hard." I raised my glass to her, she raised hers to me, and we toasted the young woman she had been.

Thursday worked out just as they had wanted it; they even got warm, sunny weather for their trip. When he reached the parking lot, Hammett looked all around to make certain no one he knew was there before he stepped into Michelle's car. To keep from being seen while she drove out of Boise, he lay down in the seat with his head in her lap. Michelle said that was the part of it that later hurt her the worst to remember, driving her car with the weight of Hammett's head on her right thigh.

She said that as she drove, they talked, mostly about their families and the way they had been brought up, Hammett an only child in Chevy Chase, Maryland, and Michelle the second of five children in Spirit Lake. His mother worked for the Department of Interior, his father for the Justice Department; her father, with two of her uncles, ran the biggest building supplies business in northern Idaho. So much did Michelle like the talking with Hammett that she asked him not to sit up even after they were well out of town. That way, she didn't think he'd notice when she started driving slower to make the trip last longer.

Little Sawtooth Falls was a tiny park tucked away in the side of a fair-sized mountain. The state had put up only a couple of small signs marking the turnoffs to it and had cleared out a ten-space parking area. When they stepped out of the car and stretched in the warm air, it was just as Michelle had thought it would be; they had the park to themselves. Hammett came around to her side, grinning at her. A small sign pointed toward the path to the falls. She touched his arm and turned him in that direction. They walked slowly out of the late afternoon sunlight into the deep Aspen shade and the smell of the mountain water.

The path wound along a stream that a rock formation prevented them from seeing, but the stream's noise grew louder as they moved through the trees. They descended a set of stone steps to a small wooden bridge. Standing there in the middle of the bridge and looking back up the way they'd come, the whole of Little Sawtooth Falls opened up to them, this immense, narrow chasm through which water billowed in tiers down to a pool spilling over right at eye level, then plunging to another deep green pool immediately below the bridge. Sunlight shafted through the trees; mist rose from the white water and the pools; high walls of gray rock jutted up to the sky.

For long minutes they stood there, Hammett just smiling and looking around them and she pretending to look down at the water, but mostly sneaking looks at him.

In noticing his glasses, she remembered how alive he was in class without them; so she reached up to take them off him. He seemed very boyish to her then. Hammett smiled at her and said she'd have to help him navigate.

Hammett's depending on her to help him move appealed to Michelle. She put his glasses in her skirt pocket, took his hand, and led him up the path on the other side of the bridge. Over there was a steep set of stone steps leading to a single bench where they could sit, where they could see the bridge and the stream far below them winding down through the trees and rocks away from the falls. The bench was a quirky fixture, something a ranger might have put up on his own because he'd decided that spot would be the ideal place to sit and study Little Sawtooth Falls. In front of Hammett and Michelle, maybe fifteen yards away, a powerful column of water caught the last sunlight of the day in a cloud of rising mist.

That bench was one reason why Michelle claimed a spiritual ownership of the place: Every other time she'd come to Little Sawtooth Falls, it had been unoccupied. Sitting there with Hammett was utterly natural to her; in no place in the world would she have felt more at home. She joked with him that this was her office, and now she was holding office hours.

With their talking and stopping to kiss and touch each other, the time passed without their noticing it. Hammett didn't have to be back home, because his family was in Portland. And Michelle's suitemates might have wondered where she was, but even if she did still live in a dorm, she was a senior and could do what she wanted. She figured her suitemates would be delighted if she stayed out late for the first time since they'd known her.

The light very slowly sifted up out of the woods around them, so that when they first noticed it, they were softly encased in a deep blue grayness, but they could look up through the leaves and limbs and still see a lighted sky. They were pleased with themselves for having forgotten about time. The darkness brought them still closer to each other.

She kept thinking that she was embarrassed by what they began to do, but instead of holding her back, the embarrassment fueled her desire to go further, to do more. It wasn't something either one of them would have even thought possible, but somehow they managed to have intercourse on that bench. This wasn't easy for her to tell me about—there was a lot of stopping on her part and a lot of questioning from me, but finally she made it clear to me how things went. It was Michelle's first real sex, and though aroused, she wasn't as satisfied by it as apparently Hammett was. But she was able to give herself over to the deep twilight, the sound of the water, the smell of the woods, the absolute aloneness and intimacy of the two of them.

When they stood up to leave, they realized they might as well have been blind. No light came from the sky, from the water, from the road, no light came from anywhere: it was the darkest kind of dark.

The situation was funny to them, a little trick they'd played on themselves—or rather a trick desire had played on them. When they started inching their way down the hill in the direction of the bridge, they were holding onto each other's hands and even giggling nervously. Their feet hadn't located the stone steps that had brought them up there—those steps had probably been set by hand into the mountainside by the ranger who'd installed the bench in the first place, but that ranger had probably never imagined two people getting themselves stuck up there in the dark.

Hammett was in front, stepping gingerly and teasing Michelle about having stolen his glasses. She was teasing him back, saying that if he had them, he'd just be worse off because it would only mean that he'd have a clearer vision of the dark.

Michelle realized she was shivering; she knew some of it was because of that mountain coolness that rises up out of the ground. She also realized how all of her senses had opened up, so that she was like this night-blooming plant that had become sensitive to even the slightest current of air.

She was a little scared, but mostly she was excited by the adventure, by the sheer craziness of what she and Hammett were doing. Until recently, she could not have dreamed of moving through absolute dark in the company of a man with whom she'd just made love.

The sound of the water was clearly audible; all they had to do was slowly make their way down the slope in that direction; eventually they'd find the little bridge. Then the path up the other side would be easy.

While Michelle was imagining their coming down to the bridge, imagining the way their footsteps would sound on the flat wooden planks, Hammett's hand slipped out of hers.

Hammett hadn't spoken, hadn't made a sound; he was just suddenly gone.

Down the hill from her there was a little noise, a scraping like a foot sliding through loose dirt and rocks. Then from farther down the slope there came a slight brushing sound like a shoulder scraping the bark of a tree. That was it.

Michelle stood still a moment, listening. She called Hammett's name, softly at first, then louder. He wouldn't play a joke on her; if he wasn't answering, she knew he must be hurt. Fear was rising in her so that if she didn't do something to stop it, she was going to start shaking.

Getting down on her hands and knees, she crawled slowly in the direction she thought Hammett had fallen.

Almost immediately she came to a drop-off of about a foot and a half from one shelf of rock to another. Michelle encountered it with a hand reaching out and down into nothing until she was touching the ground with her shoulder. If she'd been walking, she'd have pitched forward off that shelf the same as Hammett had. So finding it that way made her feel both worse and better. She figured Hammett had knocked himself unconscious somewhere farther down the slope. That brought the fear rising back up in her. But she also figured that worming her way down the slope the way she was doing was probably safe and that going as she was, even if it took hours, finally she was sure to find him.

It did take hours—or it seemed like hours to Michelle. As she made her way downhill, the noise of the water kept getting louder. Finally she reached the top edge of a cliff-face that plummeted all the way to the water. By now she had been crawling through the dark, blind and alone and scared, for too long to be able to feel much of anything new. But when she stretched her arm down over the cliff-face, she said it was like that huge pit of rock opened up inside her. She backed away a couple of feet and lay down in the leaves and dirt, curled up tight.

Too cold to lie there any longer, she crawled back to the edge of the cliff, crawled in the upstream direction for a long way, then back in the downstream direction. When she reached the little wooden bridge, that was when she knew she had been holding onto this shred of a fantasy of finding Hammett sitting there, waiting for her.

By now she didn't know how much time had passed. She was shivering hard, sitting on the bridge, hunched over and hugging her scraped knees until it began raining. Figuring she might be in danger of going into hypothermia, she made herself stand up and start picking her way along the path back up toward the parked car.

It was just so easy to get from that bridge to her parked car. She hated how easy it was.

She'd been carrying her car keys in her skirt; taking them out, she remembered what she had in the other pocket. It hurt her whole body to remember Hammett's glasses, which she thought she could feel now, pressing ever so slightly against her upper thigh. She didn't touch them.

She got into her car, started it, turned on the heater, then sat there thinking. The clock said it was close to three. It kept raining. By the time she had warmed up enough to stop shivering, she had decided that whatever she did, it would have to be the right thing for Hammett. She tried to think what that would be. He'd avoided telling her much about his wife and children even though their pictures were on his desk and even though she'd asked him about them quite a few times. She wondered what that evasion meant—probably that he'd wanted to protect them from what he and Michelle were doing in his office. She took a deep breath and made herself think even harder about Hammett. It came to her then that he'd probably been afraid she'd want him to leave his family for her. She had a quick flash of hating him.

She wasn't sleepy, and she hoped she was thinking with a clear head. She had faced up to the likelihood that Hammett was dead, or at the very least, hurt badly. When daylight came, she'd go down there and find him.

Even after the inky blue world outside her windshield started lightening, she made herself wait longer, because she knew she'd need more than just a little bit of light. Still, the rain slowed daylight's coming; when she started down the path again, she couldn't see very far in front of her.

At the bridge there wasn't a lot she could do except stare down at the rock and water below it. The rain was soft and steady.

She made her way up the stone steps to the bench where only hours ago she and Hammett had sat. The rain had smoothed out the mud and leaves around the bench.

By guessing about what angle they would have started moving in, she found what she was pretty certain to be the rock ledge that had caused Hammett to pitch forward in the dark. She found some marks that looked like they were her knee prints from the crawling she'd done down the hill. When she came down to the side of the cliff, she couldn't see over it all the way to the bottom. Like the soul of a stone, a draft of cold air rose into her face.

Michelle wasn't about to give up. She walked downstream from the bridge until she discovered a path that led her to the water's edge. Moving beside the stream, she worked her way back toward the bridge, stepping on rocks and ledges, sometimes even wading in the foot-numbing water. "Step up here, stupid," she'd say, or, "Over there, over there!" She was aware of how tired her body was while her mind kept driving her.

She was able to maneuver herself under the bridge and all the way up to the edge of the pool where Hammett should have fallen. From that point, she was able to see all around several tiers of the falls and down into the water. Beneath the surface she saw no shape or shadow that could have been Hammett.

So she walked slowly back downstream, then up again to the bridge and from there to the parking lot and the car. She got in and started it. Now she put her hand in her skirt pocket to hold onto Hammett's glasses. There were no other cars in the parking lot; there wasn't another person around. Shivering, she sat for a while with one hand in her pocket and the other on the steering wheel. Finally she put the car into gear and headed back to school.

Around ten that morning she drove into her dormitory's parking lot. The building itself was almost empty; she saw no one who knew her by name. No one seemed to take note of her coming in, even though she was wet and her skirt was muddy. It was an hour in which almost everyone was in class; her suite was empty. When she unlocked her room—she had a single—and went in and closed the door, she stood listening to the silence, staring at the rainy light at her window. In a trance, she removed Hammett's glasses from her skirt pocket and set them in her desk drawer, at the front. Then she undressed and put on her robe. She had the shower to herself. She didn't come out until the water stopped stinging her scraped knees and palms. Back in her room, she lay down on the bed to wait.

Her mind darted in and out of sleep. She stayed where she was until well after dark. Then she dressed in her regular studying clothes and went out. She was sure her suitemates would ask her questions that would lead her to something, questions that would make her tell them what had happened or lie to them or something.

In the bathroom, a girl said hi to her; two others, chatting in the common room, smiled at her and gave her little finger-waves; Michelle felt almost invisible. She began to understand that they hadn't know she'd been gone. If they'd thought about her at all, they must have figured she was in her room, studying or sleeping or whatever they thought she usually did.

Standing in the common room leafing blindly through a magazine, Michelle had the eerie sensation of having dreamed the night that burned so vividly in her mind. She swayed on her feet. Then she felt her body sharply insisting that every bit of it had happened.

She wished that she'd had somebody she'd confided in about Hammett. There ought to have been somebody she had to answer to.

She knew she had to get out of that dormitory. When she put on her jacket, picked up her backpack of books and headed for the door, no one even asked her where she was going. She was already outside before she heard somebody call out to her, "Bye, Michelle."

In a snack-bar booth with her Shakespeare text open on the table in front of her so that she'd be less likely to be bothered, Michelle worked it through in her mind to the point where she saw that it wasn't likely that anybody would connect her with Hammett's disappearance. She sipped her coffee. If anybody was even going to mention her name with his, she would have to be the one.

She tried to read the signs of everything she'd been through since that moment in class she'd found Hammett looking into her eyes. She could feel herself wanting to tell it all to somebody, tell it just so that it wouldn't evaporate. But she couldn't help feeling that telling somebody would be indulging herself. She knew she had to discern the answer to one simple question: Should she walk out to the pay phone in the hallway, make a call, and tell someone what had happened? Staring at the back of her hand, she stopped it from shaking. A vision came to her, of Hammett Wilson sitting in his office waiting for her to come visit him and smiling at the pictures of his wife and sons on his desk.

So she decided. And walking back to her dormitory that night Michelle wrapped that secret around herself like some kind of invisible coat. She understood that holding it to herself made her experience with Hammett something that was hers and only hers. She set her mind to what she knew wouldn't be easy, carrying herself in such a way that no one would suspect how her life had been changed.

Something she never did tell me about, though I asked her, was what it was like at school when Hammett didn't show up for his classes or what it was like at his house when his wife and boys showed up and he wasn't there. She shook her head, as if she didn't want to say. "But, Michelle, wasn't there a huge investigation?" I asked her.

"Yes, there was," she said, nodding, but she went no further than that.

The last week of school that spring, Michelle made excuses not to go with me to the Moscow Hotel for our evening drinks. When I stopped by her place, she was polite enough in her refusals—saying she had vast amounts of work to accomplish in order to finish the semester. I was preoccupied with schoolwork, too, and so I didn't press her.

On my last morning in town, I called Michelle to try to persuade her to have breakfast with me over at the Moscow Hotel. She didn't need any persuading. She said she'd been planning to see me before I went back east.

The morning was bright, and we were both a little giddy at having finished up our school work. Over our last cups of coffee, we were chatting very pleasantly, I thought, when Michelle startled me by taking Hammett's glasses out of her purse.

"You remember these," she said, holding them in front of her.

I nodded.

"These have been with me all this time." She curled her fingers around them. "I've kept them in my purse or else in my desk drawer, near the front, where you found them that time. I decided that if anyone ever asked me about them, I'd tell them the story, as best I could. That was how I worked it out: I wouldn't ever volunteer to tell anybody, but I wouldn't try to protect myself either." She spoke very softly, with her eyes almost closed. We were sitting in a dark corner but near a window that cast Michelle in a bright beam of sun, with flecks of dust floating all around her in the light. Her skin was clear and pale as a cup of fresh milk.

She leaned forward and asked in a near whisper, "But you know what?"

I shook my head.

She didn't seem to see me, but she went on anyway, still whispering. "I hated every single word I told you." She paused before she spoke again, this time so softly it was more like a message to herself than to me. "And I won't ever tell it again." She kept her eyes on the glasses in her hand on the table.

While we sat there, I had the oddest sensation of being with her and not with her. I had a sense of her making important decisions, and there was a crazy moment when I thought maybe she was getting ready to ask something of me; though I couldn't imagine what it might be, I felt a vague dread about it. I was pretty sure I would let her down because I wasn't ready that morning to be responsible for anyone but myself. But Michelle kept her silence, and we sat still until the window's shaft of sunlight had moved well past her. When we stood up, she quickly tucked the glasses back into her purse, as if she'd just stolen them. She came around the table toward me, meaning to give me a hug, I guess, but I wasn't ready for that either, because I backed away, facing her with no suitable gesture to make except a stupid handshake.

Michelle and I hadn't pretended we'd write to each other or keep in touch. Watching her walk away from me, I couldn't help thinking about Hammett's glasses riding along with her in her purse; the thought came to me that she was going to drop them in the first trash can she came to. I shook off that notion, but at a distance, I followed her out onto the street and watched her dark figure steadily diminish as she walked away. With my hands in my pockets, I stood out there in the spring sunlight until I couldn't see her any more.

Lately Michelle's story has been coming back to me, not the way it came, through her twangy Idaho voice, but with such a visual clarity that it might have been a movie I saw lots of times years ago. The telling of it those nights in the bar of the Moscow Hotel seemed to make her cold, and I guess it made me cold, too. I remember the two of us hunkering over the table, hugging ourselves and shivering.

But when Michelle enters my thinking now, I welcome her almost as if she's a source of warmth. I understand how her telling me her story released me into the world where every day people carry out their lives with their stories locked inside themselves.

At the time, I didn't realize how she was affecting me, and I'm ashamed to say that I don't have the slightest idea what happened to Michelle. I can't imagine where she would have gone or what she would have done with her life. In my first years of teaching, I hardly thought of her. But as I gradually settled into my writing life, she began paying me more and more visits; I feel as if I have finally begun to be able to receive whatever signals her story means to send me.

Nowadays, my mornings of solitude are powerfully informed by Michelle Gonyaw and Hammett Wilson. More than once the thought has occurred to me that they may be the shades who inhabit the wing chairs that sit opposite me, while I tap out my sentences on my computer. If Michelle is alive, I know that she must spend some part of every day of her life on her hands and knees, crawling over cold dirt and moss and reaching out into the dark. And I know that thanks to her, I spend some part of almost every day of my life lost only in my writing, while light makes its way into my living room.

Acknowledgments

ESSAYS

"Let's Say You Wrote Badly This Morning," "The Writing Habit," and "What You Get for Good Writing" are reprinted from *The Writing Habit* by permission of Gibbs Smith, Publisher.

"Do You Wanna Dance?" first appeared in *The Southern Review*.

"Ingrained Reflexes" was originally published as "About Men: Ingrained Reflexes." Copyright © 1986 by The New York Times Company. Reprinted by permission.

"Just Looking, Thank You" was originally published as "Here's Looking at You" in *Playboy* magazine.

"Fire in the House" originally appeared in *Sunshine* magazine.

POEMS

"Gregory's House," "Miss Florence Jackson," "Jeep Alley, Emperor of Baseball," "Janie Swecker and Me and Gone with the Wind," "Mrs. Green," and "My Brother Flies Over Low": Reprinted from *Paper Boy*, by David Huddle, by permission of the University of Pittsburgh Press. © 1979 by David Huddle.

"Theory," "Bac Ha," "Words," "Them," "Cousin," "Vermont," "Music," "The Field," "The School," "Croquet," "Icicle," "Sunday Dinner," and "Stopping by Home" are reprinted from *Stopping by Home*; and "Local Metaphysics," "Inside the Hummingbird Aviary," "The Snow Monkey Argues with God," "Love and Art," "Upstairs Hallway," "5 A.M.," and "Thinking About My Father" are reprinted from *The Nature of Yearning*; by permission of Gibbs Smith, Publisher.

"Poem at Fifty, Mostly in Long Lines," "This Poem Is the End of a Long Story," and "Mother Encounters Monkey at the Post Office" originally appeared in *The Iron Mountain Review*.

STORIES

"Summer of the Magic Show," "The Undesirable," and "Only the Little Bone" are reprinted from *Only the Little Bone*; "Playing" and "The Beautiful Gestures" are reprinted from *The High Spirits*; and "Little Sawtooth" is reprinted from *Intimates*; by permission of David R. Godine, Publisher.

UNIVERSITY PRESS OF NEW ENGLAND publishes books under its own imprint
and is the publisher for Brandeis University Press, Brown University Press, University of Connecticut, Dartmouth College, Middlebury College Press, University
of New Hampshire, University of Rhode Island, Tufts University, University of
Vermont, and Wesleyan University Press.

LIBRARY OF CONGRESS CATALOGING-IN-PUBLICATION DATA

Huddle, David, 1942–
    [Selections. 1993]
    A David Huddle reader : selected prose and poetry / David Huddle.
       p.   cm. — (Bread Loaf series of contemporary writers)
    ISBN 0–87451–652–8 (hard). — ISBN 0–87451–644–7 (pbk.)
    I. Title. II. Series.
PS3558.U287A6 1993
818′ .5409—dc20   93–13607
∞